A Child's History of the World

by

V. M. HILLYER

FIRST HEAD MASTER OF CALVERT SCHOOL

With many illustrations by
CARLE MICHEL BOOG
and
MARY SHERWOOD WRIGHT

List of Stories

This page is not for you, boys and girls. It is for that old man or woman — twenty, thirty, or forty years old, who may peek into this book; and is what they would call the

Preface

To give the child some idea of what has gone on in the world before he arrived;

To take him out of his little self-centered, shut-in life, which looms so large because it is so close to his eyes;

To extend his horizon, broaden his view, and open up the vista down the ages past;

To acquaint him with some of the big events and great names and fix these in time and space as a basis for detailed study in the future;

To give him a chronological file with main guides, into which he can fit in its proper place all his further historical study—

Is the purpose of this first SURVEY OF THE WORLD'S HISTORY.

About the Preface and Introduction: This edition contains Virgil Hillyer's unedited Preface and Introduction as they appeared in the original 1924 publication.

This part is not for you, either. It is for your father, mother, or teacher, and is what they would call the

Introduction

In common with all children of my age, I was brought up on American History and given no other history but American, year in and year out, year after year for eight or more years.

So far as I knew 1492 was the beginning of the world. Any events or characters before that time, reference to which I encountered by any chance, were put down in my mind in the same category with fairy-tales. Christ and His times, of which I heard only in Sunday-school, were to me mere fiction without reality. They were not mentioned in any history that I knew and therefore, so I thought, must belong *not* to a realm in time and space, but to a spiritual realm.

To give an American child only American History is as provincial as to teach a Texas child only Texas History. Patriotism is usually given as the reason for such history teaching. It only promotes a narrow-mindedness and an absurd conceit, based on utter ignorance of any other peoples and any other times—an intolerant egotism without foundation in fact. Since World War I, it has become increasingly more and more important that American children should have a knowledge of other countries and other peoples in order that their attitude may be intelligent and unprejudiced.

As young as nine years of age, a child is eagerly inquisitive as to what has taken place in the ages past and readily grasps a concept of World History. Therefore, for many years Calvert School nine-year-old pupils have been taught World History in spite of academic and parental skepticism and antagonism. But I have watched the gradual drift toward adoption of this plan of history teaching, and with it an ever-increasing demand for a textbook of general history for young children. I have found, however, that all existing textbooks have to be largely abridged and also supplemented by a running explanation and comment, to make them intelligible to the young child.

The recent momentous studies into the native intelligence of children show us what the average child at different ages can understand and what he cannot understand—what dates, figures of speech, vocabulary, generalities, and abstractions he can comprehend and what he cannot comprehend—and in the future all textbooks will have to be written with constant regard for these intelligence norms. Otherwise, such texts are very likely to be "over the child's head." They will be trying to teach him some things at least that, in the nature of the case, are beyond him.

In spite of the fact that the writer has been in constant contact with the child mind for a great many years, he has found that whatever was written in his study had to be revised and rewritten each time after the lesson had been tried out in the classroom. Even though the first writing was in what he considered the simplest language, he has found that each and every word and expression has had to be subjected again and again to this classroom test to determine what meaning is conveyed. The slightest inverted phraseology or possibility of double meaning has oftentimes been misconstrued or found confusing. For instance, the statement that "Rome was on the Tiber River" has quite commonly been taken to mean that the city was literally built on top of the river, and the child has had some sort of fantastic vision of houses built on piles in the river. A child of nine is still very young—he may still believe in Santa Claus—younger in ideas, in vocabulary and in understanding than most adults appreciate—even though they be parents or teachers—and new information can hardly be put too simply.

So the topics selected have not always been the most important—but the most important that can be understood and appreciated by a child.

Introduction

Most political, sociological, economic, or religious generalities are beyond a child's comprehension, no matter how simply told. After all, this History is only a preliminary story.

Excellent biographies and stories from general history have been written. But biographies from history do not give an historic outline. They do not give any outline at all for future filling in; and, indeed, unless they themselves are fitted into such a general historical scheme, they are nothing more than so many disconnected tales floating about in the child's mind with no associations of time or space.

The treatment of the subject in this book is, therefore, chronological— telling the story of what has happened century by century and epoch by epoch, not by nations. The story of one nation is interrupted to take up that of another as different plots in a novel are brought forward simultaneously. This is in line with the purpose, which is to give the pupil a continuous view or panorama of the ages rather than Greek History from start to finish then, retracing the steps of time, Roman History, and so on. The object is to sketch the whole picture in outline, leaving the details to be gradually filled in by later study, as the artist sketches the general scheme of his picture before filling in the details. Such a scheme is as necessary to orderly classification of historical knowledge as is a filing system in any office that can function properly or even at all.

The Staircase of Time is to give a visual idea of the extent of time and the progressive steps in the History of the World. Each "flight" represents a thousand years, and each "step" a hundred—a century. If you have a spare wall, either in the play-room, attic, or barn such a Staircase of Time on a large scale may be drawn upon it from floor to reaching height and made a feature if elaborated with pictures or drawings of people and events. If the wall faces the child's bed so much the better, for when lying awake in the morning or at any other time, instead of imagining fantastic designs on the wallpaper, he may picture the crowded events on the Staircase of Time. At any rate, the child should constantly refer either to such a Staircase of Time or to the Time Table as each event is studied, until he has a mental image of the Ages past.

At first a child does not appreciate time values represented by numbers or the relative position of dates on a time line and will wildly say twenty-five hundred B.C. or twenty-five thousand B.C. or twenty-five million B.C. indiscriminately. Only by constantly referring dates to position on the Staircase of Time or the Time Table can a child come to visualize dates. You may be *amused*, but do not be *amazed*, if a child gives 776 thousand years A.D. as the date for the First Olympiad, or says that Italy is located in Athens, or that Abraham was a hero of the Trojan War.

If you have ever been introduced to a roomful of strangers at one time, you know how futile it is to attempt even to remember their names to say nothing of connecting names and faces. It is necessary to hear something interesting about each one before you can begin to recall names and faces. Likewise an introduction to World History, the characters and places in which are utterly unknown strangers to the child, must be something more than a mere name introduction, and there must be very few introductions given at a time or both names and faces will be instantly forgotten. It is also necessary to repeat new names constantly in order that the pupil may gradually become familiarized with them, for so many strange people and places are bewildering.

In order to serve the purpose of a basal outline, which in the future is to be filled in, it is necessary that the Time Table be made a permanent possession of the pupil. This Time Table, therefore, should be studied like the multiplication tables until it is known one hundred per cent and for "keeps," and until the topic connected with each date can be elaborated as much as desired. The aim should be to have the pupil able to start with Primitive Man and give a summary of World History to the present time, with dates and chief events without prompting, questioning, hesitation, or mistake. Does this seem too much to expect? It is not as difficult as it may sound, if suggestions given in the text for connecting the various events into a sequence and for passing names and events in a condensed review are followed. Hundreds of Calvert children each year are successfully required to do this very thing.

The attitude, however, usually assumed by teachers, that "even if the pupil forgets it all, there will be left a valuable impression," is too often an apology for superficial teaching and superficial learning. History may be made just as much a "mental discipline" as some other studies, but only if difficulties of dates and other abstractions are squarely met and overcome by hard study and learned to be remembered, not merely to be forgotten after the recitation. The story part the child will easily remember, but it is the "who and when and where and why" that are important, and this part is the serious study. Instead of, "A man, once upon a time," he should say, "King John in 1215 at Runnymede because—"

This book, therefore, is not a supplementary reader but a basal history study. Just enough narrative is told to give the skeleton flesh and blood and make it living. The idea is not how much but how little can be told; to cut down one thousand pages to less than half of that number without leaving only dry bones.

No matter how the subject is presented it is necessary that the child do his part and put his own brain to work; and for this purpose he *should be required to retell each story after he has read it* and should be repeatedly questioned on names and dates as well as stories, to make sure he is retaining and assimilating what he hears.

I recall how once upon a time a young chap, just out of college, taught his first class in history. With all the enthusiasm of a full-back who has just kicked a goal from field, he talked, he sang; he drew maps on the blackboard, on the floor, on the field; he drew pictures, he vaulted desks, and even stood on his head to illustrate points. His pupils attended spellbound, with their eyes wide open, their ears wide open, and their mouths wide open. They missed nothing. They drank in his flow of words with thirst unquenched; but, like Baron Munchausen, he had failed to look at the other end of the drinking horse that had been cut in half. At the end of a month his kindly principal suggested a test, and he gave it with perfect confidence.

There were only three questions:

1) Tell all you can about Columbus.
2)   "   "   "   "   "   Jamestown.
3)   "   "   "   "   "   Plymouth.

And here are the three answers of one of the most interested pupils:

1) He was a *grate* man.
2)   "   "   "   "   "
3)   "   "   "   "   "   *to.*

Introduction

Here is the

Staircase of Time

IT starts far, far below the bottom of the pages and rises up, UP, UP to where we are NOW—each step a hundred years, each flight of steps a thousand. It will keep on up until it reaches high heaven. From where we are NOW let us look down the flights below us and listen to the story of what has happened in the long years gone by.

A Child's History of the World

begins here

1

How Things Started

ONCE upon a time there was a boy —

Just like me.

He had to stay in bed in the morning until seven o'clock until his family was ready to get up.

So did I.

As he was always awake long before this time, he used to lie there and think about all sorts of curious things.

So did I.

One thing he used to wonder was this:

What would the world be like if there were —

No fathers and mothers,

No uncles and aunts,

No cousins or other children to play with,

No people at all, except himself in the whole world!

Perhaps you have wondered the same thing.

So did I.

At last he used to get so lonely, just from thinking how dreadful such a world would be, that he could stand it no longer and would run to his parents' room and jump into bed by their side just to get this terrible thought out of his mind.

So did I—for *I was the boy.*

Well, there *was* a time long, long, long ago when there were no men or women or children, NO PEOPLE of any kind, in the whole world. Of course there were no houses, for there was no one to build them or to live in them, no towns or cities—nothing that people make. There were just animals—mastodons and dinosaurs, birds and butterflies, frogs and snakes, turtles and fish. Can you think of such a world as that?

Then,
    long, long, long,

before that, there was a time when there were NO PEOPLE, and NO ANIMALS of any sort in the whole world; there were just growing plants. Can you think of such a world as that?

Then,
    long, long, long,
    long, long, long,

before that, there was a time when there were NO PEOPLE, NO ANIMALS, NO PLANTS, in the whole world; there was just bare rock and water everywhere. Can you think of such a world as that?

Then,
    long, long, long,
    long, long, long—you might
        keep on saying—
            "long, long, long," all day, and
            tomorrow, and all

next week, and next
month, and next
year, and it would
not be long enough —

before this, there was a time when there was NO WORLD AT ALL!

No world at all! Only the stars, and God, who made the stars.

Now, real stars are not things with points like those in the corner of a flag or the gold ones you put on a Christmas tree. The real stars in the sky have no points. They are huge burning balls of fire—balls of fire. Each star, however, is so huge that there is nothing in the world now anywhere nearly as big. One little bit, one little scrap of a star is bigger than our whole world—than our whole world.

One of these stars is our sun—yes, our sun. The other stars would look the same as the sun if we could get as close to them. But at that time, so long, long ago, our sun was not just a big, round, white, hot ball as we see it in the sky today. It was then more like the fireworks you may have seen on the

The sun sputtering and throwing off sparks

Fourth of July. It was whirling and sputtering and throwing off sparks.

One of these sparks, which the sun threw far off, got cool just as a spark from a crackling log in a fireplace gets cool, and this cooled off spark was—

What do you suppose?

See if you can guess—

It was our world!—yes, the world

on which we now live.

At first, however, our world, or Earth, was nothing but a ball of rock. This ball of rock was wrapped around with steam, like a heavy fog.

Then the steam turned to rain, and it rained on the world,

a a a
n n n
d d d

i i i
t t t

r r r
a a a
i i i
n n n
e e e
d d d

until it had filled up the hollows and made enormously big puddles. These puddles were the oceans. The dry places were bare *rock*.

Then, after this, came the first living things—tiny plants that you could only have seen under a microscope. At first they grew only in the water, then along the water's edge, then out on the rock.

Then dirt, or soil, as people call it, formed all over the rock and made the rock into land, and the plants grew larger and spread farther over the land.

Then, after this, came the first tiny animals in the water. They were wee specks too small, like the first plants, to be seen without the help of a microscope.

Then, after this, in the water came larger animals like *Jellyfish* and clams and horseshoe crabs.

Then, after this, came *Insects*, some that live *in* the water, some on the water, some *on* the land, like cockroaches, and some *in* the air.

Then, after this, came *Fish* that live only in the water.

Then, after this, came animals like frogs called *Amphibians* that live in the water and also on the land.

Then, after this, came *Reptiles*, like snakes, turtles, lizards, and huge dinosaurs.

Then, after this, came *Birds* that lay eggs, and *Mammals*, like foxes and monkeys and cows, that nurse their babies when they are born.

Then, last of all, came—what do you suppose? Yes—*People*—men, women, and children. Here are the steps; see if you can take them:

STARS,

    SUN,

        SPARK,

            WORLD,

                STEAM,

                    RAIN,

                        OCEANS,

                            PLANTS,

ANIMALS,

     JELLYFISH,

          INSECTS,

               FISH,

                    AMPHIBIANS,

                         REPTILES,

                              BIRDS,

                                  MAMMALS,

PEOPLE.

    And here we are!

What do you suppose will be next?

2

People Who Lived in Caves

How do you suppose I know about all these things that took place so long ago?

I don't.

I'm only guessing about them.

But there are different kinds of guesses. If I hold out my two closed hands and ask you to guess which one has the penny in it, that is one kind of a guess. Your guess might be right or it might be wrong. It would be just luck.

But there is another kind of guess. When there is snow on the ground and I see tracks of a boot in the snow, I guess that a person must have passed by, for boots don't usually walk without someone in them. That kind of guess is not just luck but common sense.

So we can guess about a great many things that have taken place long ago, even though there was no one there at the time to see them or tell about them.

We have dug down deep under the ground in different parts of the world and have found there—what do you suppose?

I don't believe you would ever guess.

We have found the heads of arrows and spears and hatchets.

The peculiar thing about these arrows and spears and hatchets is that they are not made of iron or steel, as you might expect, but of stone.

Now, we are sure that only human beings could have made and used such things, for birds and fish or other animals do not use hatchets or spears. We are also sure that these people must have lived long, long years ago before iron and steel were known, because it must have taken long, long years for these things to have become covered up so deep by dust and dirt. We have also found the bones of the people themselves, who died several million years ago, long before anyone began to write down history. The oldest bones we have ever found were in East Africa. We know that people long ago were working and playing, eating and fighting—doing many of the same things we are today—especially the fighting.

This time in the prehistory of the world, when people used such things made of stone, is therefore called the Stone Age.

Life was hard for Stone Age people. They didn't have all the things we are used to having today.

Some wild animals make houses. Foxes dig holes, beavers make houses of sticks and mud. These first people probably had no houses of any sort in which to live. They simply found any shelter they could. They found caves in the rocks or in the hillsides where they could get away from the cold and storms and wild animals. So men, women, and children of this time were called *Cave People.*

They spent their days hunting some animals and running and hiding from others. They caught animals by trapping them in a pit covered over with bushes, or they killed them with a club or a rock if they had a chance, or with stone-headed arrows or hatchets. They even painted or cut pictures of these animals on the walls of their caves. Some of these pictures we can still see today.

They lived on berries and nuts and seeds. They robbed the nests of birds for the eggs, which they ate raw, for at first they had no fire with which to cook. They liked to drink the warm blood of animals they killed, as you would a glass of milk.

They talked to each other by some sort of grunts or very simple words. They made clothes of skins of animals they killed, for there was no such thing as cloth.

These early people must have spent most of their time hunting for food or trying to get away from animals hunting *them* for food. They had no thick hide like an elephant to protect them; they did not grow a coat of fur like a bear to keep them warm; they could not run very fast, like a deer to escape their enemies; they were no match for an animal with sharp teeth and claws and strong muscles like a lion. It's a wonder any of them lived to grow up.

Stone Age people had two things that helped them more than sharp claws, or strong muscles, or tough skins. They had better brains than the animals. And they had hands instead of front feet. With their brains they could *think*. They could *think* of ways of doing things better.

With their brains they could *think* of using tools. With their hands they could make tools and use them. Instead of sharp teeth, men could use spears. In place of a furry skin to keep them warm, men could use the skins of animals.

Suppose you had been a boy or a girl in the Stone Age. I wonder how you would have liked the life.

When you woke up in the morning, you would not have bathed or even washed your hands and face or brushed your teeth or combed your hair.

You ate with your fingers, for there were no knives or forks or spoons or cups or saucers, only one bowl—which your mother had made out of mud and dried in the sun to hold water to drink—no dishes to wash and put away, no chairs, no tables, no table manners.

There were no books, no paper, no pencils.

There was no Saturday or Sunday, January or July. Except that one day was warm and sunny or another cold and rainy, they were all alike. There was no school to go to.

There was nothing to do all day long but make mud pies or pick berries or play tag with your brothers and sisters.

I wonder how you would like that kind of life!

"Fine!" do you think?—"a great life—just like camping out"?

But I have only told you part of the story.

The cave would have been cold and damp and dark, with only the bare ground or a pile of leaves for a bed. There would probably have been bats and big spiders sharing the cave with you.

You might have had on the skin of some animal your father had killed, but as this only covered part of your body and as there was no fire, you would have felt cold in winter, and when it got very cold you might have frozen to death.

For breakfast you might have had some dried berries or grass seed or a piece of raw meat, for lunch the same thing, for dinner still the same thing.

You would never have had any bread or cheese or griddlecakes with syrup, or oatmeal with sugar on it, or apple pie or ice cream.

There was nothing to do all day long but watch out for wild animals—bears and tigers; for there was no door with lock and key, and a tiger, if he found you out, could go wherever you went and "get you" even in your cave.

And then some day your father or brother, who had left the cave in the morning to go hunting, would not return, and you would know he had been torn to pieces by some wild beast, and you would wonder how long before your turn would come.

Do you think you would like to have lived then?

3

Fire! Fire! Fire!!

THE first things are usually the most interesting—the first baby, the first tooth, the first step, the first word, the first spanking. This book will be chiefly the story of first things; those that came second or third or fourth or fifth you can read about and study later.

Primitive people did not at first know what fire was. They had no matches nor any way of making a light or a fire. They had no light at night. They had no fire to warm themselves by. They had no fire with which to cook their food. Somewhere and sometime, we do not know exactly when or how, they found out how to make and use fire.

If you rub your hands together rapidly, they become warm. Try it. If you rub them together still more rapidly, they become hot. If you rub two sticks together rapidly, they become warm. If you rub them together still more rapidly, they become hot. If you rub two sticks together very, very, very rapidly, they become hot and at last, if you keep it up long enough and fast enough, are set on fire. Native Americans and Boy Scouts and Girl Scouts do this and make a fire by twisting one stick against another.

This was one of the first inventions, and this invention was as remarkable for them at that time as the invention of electric light in our own times.

People of the Stone Age had hair and beards that were never cut, because they had nothing to cut them with, even had they wanted them short, which they probably didn't.

They had no clothes made of cloth, for they had no cloth and nothing with which to cut and sew cloth if they had.

They had no saws to cut boards, no hammer or nails to fasten them together to make houses or furniture.

They had no forks nor spoons; no pots nor pans; no buckets nor shovels; no needles nor pins.

The people of the Stone Age had never seen or heard of such a thing as iron or steel or tin or brass or anything made of these metals. For

A cave man discovering copper

thousands and thousands of years primitive people got along without any of the things that are made of metal.

Then one day a Stone Age man found out something by accident; a *discovery* we call it.

He was making a fire; and a fire, which is to us such a common, everyday thing, was still to him very wonderful. Round his fire he placed some rocks to make a sort of campfire stove. Now, it happened that this particular rock was not ordinary rock but what we now call "ore," for it had copper in it. The heat of the fire melted some of the copper out of the rock, and it ran out on the ground.

What were those bright, shining drops?

He examined them.

How pretty they were!

He heated some more of the same rock and got some more copper.

Thus was the first metal discovered.

At first people used the copper for beads and ornaments, for it was so bright and shiny. But they soon found out that copper could be pounded into sharp blades and points, which were much better than the stone knives and arrow-heads they had used before.

Notice that it was not iron they discovered first; it was copper.

We think people next discovered tin in somewhat the same way. Then, after that, they found out that tin when mixed with copper made a still harder and better metal than either alone. This metal, made of tin and copper together, we now call bronze; and for two or three thousand years people made their tools and weapons out of bronze. We call the time when men used bronze tools, and bronze weapons for hunting and fighting the Bronze Age.

At last somebody discovered iron, and soon people saw that iron was better for most useful things than either copper or bronze. The Iron Age lasted three thousand years.

People who lived in the Bronze and Iron Ages were able, after the discovery of metal, to do many things they could not possibly have done before with only stone.

You may have heard in your mythology or fairy tales of a *Golden Age* also, but by this is meant something quite different. The Golden Age means a time when everything was beautiful and lovely and everybody wise and good. There have been times in the world's history which have been called the Golden Age for this reason.

But I am afraid there never has been really a Golden Age—only in fairy tales.

4

From an Airplane

PEOPLE of the Bronze and Iron Ages thought the world was flat, and they knew only a little bit of the world, the small part where they lived; and they thought that if you went too far the world came to an end where you would

TU
  M
   B
    L
   E

     O
      F
      F

If we should go up in an airplane and look down on the world at the place where the first civilized people once lived, we should see several rivers, seas, and a gulf, and from so high up in the air they would look something like this:

Map of Mesopotamia[1] and Mediterranean

Now, you probably have never even heard of these rivers and seas, and yet they have been known longer than any other places in the world. One of these rivers is the Tigris River, and another is the Euphrates.[2] They run along getting closer and closer together until at last they join each other and flow into what is called the Persian Gulf.

You might make these two rivers in the ground of your yard or garden or draw them on the floor if your mother will let you. Just for fun you might name your drinking cup *Tigris* and your glass *Euphrates*. Then you might call your mouth, into which they both empty, the *Persian Gulf*, for you will hear a great many new names by and by, and as grown-up people give names to their houses and boats, to their horses and dogs, why shouldn't you give names to things that belong to you? For instance, you might call your chair, your bed, your table, your comb and brush, even

---

[1] Mesopotamia [mes ə pə tā′ mi ə]   [2] Euphrates [yōō frā′ tēz]

your hat and shoes, after these strange names.

Then, if we flew in our airplane to the west, we should in the northeast corner of Africa see a country called Egypt, a river called the Nile, and a sea now named the Mediterranean. Mediterranean simply means *between the land*, for this sea is surrounded by land. It is, indeed, almost like a big lake. It is supposed that long, long ago in the Stone Age, there was no water at all where this sea now is, only a dry valley, and that people once lived there.

Along the Nile in what is now Egypt, and along the Tigris and Euphrates in what was then Babylon,[3] Assyria,[4] and Syria, lived people who were recording their activities in writing and pictures that have survived to this day.

Certainly there were cave men and other primitive peoples who were drawing pictures of their way of life. But because travel was not easy in those days, people in one region didn't know a great deal about people in another part of the world. This was soon to change.

Many different groups of people lived in the country of the Tigris and Euphrates and along the Nile, and all of them wanted to own the best land. There were many battles. People moved around a lot—because they lost a battle and had to move or just because they were looking for a better place to live.

One group or family of people called Semites[5] lived in the land that today we call the Middle East, near the Mediterranean Sea and the Tigris and Euphrates. Modern Arabs and Jews are Semites. They speak Semitic languages that are part of one language family and sound very similar. Here's an example. In Hebrew, the word for peace is *shalom*. In Arabic, the word for peace is *salaam*.

Another group of people lived along the Nile. In Egypt and other parts of North Africa, Egyptians and people called Berbers[6] were related to the

---

[3] Babylon [bab′ ə lon]
[4] Assyria [ə sir′ ē ə]

[5] Semites [sem′ ĭtz]
[6] Berbers [bûr′ bərz]

Middle Eastern Semites. Nubians who came from the part of Africa south of Egypt belonged to a group of people called Nilo-Saharans.[7] If you look at a map, you can see how they got this name. They lived along the Nile River and near the Sahara[8] Desert. These Nubians traveled northward along the Nile Valley into Egypt. And sometimes Egyptians traveled south into Nubia.

Another group of people came from the area that is now Iran. They are called Indo-Europeans, and they spread eastward into northern India and westward into Europe. Today, people in Europe, Iran, and India are descended from these early Indo-Europeans. Just like the Semites, they speak languages that are related to each other.

We know now that these ancient peoples moved around a lot more than we used to think they did. They taught each other to grow different kinds of food. They exchanged goods with each other. And sometimes people settled down in the new land and stayed there. Just as the United States has seen many nationalities of people move here and become Americans, people in ancient times also migrated and settled down in a new land.

---

[7] Nilo-Saharans [ni´ lō sə har´ ənz]   [8] Sahara [sə har´ ə]

5

Real History Begins

You can remember the big things that have happened in your own lifetime.

Perhaps you may have heard your grand-parents or your parents tell about things that happened in their own lives—things like World War II or the wars in Korea[1] or Vietnam.[2]

And your grandparents, of course, had parents and grandparents and great grandparents, just like you.

Perhaps your

> great,
>> great,
>>> great,
>>>> grandparents

may have been living when Washington was President, and *his*

> great
>> great,
>>> great,
>>>> great,
>>>>> great,
>>>>>> grandparents

---

[1] Korea [kə rē′ ə]   [2] Vietnam [vē et näm′]

were living in the days of Julius Caesar.[3]

Although these ancestors, as they are called, are dead long since, the story of what did happen in all their lifetimes 'way, 'way back has been written down in books and this story is history—*his story* one boy named it.

Christ was living in the Year 1—no, not the first year of the world, of course.

Do you know how many years ago that was?

You can tell if you know what year this is now.

If Christ were living today, how old would He be?

Two thousand years may seem a long time. But perhaps you have seen or heard of a man or a woman who was a hundred years old. Have you?

Well, in two thousand years only twenty people, each a hundred years old, might have lived one after the other—twenty people one after the other since the time of Christ—and that doesn't seem so long after all!

Everything that happened *before* Christ was born is called B.C., which you can guess are the initials of Before Christ, so B.C. stands for Before Christ. So much is easy.

Everything that has happened in the world *since* the time of Christ is called A.D. This is not so easy, for though A. might stand for After, we know D. is not the initial of Christ.

As a matter of fact, A.D. are the initials of two Latin words, *Anno Domini.*[4] Anno means *in the year*, Domini *of the Lord*, which in ordinary, everyday language means of course *since the time of Christ*.

I have told you about things I have had to guess at. We call these things *before-history*, or *pre-history*, which means the same thing. But the things that have happened in the lifetime of people who wrote them down—the stories I don't have to guess at—we call history. The first history that we feel fairly sure is true begins with the people in North

---

[3] Julius Caesar [jōōl′ yəs sē′ zər]   [4] Anno Domini [an′ ō dom′ə ni]

Africa and the Middle East.

Some people began writing down their stories thousands of years ago. What's interesting is that different peoples in parts of the world that were really far apart figured out all by themselves how to write, and they did this at different times. Ancient people in the Middle East invented a written language called cuneiform.[5] Ancient people in Egypt wrote in hieroglyphics.[6] Centuries ago, people in India were writing in Sanskrit.[7] People as far away as China, Nubia,[8] and Central America invented their own writing. So did people on the island of Crete in the Mediterranean Sea, halfway between Egypt and Greece.

Today, we know how to read some of these languages from several thousand years ago. But other languages are like an unsolved puzzle. We see the writing, but we don't have any idea what it means.

If you think about all these early civilizations, which ones do you suppose we know the most about? The ones whose writing we can read, or the others? Well, I'll bet you all guessed the right answer to that question! Of course, we know the most about places whose stories *we can read.*

Four places whose early stories we can read about are Egypt, Mesopotamia, India, and China. We can read their writing, so we know what people were there during all those long years ago. We're not as good on the writing of Nubia or Central America or Crete, so we don't know as much about what was happening in those places long, long ago.

What's really interesting is what we *do* know about the places whose history we *can* read. We know that all four of those ancient civilizations grew up along river valleys.

Egypt was built along the Nile River valley. And Mesopotamia grew along the valleys of two rivers—the Tigris and the Euphrates. But you already know about those rivers.

---

[5] cuneiform [kyoo nē′ ə fôrm]
[6] hieroglyphics [hī ər ə glif′ iks]
[7] Sanskrit [san′ skrit]
[8] Nubia [noo′ bē ə]

Now here are two new rivers for you. India's first history took place along the valley of the Indus[9] River and China's along the Huang[10] River. The Huang River is sometimes called the Yellow River because the river's bottom is thick yellow mud.

Even though they lived far apart, the peoples who lived along these rivers did a lot of the same things. This isn't too surprising when you think about it. You may never have visited Africa or India or China today, but you can guess that girls and boys there play games, and that mothers cook, and so on. Even in ancient times, people around the world did many of the same things.

The river valleys were a good place to live because food was plentiful. There was lots of water for animals to drink, and to use to water plants. So men and women and boys and girls all settled down next to the rivers—in Egypt, in Mesopotamia, in India and in China.

Soon enough people were living so close together that they were living in what we call a town. Then people in these towns began to build little boats, then bigger boats. Soon the boats were sailing up and down the river to the next town and to towns farther away. The towns began to trade with each other. And sometimes the towns began to fight with each other.

One of the best ways to stop the towns from having little wars was to put them all under the rule of one person. So, in place

Trading boat of river valley town

---

[9] Indus [in′ dəs]   [10] Huang [hwäng]

after place, a *government* grew up. Sometimes the towns agreed to get together. Other times they were united when one strong man conquered his neighbors. Either way, a king, or emperor, or pharaoh[11] was in charge of the government and was ruler of what we now call a nation.

So, if you look back at these river civilizations, you can see a piece of history that is really quite remarkable. At a time when many people were still hunters and gatherers, maybe even living in caves, something new and exciting was happening first in Egypt and Mesopotamia and soon afterwards in India and China. People settled down and farmed, then built towns, then traded with each other, and then built nations. And, sometime during all this, they figured out that it would be a great thing to write— and so they wrote down their history for us to read today.

---

[11] pharaoh [fâr· ō]

6

The Puzzle Writers in Egypt

EGYPT was one of the first places where people began to write. The Egyptians did not write with letters like ours, but with signs that looked like little pictures—a lion, a spear, a bird, a whip. This picture-writing was called hieroglyphics—see if you can say *hi-er-o-glyph-ics*. Perhaps you have seen, in the puzzle sections of a newspaper, stories written in pictures for you to guess the meaning. Well, hieroglyphics were something like that.

Here is the name of an Egyptian queen written in hieroglyphics. You would never guess her name from this funny writing. Her name was Hatshepsut. Can you say it? It's not as hard as it looks at first. *Hat SHEP sut*. She was the first woman ruler known to history.

A king's or queen's name always had a line drawn around it, like the one you see around the name of Hatshepsut, in order to mark it more prominently and give it more importance. It was something like the frame that we put around a fine picture to make it look better where it hangs on the wall.

Hatshepsut in hieroglyphic writing

There was no paper in those days and so the Egyptians wrote on the stalks of a plant called papyrus that grew in the water. They pressed the thick stalks until they were thin and flat and looked like paper. It is from this name *papyrus* that we get the name *paper*. Can you see that *paper* and *papyrus* look and sound something alike? The Egyptians' books were written by hand, of course, but they had no pencils nor pens nor ink with which to write. For a pen they used a reed, split at the end, and for ink a mixture of water and soot.

Their books were not made of separate pages like our books, but from long sheets of papyrus pasted together. This was rolled up to form what was called a scroll, something like a roll of wallpaper, and was read as it was unrolled.

Stories of their kings and battles and great events in their history they used to write on the walls of their buildings and monuments. This writing they carved into the stone, so that it would last much longer than that on the papyrus leaves.

All the old Egyptians, who wrote in hieroglyphics and knew how to read this writing, had died long since, and for a great many years no one knew what such writing meant. But a man found out by accident how to read and understand hieroglyphics once again. This is the way he happened to do so.

The Nile separates into different streams before it flows into the Mediterranean Sea. At the mouth of one of these streams is a port called Rosetta.[1]

One day some soldiers were digging near Rosetta when they found a stone, something like a tombstone with three kinds of writing on it. The top writing was in pictures, which we now call hieroglyphics, and no one understood what it meant. Below this was written what was supposed to be the same story in the Greek language, and a great many people do understand Greek. All one had to do, therefore, to find out the meaning

[1] Rosetta [rō zet′ ə]

of the hieroglyphics, was to compare the two writings. It was like reading secret writing when we know what the letters stand for. You may have tried to solve a puzzle in the back of your magazine, and this was just such an interesting puzzle, only there was no one to tell the answers.

The puzzle was not as easy as it sounds, however, for it took a clever man almost twenty years to solve it. That is a long time for anyone to spend in trying to solve a puzzle, isn't it? But after this *key* to the puzzle was found, men were able to read all of the hieroglyphics in Egypt and so to find out what happened in that country long ago.

This stone is called the Rosetta Stone. It is now in the great British Museum in London and is very famous, because from it we were able to learn so much history that we otherwise would not have known.

We know that Egypt was a fine place to live. It was chiefly on account of a habit of the river Nile—a bad habit you might at first think it—a habit of flooding the country once a year.

It rained so hard that the water filled up the river Nile, overflowed its banks, and spread water and mud far out over the land, but not very deep.

The people knew when the overflow was coming. They invented a calendar to keep track of it. After most of the water dried up, it left a layer of rich, dark, moist earth over the whole valley. This was a natural fertilizer, like compost that some of your families may use in your own gardens. This fertile soil made it easy to grow dates, wheat, and other good things to eat.

We know also that Egypt was ruled by a king who was called a pharaoh. The first Egyptian king whose name we know was Menes.[2] He came from southern Egypt and conquered the north. He united the country under his rule. He also declared that he was a god. So Egyptians believed that they should obey him both because he was king and because he was a god. Menes lived around 3100 B.C.

Menes, 3100 B.C.

[2] Menes [mē′ nēz]

People in Egypt were divided into classes. Children in each class usually became what their parents had been. Only a very few ever got to move up.

The highest class of people were called priests. They were not like priests or ministers of a church nowadays, however, for there was no church at that time. The priests made the religion and rules, which everyone had to obey as everybody does the laws of our land.

The priests were not only priests; they were doctors and lawyers and engineers, as well. They were the best-educated class, and they were the only people who knew how to read and write, for it was very difficult, as you might suppose, to learn how to read and write hieroglyphics.

The next highest class to the priests were the soldiers, and below these were the lower classes—farmers, shepherds, shopkeepers, merchants, mechanics, and last of all the swineherds.

The Egyptians did not worship one God as we do. They believed in hundreds of gods and goddesses, and they had a special god for every sort of thing, who ruled over and had charge of that thing— a god of the farms, a god of the home, and so on. Some of their gods were good and some were bad, but the Egyptians prayed to them all.

Osiris[3] was the chief god, and Isis[4] was his wife. Osiris was the god of farming and judge of the dead. Their son, Horus,[5] had the head of a falcon.

Many of their gods had bodies of men with heads of animals, animals they thought sacred. The dog and the cat were sacred animals. The ibis, which is a bird like a stork, was another. Then there was the beetle, which was called a scarab. If anyone killed a sacred animal he was put to death, for the Egyptians thought it much worse to kill a sacred and holy creature than to kill even a human being.

[3] Osiris [ō sī′ ris]   [5] Horus [hôr′ əs]
[4] Isis [ī′ sis]

7

The Tomb Builders

THE Egyptians believed that when they died, their souls stayed near by their bodies. So when a person died, they put in the tomb with him all sorts of things that he had used in daily life—things to eat and drink, furniture and dishes, toys and games. They thought the soul would return to its own body at the day of judgment. They wanted their bodies to be kept from decaying until judgment day, in order that the soul

Tutankhamen's¹ tomb showing foods preserved

might then have a body to return to. So they pickled the bodies of the dead by soaking them in a mineral called natron and wrapping them round and round and round with a cloth like a bandage. A dead body pickled in this way is called a *mummy*, and after thousands of years the mummies of the Egyptians may still be seen. Most of them are not, however, in the tombs where they were at first placed. They have been

¹ Tutankhamen [to͞ot äng kä΄ mən]

moved away and put in museums, and we may see them there now. Although they are yellow and dried up, they still look like

Little old men
All skin and bones.

At first only kings or important people of the highest classes were made mummies, but after a while all the classes, except perhaps the lowest, were treated in the same way. Sacred animals from beetles to cows were also made into mummies.

When an Egyptian died, his friends heaped up a few stones over his body just to cover it up decently and keep it from being stolen or destroyed by those wild animals that fed on dead bodies. But a king or a rich man wanted a bigger pile of stones over his body than just ordinary people had. To make sure that his pile would be big enough, a king built it for himself before he died. Each king tried to make his pile larger than anyone else's until at last the pile of stones became so big it was a hill of rocks and called a *pyramid*. The pyramids therefore were tombs of the kings, who built them while they were alive, to be monuments to themselves when they were dead. In fact a king was much more interested in building a home for his dead body than he was in a home for his live body. So, instead of palaces, kings built pyramids. There are many of these pyramids built along the bank of the Nile, and most of them were built, we think, just after 3000 B.C.

In Nubia, up the Nile farther south in Africa, in what is now the modern nation of Sudan, kings also built pyramids for themselves. This is not surprising since Egyptians and Nubians shared many of the same religious beliefs.

When a building is being put up nowadays, men use derricks and cranes and engines to haul and raise heavy stones and beams. But the Egyptians had no such machinery, and though they used huge stones to build the pyramids, they had to drag these stones for many miles and raise them into place simply by pushing and pulling them. The three biggest of all the pyramids are near the city of Cairo.[2] The largest one of them, which is called the Great Pyramid, was built by a king named Cheops.[3] That name is pronounced just like *KEY ops*. Here is his date:

Cheops.............................2900 B.C.

It is said that one hundred thousand men worked twenty years to build his pyramid. It is one of the largest buildings in the world, and some of the blocks of stone themselves are

Cheops building his pyramid

as big as a small house. I have been to the top if it, and it is like climbing a steep mountain with rocky sides. I have also been far inside to the cave-like room in the center where Cheops's mummy was placed. There is nothing in there now, however, except bats that fly about in the darkness, for the mummy has disappeared—been stolen, perhaps.

Near the Pyramid of Cheops is the Sphinx.[4] It is a huge statue of a lion with a man's head. Although it is big, it was carved out of one single rock. The Sphinx is a statue of the god of the morning, and the head is that of one of the Egyptian pharaohs who built a pyramid near that of Cheops. The desert sand has covered the paws and most of the body.

---

[2] Cairo [kī´ rō]   [3] Cheops [kē´ ops]   [4] Sphinx [sfingks]

Though the sand has been dug away from time to time, the wind quickly covers the body with sand again.

The Egyptians carved other large statues of men and women out of rock. These figures are usually many times bigger than life-size, and sit or stand stiffly erect with both feet flat on the ground and hands close to the body in the position some children take when they *sit* for their photograph.

They built huge houses for their gods. These were called temples. These temples had gigantic—that's the way it is spelled, though it means *giant-ic*—columns and pillars. Ordinary people standing beside them look like dwarfs.

Egyptian Temple

Here is one of these temples, and you can see how different it is from a church.

They decorated their temples and pyramids, and the cases in which the mummies were put, with paintings. They did not try to make these paintings look real, however. For example, when they wanted to make a picture of water, they simply made zigzag lines to represent waves and colored them blue-green. When they wanted to draw a row of men behind a row in front, they put those in back *on top* of those in front. To show that a man was a king, they made him larger than the other men in the picture.

The Egyptians used bright colors in their pictures. They used a lot of red, yellow, and brown. You can see in their pictures that some people had dark skin and some had light tan skin. At first people from southern Egypt had darker skin, and people from near the Mediterranean had lighter skin. Over the years, people moved all over Egypt and then you could no longer tell where a person came from by the color of his or her skin.

8

A Rich Land Where
There Was No Money

YOU have read in fairy tales of a land where cakes and candy and sugarplums grow on trees, where everything you want to eat or to play with can be had just by picking it. Well, long, long ago people used to think there had been really such a country, and where do you suppose they said it was? Somewhere near the Tigris and Euphrates Rivers—those rivers with the strange names I asked you to learn—and they called this spot the Garden of Eden. We do not know exactly where it was, for there is no such place now quite as wonderful as the Garden of Eden was supposed to be.

Egypt was a land of one river, the Nile. The land of the Two Rivers had several names.

Let us suppose we are flying over the country in an airplane and looking down at the land between these two rivers. It is called Mesopotamia, which is two Greek words simply meaning *between the rivers.*

See the land over there by the upper Tigris. It is called Assyria.

See the land near where the rivers join each other. That is called Babylonia.[1]

See the land near where they empty. That is called Chaldea.[2]

---

[1] Babylonia [bab ə lōʹ nē ə]   [2] Chaldea[kal dēʹ ə]

The ancient Mediterranean world

And see over there is Mount Ararat,[3] where it is supposed Noah's Ark rested after the flood.

Here are a lot of new names. A young friend of mine had a train of toy cars. He had noticed that the cars on which he had ridden had names, and so he gave his toy cars names also. He called them:

ASSYRIA	MESOPOTAMIA
BABYLONIA	ARARAT
CHALDEA	EUPHRATES

[3] Ararat [ar′ ə rat]

Babylonia was a very rich country, for the two rivers brought down and dropped great quantities of earth just as the Nile did in Egypt, and this made very rich soil. Wheat, from which we make bread, is called the staff of life. It is the most valuable of all foods which grow. It is supposed that wheat first grew in Babylonia. Dates in that part of the world are almost as important a food as wheat. Dates, too, grow there very plentifully. Now, you may think dates are something to be eaten almost like candy, but in Babylonia dates took the place of oatmeal. In the rivers there were quantities of good fish, and as fishing was just fun, you see that the people who lived in Babylonia—the Babylonians, as they were called—had plenty of good food. No one had any money in those days; people had pigs and sheep and goats, and a man was rich who had much of these goods. Early on, if a man wanted to buy or sell, he had to buy or sell by trading something he had for something he wanted.

Somewhere in Babylonia the people built a great tower called the *Tower of Babel*, which you have probably heard about. It was more like a mountain than a tower. They built other towers, too. Some say the Tower of Babel and towers like it were built so that the people might have a high place to which they could climb in case of another flood. Others give a different reason. They say that the people who built these towers came to Babylonia from farther north where there were mountains. In this northern land they had always placed their altars on the top of a mountain, to be close to heaven. So when they moved to a flat country like Mesopotamia and Babylonia, where there were not mountains, they *built* mountains in order to have a high place for the altar on top. To reach the top of these mountains or towers, they made, instead of a staircase on the inside, a slanting roadway that wound around the outside in somewhat the way a road winds around a mountain.

There was hardly any stone either in or near Babylonia as there was in

Egypt, and so the Babylonians built their buildings of bricks, which were made of mud formed into blocks and dried in the sun. In the course of time, bricks of this sort crumble and turn back into dust again, just as mud pies that you might make would do. This is the reason why all that is left of the towers and the other buildings that were put up so long ago are now simply hills of clay into which the brick has turned.

The Egyptians wrote on papyrus or carved their history in stone, but the Babylonians had neither papyrus nor stone. All they had were bricks. So they wrote on bricks before they were dried, while they were still soft clay. This writing was made by punching marks into the clay with the end of a stick. It was called *cuneiform*, which means wedge-shaped, for it looked like little groups of wedge-shaped marks, like chicken-tracks, made in the mud. I have seen boys' writing that looked more like cuneiform than it did like English.

As the Babylonians watched their flocks by day and night, they watched also the sun and the moon and the stars moving across the sky. So they came to know a great deal about these heavenly bodies.

Did you ever see the moon in the daytime?

Oh, yes, you can.

Well, every once in a great while the moon as it moves across the sky gets in front of the sun and shuts out its light—just as, if you should put a plate in front of an electric lamp, the plate would block the light from the lamp. It may be ten o'clock in the morning and broad daylight, when suddenly the sun is covered up by the moon, and it becomes night and the stars shine out, and chickens, thinking it is night, go to roost. But in a few moments the moon passes by and the sun shines out once again. This is called an *eclipse* of the sun.

Now you may never have seen an eclipse of the sun, but some day you may. If you do, I hope you do not think the way ignorant people always

have: they think that
something dreadful is
going to happen—the
end of the world,
perhaps, just because
they have never seen
such a strange sight
before and do not
know that it is a thing
that happens regularly
and that no harm
comes from it.

Babylonians watching eclipse

Well, nearly twenty-three hundred years before Christ, in 2300 B.C., the Babylonians told beforehand just when there was going to be an eclipse of the sun. They had watched the moon moving across the sky and they had figured out how long it would be before it would catch up with the sun and cross directly over it. You see how much the old Babylonians knew about such things. Men who study the stars and other heavenly bodies are called *astronomers*, and the Babylonians, therefore, were famous astronomers. The Babylonians worshiped these wonderful heavenly bodies the sun, moon, and stars—that they knew so well.

The first king of Babylonia whom we know much about—and that much is very little—was Sargon I,[4] who may have lived about the same time that the pyramids were built in Egypt.

About 1770 B.C. Babylonia had a king known far and wide for the laws he made. His name was Hammurabi,[5] and we still have the code of laws he made though we no longer obey them. They were carved into a stone

---

[4] Sargon I [sär′ gon]

[5] Hammurabi [hä moo′ rä′ bē]

in cuneiform, and we have the stone. Sargon and Hammurabi are strange names like no one's name you ever heard before, yet they are real names of real kings who ruled over real people.

9

The Jews Search for a Home

YOU are spells *Ur.* It is one of the shortest names I know. It is the name of a little place in that part of Babylonia called Chaldea. In this place—about nineteen hundred years B.C.—there lived a man named Abraham.[1] Abraham had a very large family and though he had no money, he was rich. He had large herds of sheep and goats, and these were the chief riches in those days. Now Abraham believed in one God, as we do, while his neighbors, the Babylonians, worshiped many gods and the heavenly bodies, such as the sun, moon, and stars, as I have just said. Abraham did not agree with his neighbors for this reason; and his neighbors didn't agree with him, either, for they thought his ideas were peculiar or even crazy. So, about nineteen hundred years before Christ, Abraham took his large family, his flocks, and his herds and moved to a land called Canaan,[2] far away near the Mediterranean Sea.

Abraham lived to be a very old man, and he had a large family. One of his grandsons named Jacob, who was also known by the name of Israel,[3] had a son Joseph. You probably remember the Bible story of Jacob's favorite son Joseph with the coat of many colors. Joseph's brothers were jealous of him, as children and even dogs are apt to be jealous of anyone who is liked better than they are. So they put Joseph into a well and then

---

[1] Abraham [ā′ brə ham]   [2] Canaan [kā′ nən]   [3] Israel, Israelites [iz′ rē əl, iz′ rē əl ĭt]

sold him as a slave to
some Egyptians who
were passing by. Then
they told their father
Jacob that Joseph
had been killed by
wild animals. The

Abraham leaving Ur, 1900 B.C.

Egyptians took Joseph to far-off Egypt—far away from Canaan.

As I told you, it was very difficult for anyone to work his way up out of his class to a higher class. Nevertheless, Joseph was a slave in Egypt, and he was so bright that at last he became one of the rulers in Egypt.

At that time when he was ruler, there came a famine in Canaan and there was no food. In Egypt, however, there was plenty of food stored up. So Joseph's wicked brothers went down to Egypt to beg the rulers for bread. They probably thought by that time their brother was dead. They did not know that he had become such a great man and that he was now the ruler from whom they were begging food. You can imagine how surprised they were and how ashamed they must have felt when they found out that the great ruler was their own brother, whom they had planned to kill and then had sold as a slave.

Joseph might have let his brothers starve to death or put them in prison, or sent them back to Canaan without anything, if he had wanted to revenge himself on them. Instead of doing any of these things, he gave them not only all the food they wanted and more to take back home, but made them rich presents besides. Then he told them to go back and get the rest of his family and return with them to Egypt, and he promised to give them a piece of land called Goshen where there would be no famines and they might live happily. They did as they were told, and Israel and his sons and all their families came down and settled in Goshen about

1700 B.C. They were called Israelites, which means of course the children of Israel. These are the people we now call the Jews.

After Joseph, who was of course an Israelite himself, died, the kings or Pharaohs of Egypt did not like these foreign people and treated them very badly, as other peoples have often treated the Jews badly ever since. Though the Jews and their children and children's children lived in Egypt for about four hundred years, they were enslaved by the Egyptians.

Now about four hundred years from the time the Jews first came into Egypt—400 from 1700 is 1300 B.C.—there was a ruler of Egypt called Rameses[4] the Great.

Rameses's mummy

Rameses so feared the growing number of Jews that finally he gave orders to have every Jewish boy baby killed. In this way he thought to control these people. One little Jewish boy named Moses, however, was saved, and when he grew up he became the greatest leader of his people. Moses wanted to get the Jews out of this hostile country where the people worshiped false gods. At last he led all his people out of Egypt across the Red Sea. This was called the *Exodus*,[5] and it took place about 1300 B.C.

After the Jews had left Egypt, they first stopped at the foot of a mountain called Mount Sinai,[6] while Moses went up to the top where he could be by himself and learn what God wanted him and the Jews to do. Moses spent forty days praying on top of the mountain. When he came down from the mountain-top, he brought with him the Ten Commandments, the same Ten Commandments you may have learned in Sunday school. But Moses had been gone so long that when he came

---

[4] Rameses [ram´ ə sēz]   [5] Exodus [ek´ sə dəs]   [6] Sinai [sī´ nī]

Rameses the Great

back again to his people, he found them worshiping a golden calf as the Egyptians had done. They had lived in Egypt until they had come to think it was all right to worship idols.

Moses was very angry. It was high time, he thought, that they should get rid of the bad influence of their old Egyptian neighbors. At last he succeeded in making them worship God again and gave them the Ten

Commandments for their rule of life. So Moses is called a lawgiver and the first teacher of the Jewish religion. The Jews wandered from place to place for a great many years before Moses died. Then Joshua, their new leader, led them into Canaan.

The Jews had no kings. They were ruled by men called judges, but the judges lived very simply, just like everyone else and not like kings in palaces with servants and fine robes and rich jewels. But the Jews thought it would be better to have a real king like their neighbors had.

At last a judge who was named Samuel said they should have a king, and Saul was chosen. Then Samuel poured olive-oil over Saul's head. To us this seems a strange thing to do, but it took the place of putting a crown on his head and was a sign that he was to be king. Samuel, therefore, was the last one of their judges, and Saul was their first king.

All other nations at that time believed as the Egyptians and Chaldeans did, in many different gods. The Jews alone believed in one God and lived by laws they believed God had given them. They had a holy book that contained these laws and recorded their early history. This book is also known as the Old Testament and has been made a part of the Christian Bible. Many Old Testament stories also appear in the Koran,[7] the Muslims'[8] holy book.

This is the story of the Jews, who gave us the Old Testament and the Ten Commandments, and here is the way they wandered:

From Ur to Canaan—1900 B.C.

From Canaan to Egypt—1700 B.C.

From Egypt back to Canaan—1300 B.C. You can see that they finally settled down in Canaan, and then they called that land their home.

---

[7] Koran [kə rän'] (Qur'an)   [8]Muslims [muz' limz]

10

Fairy-Tale Gods

THERE was once a man named Hellen—strange-sounding name for a man, isn't it? He had a great many children and children's children, and they called themselves Hellenes. They lived in a little scrap of a country that juts into the Mediterranean Sea, and they called their land Hellas.[1] I once upset a bottle of ink on my desk, and the ink ran out into a wriggly spot that looked exactly as Hellas does on the map. Though Hellas is hardly any bigger than one of our states, its history is more famous than that of any other country of its size in the world. We call Hellas *Greece* and the people who lived there *Greeks*.

About the same time, the Jews were leaving Egypt, about the time when people were beginning to use iron instead of bronze, that is, about 1300 B.C., we first begin to hear of Hellas and the Hellenes, of Greece and the Greeks.

The Greeks believed in many gods, not in one God, as we do and as the Jews do, and their gods were more like people in fairy tales than like divine beings. Many beautiful statues have been made of their different gods, and poems and stories have been written about them.

There were twelve—just a dozen—chief gods. Six of these were female gods, known as goddesses. They were supposed to live on Mount Olympus, which was the highest mountain in Greece. These gods were not always good, but often quarreled and cheated and did even worse things. The gods lived on a kind of food that was much more delicious

---

[1] Hellas [hel′ əs]

than what we eat. It was called nectar and ambrosia, and the Greeks thought it made those who ate it immortal; that is, so that they would never die.

Let me introduce you to the family of the gods. I know you will be pleased to meet them. Most of them are known by two names; the first name is Greek, the second is Roman.

Zeus[2] or *Jupiter* is the father of the gods and the king who rules over all human beings. He sits on a throne and holds a zigzag flash of lightning called a thunderbolt in his hand. An eagle, the king of birds, is usually by his side.

Hera[3] or *Juno* is his wife and the queen of the gods. She carries a scepter, and her pet bird, the peacock, is often with her.

Poseidon[4] or *Neptune* is one of the brothers of Zeus. He rules over the sea. He rides in a chariot drawn by sea-horses and carries in his hand a trident, which looks like a pitchfork with three points. He can make a storm at sea or quiet the waves simply by striking them with his trident.

Hephaestus[5] or *Vulcan* is the god of fire. He is a lame blacksmith and works at a forge. His forge is said to be in the cave of a mountain, and as smoke and fire come forth from some mountains they are called volcanoes after the god Vulcan inside.

Apollo[6] is the most beautiful of all the gods; his name is the same to both Greeks and Romans. Apollo is the god of the sun and of song and music. Every morning—so the Greeks said—he drives his sun-chariot across the sky from the east to the west, and this makes the sunlighted day.

Artemis[7] or *Diana* is the twin sister of Apollo. She is the goddess of the moon and of hunting.

---

[2] Zeus [zoos]
[3] Hera [hēr′ ə]
[4] Poseidon [pō sīd′ n]
[5] Hephaestus [hi fes′ təs]
[6] Apollo [ə pol′ ō]
[7] Artemis [är′ tə mis]

Ares[8] or *Mars* is the terrible god of war, who is only happy when a war is going on—so that he is happy most of the time.

Hermes[9] or *Mercury* is the messenger of the gods. He has wings on his cap and on his sandals, and he carries in his hand a wonderful winged stick or wand, which, if placed between two people who are quarreling, will immediately make them friends. One day Hermes saw two snakes fighting and he put his wand between them, whereupon they twined around it as if in a loving hug, and ever since the snakes have remained entwined around it. This wand is called a *caduceus*.

Athena[10] or *Minerva* is the goddess of wisdom. She was born in a very strange way. One day Zeus had a terrible headache—what we call a *splitting* headache. It got worse and worse, until at last he could stand it no longer, but he took a very strange way to cure it. He called Hephaestus, the lame blacksmith, and told him to hit him on the head with his hammer. Though Hephaestus must have thought this a funny request, of course he had to obey the father god. So he struck Zeus a terrible blow on the head, whereupon there sprang forth Athena in all her armor, and the headache, of which she had been the cause, had gone. So she was born from his brain; that is why Athena is the goddess of wisdom. She founded a great city in Greece and named it Athens, after herself. She is supposed to look out for this city as a mother does for her child.

Aphrodite[11] or *Venus* is the goddess of love and beauty. She is the most beautiful of the goddesses, as Apollo is the most beautiful of the gods. She is said to have been born from the sea foam. Eros or Cupid, her son, is a chubby boy with a quiver of arrows on his back. He goes about shooting his invisible arrows into the hearts of human beings, but instead of dying when they are hit, they at once fall in love with someone. That is why we put hearts with arrows through them on valentines.

---

[8]Ares [âr´ ēz]
[9]Hermes [her´ mēz]

[10]Athena [ə thē´ nə]
[11]Aphrodite [af r ədī´ tē]

Birth of Minerva or Athena

Hestia or *Vesta* is the goddess of the home and fireside, who looks out for the family.

Demeter[12] or *Ceres*[13] is the goddess of the farmer.

These are the twelve gods and goddesses of the Olympian family.

Hades or *Pluto* is a brother of Zeus. He rules the world underground and lives down there.

There are many other less important gods and goddesses as well as some gods that are half human, such as the three Fates, the three Graces, and the nine Muses.

Some of the planets in the sky that look like stars are still called by the names of these gods. Jupiter is the name of the largest planet. Mars is the name of one that is reddish—the color of blood. Venus is the name of one

---

[12] Demeter [di mē′ tər]   [13] Ceres [sēr′ ēz]

that is very beautiful. There is also a Mercury, a Neptune, and a Pluto.

The Greeks' prayers to their gods were not like ours. Instead of kneeling and closing their eyes as we do, they stood up and stretched their arms straight out before them. They did not pray to be forgiven for their sins and to be made better. They prayed for victory over their enemies or to be protected from harm.

When they prayed, they often made the gods an offering of animals, fruit, honey, or wine in order to please them so that the gods or goddesses would grant their prayer. The wine they poured out on the ground, thinking the gods would like to have them do this. The animals they killed and then burned by building a fire under them on an altar. This was called a *sacrifice*. Their idea seemed to be that even though the gods could not eat the meat of the animals nor drink the wine themselves, they liked to have something *given up* for them. Even today we say a person makes a sacrifice when he *gives up* something for another person.

When the Greeks were sacrificing, they usually looked for some sign to tell whether the gods were pleased with the sacrifice and whether they would answer the prayer and do what was asked. A flock of birds flying overhead, a flash of lightning, or any unusual happening they thought was a sign which meant something. Such signs were called *omens*. Some omens were good and showed that the god would do what he was asked, and some omens were very much like some of the signs that people believe in even today when they say it is a good sign or good luck if you see the new moon over the right shoulder, or a bad sign or bad luck if you spill the salt.

Not so very far from Athens is a mountain called Mount Parnassus.[14] On the side of Mount Parnassus was a town called Delphi.[15] In the town of Delphi there was a crack in the ground, from which gas came forth, somewhat as it does from cracks in a volcano. This gas was supposed to be the breath of the god Apollo, and there was a woman priest called a priestess, who sat on a three-legged stool or tripod over the crack so as to breathe the gas. She would become delirious, as some people do when

---

[14] Parnassus [pär nas′ əs]   [15] Delphi [del′ fī]

they are sick with fever and we say they are *out of their heads*, and when people asked her questions she would mutter strange things and a priest would tell what she meant. This place was called the Delphic Oracle, and people would go long distances to ask the oracle questions, for they thought Apollo was answering them.

The Greeks went to the oracle whenever they wanted to know what to do or what was going to happen, and they firmly believed in what the oracle told them. Usually, however, the answers of the oracle were like a riddle, so that they could be understood in more than one way. For instance, a king who was about to go to war with another king asked the oracle who would win. The oracle replied, "A great kingdom will fall." What do you suppose the oracle meant? Such an answer, which you can understand in two or three ways, is still called *oracular*.

11

A Fairy-Tale War

THE history of countries usually begins—and also ends—with war. The first great happening in the history of Greece was a war. It was called the Trojan War and was supposed to have taken place about twelve hundred years before Christ, or not long after the beginning of the Iron Age. But we are not only unsure of the date; we are not even sure that there ever was such a war, for a great deal of it, we know is simply fairy tale. This is the way the tale goes.

Once there was a wedding feast of the gods and goddesses on Mount Olympus, when suddenly a goddess who had not been invited threw a golden apple on the table. On the apple were written these words:

TO THE FAIREST.

The goddess who had thrown the apple was the goddess of quarreling; and true to her name she *did* start a quarrel, for each of the goddesses, like vain human beings, thought she was the fairest and should have the apple. At last they called in a shepherd boy named Paris to decide who was the fairest.

Each goddess offered Paris a present if he would choose her. Hera, the queen of the gods, offered to make him a king; Athena, the goddess of wisdom, offered to make him wise; but Aphrodite, the goddess of beauty, offered to give him the most beautiful girl in the world for his wife.

Now, Paris was not really a shepherd boy but the son of Priam,[1] the king of Troy, which was a city on the seashore opposite Greece. When he was a baby, Paris had been left on a mountain to die, but he had been found by a shepherd and was brought up by him as his own child.

Paris didn't care about being wise; he didn't care about being king; what he did want was to have the most beautiful woman in the world for his wife, and so he gave the apple to Aphrodite.

Now the most beautiful woman in the world was named Helen, and she was already married to Menelaus,[2] the king of Sparta. In spite of that fact, Aphrodite told Paris to go to Sparta in Greece, where he would find Helen, and then run away with her. So Paris went to Sparta to visit King Menelaus and was royally entertained by him. And then Paris, although he had been treated so kindly and had been trusted, one night stole Helen away and carried her off across the sea to Troy.

Menelaus and the Greeks were naturally very angry and immediately prepared for war and sailed off for Troy to get Helen back. Now, in ancient times all cities had walls built around them to protect them from the enemy. As there were no cannons nor guns nor deadly weapons such as are used in war nowadays, it was very hard to get into a walled city or capture it. Troy was protected in this way by walls; and though the Greeks tried for ten years to capture it, at the end of the ten years Troy was still unconquered.

At last the Greeks decided to try a trick to get into the city. They built a huge horse of wood, and inside this wooden horse they put soldiers. They placed the horse in front of the city walls and then sailed away as if at last they were giving up the war. The Trojans were told by a spy that

---

[1] Priam [prī′ əm]   [2] Menelaus [menl ā′ ə s]

the horse was a gift of the gods and that they ought to take it into the city. A Trojan priest named Laocoon,[3] however, told his people not to have anything to do with the horse, for he suspected a trick. But people seldom take advice when told *not* to do what they want to do.

Just then some huge snakes came out of the sea and attacked Laocoon and his two sons and, twining around them, strangled them to death. The Trojans thought this was a sign from the gods, or an omen as they would have said, that they should not believe Laocoon; so they determined to take the horse into the city against his advice. The horse was so big, however, that it would not go through the gates, and in order to get it inside the walls they had to tear down part of the wall itself. When night fell, the Greek soldiers came out of the horse and opened the gates of the city. The other Greeks, who had been waiting just out of sight, returned and entered through the gates and the hole the Trojans had made in the wall. Troy was easily conquered then, and the city was burned to the ground, and Helen's husband carried her back to Greece. Because of this horse trick, we still have a saying, "Beware of Greeks bearing gifts," which is as much as to say, "Look out for an enemy who brings you a present."

The story of the Trojan War was told in two long poems. Some people think they are the finest poems that were ever written. One of these poems is called the *Iliad*, from the name of the city of Troy, which was also known as Ilium. The *Iliad* describes the Trojan War itself. The other poem is called the *Odyssey*[4] and describes the adventures of one of the Greek heroes on his way home after the war was over. The Greek hero's name was Odysseus,[5] which gives the name Odyssey to the book, but he was also called Ulysses.[6] These poems, the *Iliad* and the *Odyssey*, were composed by a Greek poet named Homer, who is supposed to have lived at some time before 700 B.C.

Homer may have been a bard; that is, a singing poet who went about

---

[3] Laocoon [lā ok′ ō on]
[4] Odyssey [od′ ə sē]
[5] Odysseus [ō dis′ ē əs]
[6] Ulysses [yoo lis′ ēz]

from place to place and sang his songs to the people. He probably collected old legends and made his poems from them. Usually a bard played on a lyre as he sang, and the people gave him something to eat or a place to sleep to pay him for his songs.

People enjoyed hearing Homer's songs. They learned them by heart, and mothers taught them to their children after Homer had died. The poems are written down in Greek, and you may some day read them in Greek, if you study that language, or at least in an English translation.

I have told you that Homer probably made his songs out of old legends. There were many legends, too, about Homer himself, and we don't know which are true. He was said to have been blind. Seven different cities each proudly claimed that Homer had been born in their city, so you can count six or seven legends right there!

12

The Kings of the Jews

A few centuries before Homer was singing his wonderful songs through the streets of Greece, a great king of the Jews was singing other wonderful songs in Canaan. This king was named David, and he wasn't born a king. He was only a shepherd boy in King Saul's army. This is the way he happened to become king.

At first, as you remember, the Jews had no kings; but they had asked for kings, and at last they were given one by the name of Saul.

David had killed the giant Goliath.[1] We all love this Bible story because we are always glad when the skillful little chap beats the great, big, bragging bully.

Well, King Saul had a daughter, and she fell in love with this brave and athletic young David the Giant-Killer, and at last they were married.

After Saul died, David became king, and he was the greatest king the Jews had ever had. Although Saul had been king, he had lived in a tent, not in a palace, and he didn't even have a capital city.

David eventually conquered a city in Canaan called Jerusalem and made this city the capital of the Jews.

David was not only a brave warrior and a great king; he wrote beautiful songs as well.

---

[1] Goliath [gə li· əth]

The blind poet Homer sang of his fairy-tale gods. The great King David sang of his one God.

These songs are the *Psalms*, which are still read and sung in churches and synagogues.

Nowadays even a popular song is popular for only a few months, but the songs that David wrote almost three thousand years ago are still popular today! The Twenty-third Psalm, which starts, "The Lord is my shepherd," is one of the most beautiful and a good one to learn by heart. David likens himself to a sheep and his Lord to a good shepherd, who tenderly looks out for the comfort and safety of his sheep.

David's son was named Solomon, and when David died Solomon became king.

If a good fairy had asked you what you would rather have than anything in the world, I wonder what you would have chosen. When Solomon became king, God is said to have appeared to him in a dream and asked him what he would rather have than anything else in the world. Instead of saying he wanted to be made rich or powerful, Solomon asked to be made wise, and God said He would make him the wisest man that ever lived. Here is a story that shows how wise he was.

Once upon a time two women came to Solomon with a baby, and each woman said the baby was her own child. Solomon called for a sword and said, "Cut the baby in two, and give each a half." One of the women cried out to give the baby to the other rather than do this, and Solomon then knew who was the real mother and ordered the baby to be given to her.

Solomon built a magnificent temple made of cedar-wood, from the famous forest of Lebanon, and of marble and gold and studded with jewels. Then he built himself a wonderful palace, which was so gorgeous and splendid that people came from all over the world to see it. The Bible tells us just how large this temple and palace were, not in feet but in cubits. A cubit was the distance from a man's elbow to the end of his middle finger, which is about one foot and a half.

The queen of Sheba,[2] among others, came a long distance across Arabia to hear the wise sayings of Solomon and see his palace and the temple he had built.

Although the palace and temple were considered extraordinarily magnificent at that time, you must remember that this was a thousand years before Christ.

Solomon's temple and palace have disappeared long since. But his wise sayings are preserved in many languages and read by many people all around the world. There are thousands of buildings now in the world that would make his palace, if still standing, look like a child's toy house. But no one has ever been able to say any better the things he said. Do you think you could? Suppose you try. Here are some of them. They are called proverbs.

A soft answer turneth away wrath;
but grievous words stir up anger.

What's that mean?

A good name is rather to be chosen than great
riches and loving favor rather than silver and gold.

What's that mean?

Let another man praise thee and not thine own mouth.

What's that mean?

---

[2] Sheba [shē′ bə]

Solomon was the last great king the Jews ever had. After he died the Jewish nation gradually broke up and then came back together again. Then, six hundred years later it finally went to pieces and, for about two thousand years, the Jewish people were without a king, without a capital, and without a country of their own, though they are found in many other countries of the world. Then at last they formed a new country, a country called Israel. Israel is in the land that used to be called Canaan.

13

The People Who Made Our A B C's

Long before people knew how to write, there lived a carpenter named Cadmus. One day he was at work on a house when he wanted a tool that he had left at home. Picking up a chip of wood, he wrote something on it and, handing it to his slave, told him to go to his home and give the chip to his wife, saying that it would tell her what he wanted. The slave, wondering, did as he was told. Cadmus's wife looked at the chip, and without a word handed the tool to the amazed slave, who thought the chip in some mysterious way had spoken the message. When he returned to Cadmus with the tool, he begged for the remarkable chip, and when it was given him, hung it around his neck for a charm.

Cadmus's slave and the chip

This is the story the Greeks told of the man they say invented the alphabet. We believe, however, that Cadmus was a mythical person, for the Greeks liked to make up such stories, and we think no *one* person made the alphabet. But Cadmus was a Phoenician[1] and we do know that the Phoenician people invented the alphabet on which ours is based. You

---

[1] Phoenicia, Phoenicians [fi nē′ shə, fin nē′ shənz]

probably call it your A B C's, but the Greeks had much harder names for the letters. They called A *alpha*, B *beta*, and so on. So the Greek boy spoke of learning his *alpha beta*, and that is why we call it the *alphabet*.

You may never have heard of Phoenicia or the Phoenician people. Yet, if there had been no such country as Phoenicia, you might now be learning at school to read and write in hieroglyphics or in cuneiform.

Up to this time, you know, people had very clumsy ways of writing. The Egyptians had to draw pictures, and the Babylonians made writing like chicken tracks. The alphabet that the Phoenicians invented had twenty-two letters, and from it we get the alphabet we use today.

Of course, we do not use just the same alphabet now that the Phoenicians did, but some of the letters are almost, if not quite, like those we now have after three thousand years. For instance the

Phoenician A was written on its side — ◁
E   "   "   backward — Ǝ
Z   "   "   just the same — Z
O   "   "   "   "   "   — O

The Phoenicians lived next door to the Jews; like the Jews, they were Semites. Their country was just north of the kingdom of the Jews; that is, above it on the map and lying along the shore of the Mediterranean Sea.

The Phoenicians had a great king named Hiram who lived at the same time as Solomon. In fact, Hiram was a friend of Solomon and sent him some of his best workmen to help build a temple at Jerusalem. Yet Hiram himself and the Phoenicians did not believe in the Jewish God.

The Phoenicians worshiped idols named Baal[2] and Moloch,[3] which they called gods of the sun. They also believed in a goddess of the moon named Astarte[4] and made sacrifices of live children to her idol, Fe-Fi-Fo-

---

[2] Baal [bäl]   [3] Moloch [mo′ lok]   [4] Astarte [a stär′ tē]

Fum; this is a real story and not a fairy tale. Just suppose you had been a child then!

The Phoenicians were great business people. They made many things to sell, such as objects carved from ivory, engraved gold and silver items, and beautiful glassware. They knew how to weave woolen and linen cloth, and were well known for the dyed cloth and robes that they manufactured.

They knew the secret of making a wonderful purple dye from the body of a little shell-fish that lived in the water near the city of Tyre.[5] This dye was known as Tyrian purple from the name of that city, and it was so beautiful that kings' robes were colored with it.

Tyre and Sidon[6] were the two chief cities of Phoenicia, and once upon a time they were two of the busiest cities in the world.

In order to find people to sell to, the Phoenicians traveled in boats all over the Mediterranean Sea and even went outside this sea into the Great Ocean. This opening is now called the Strait of Gibraltar, but was then known as the Pillars of Hercules.[7] They went as far as the British Isles and along the coast of Africa. Many other people in those days had not dared to go so far in boats; they thought they would come to the edge of the ocean and tumble off. But the Phoenicians had no such fear, and so they were the greatest sailors as well as the greatest traders of their times. Their ships were built from the cedar trees that grew on the slopes of their hills. The trees were called the cedars of Lebanon.

In one way, the Phoenicians were very shortsighted. They cut down all their wonderful cedar trees until almost none were left. Then no more ships—or anything else—could be made with the strong wood. Do you think we would ever do anything as foolish as that?

When the Phoenicians found good harbors for their boats, they often started little towns where they traded with the local people. Often they

---

[5] Tyre [tī′ ər]   [6] Sidon [sid′ n]   [7] Hercules [her′ kyə lēz]

drove a hard bargain, trading purple cloth worth very little for gold or silver or other things worth a great deal. On the coast of north Africa, one of these towns they started was called Carthage.[8] Carthage later grew to be very strong and wealthy—but you will have to wait a while until I come to that story.

14

Hard as Nails

OUR story goes back again to Greece, the land of Homer and the fairy-tale gods, and to Sparta, where Helen once lived.

About nine hundred years before Christ was born, there lived in Sparta a man named Lycurgus.[1] That is a hard name, and when you hear about this man you may think he was hard, too. Lycurgus wanted his city to be the greatest in the world.

First he had to find out what it was that made a city and a people great.

He started off and traveled for years and years, visiting all the chief countries of the world to see if he could learn what it was that made them great. And this is what he learned.

Wherever the people thought chiefly of fun and pleasure, of amusing themselves and having a good time—he found they were not good for much, not of much account—*not* great.

Wherever the people thought chiefly of hard work and did what they ought, whether it was pleasant or not, he found they were usually good for something—of some account—great.

So Lycurgus came back to his home Sparta and set to work to make a set of rules that he thought would make his people greater than all other people in the world. These rules were called a Code of Laws, and I think

---

[1] Lycurgus [lǐ kûr′ gəs]

you'll agree they were very hard, and they made the Spartans hard, too—as *hard as nails*. We shall see whether they made the Spartans really great, also.

To begin with, babies, as soon as they were born, were examined to see that they were strong and perfect. Whenever one was found who did not seem to be so, he or she was put out on the mountainside and left to die. Lycurgus wanted no weaklings in Sparta.

When boys were seven years old, they were taken from their mothers and put in a school, which was more like a soldiers' camp than a school, and they never lived anywhere else until they were sixty years old.

In this school they were not taught the things you are, but only the things that trained them to be good soldiers.

There were no such things as schoolbooks then.

There were no spelling books.

There were no arithmetics.

There were no geographies. No one knew enough about the world to write a geography.

There were no histories. No one knew much about things that had happened in the world before that time, and of course none of the history since then that you now study had taken place.

At certain times, the Spartan boy was whipped, not because he had done anything wrong, but just to teach him to suffer pain without whimpering. He would have been disgraced forever if he had cried, no matter how badly he was hurt.

He was exercised and drilled and worked until he was ready to drop. Still he was obliged to keep on, no matter how tired or hungry or sleepy or aching he might be, and he must never show by any sign how he felt.

He was made to eat the worst kind of food, to go hungry and thirsty for long periods of time, to go out in the bitter cold with little or no clothing, just to get used to such hardships and able to bear all sorts of discomforts. This kind of training, this kind of hardening, is therefore called *Spartan discipline*. How do you think you would have liked it?

The Spartans' food, clothing, and lodging were all furnished them, though it was very poor food and poor clothing and poor lodging. They were not allowed good things to eat, soft beds to lie on, or fine clothing to wear. Such things were called luxuries, and luxuries, Lycurgus thought, would make people soft and weak, and he wanted his people hard and strong.

The Spartans were even taught to speak in a short and blunt manner; they were taught not to waste words; they must say what they had to say in as few words as possible. This manner of speaking we call *laconic*[2] from the name Laconia, the state in which Sparta was located.

Once a king wrote to the Spartans a threatening letter, saying that they had better do what he told them to, for *if* he came and took their country, he would destroy their city and make them slaves.

The Spartans sent a messenger back with their answer, and when the letter was opened, it contained only one word:

"IF!"

Even today, we call such an answer, short but to the point, a laconic answer.

Did all this hard training and hard work make the Spartans the greatest people in the world?

Lycurgus did make the Spartans the strongest and best fighters in the world—but—

The Spartans conquered all the peoples around about them, though there were ten times as many—but—

They made these people their slaves, who did all their farming and other work—but—

---

[2] laconic [lə kon′ ik]

We shall see later whether Lycurgus's idea was right.

North of Sparta was another great city of Greece called Athens. There were, of course, many other towns in Greece, but Sparta and Athens were the most important. In Athens the people lived and thought quite differently from those in Sparta.

The Athenians[3] were just as fond of everything beautiful as the Spartans were of discipline and of everything military.

The Athenians loved athletic games of all sorts just as the Spartans did, but they also loved music and poetry and beautiful statues, paintings, vases, buildings, and such things that are known as the arts.

The Athenians believed in training the mind *as well* as the body. The Spartans believed the training of the body was the all-important thing. Which do you like better, the Athenians' idea or the Spartans' idea?

Once at a big game a very old man was looking for a seat on the Athenians' side. There was no seat empty, and no Athenian offered to give him one. Whereupon the Spartans called to the old man and gave him the best seat on their side. The Athenians cheered the Spartans to show how fine they thought this act. At this the Spartans said:

"The Athenians *know* what is right but they don't *do* it."

---

[3] Athenians [ə thē′ nē ə nz]

15

The Crown of Leaves

GREEK boys and young men and even girls loved all sorts of outdoor sports.

They didn't play football or baseball or basketball, but they ran and jumped and wrestled and boxed and threw the discus—a thing like a big, heavy dinner plate of iron.

From time to time matches were held in different parts of Greece to see who was the best in these sports.

The Big Meet, however, took place only once every four years at a place called Olympia[1] in southern Greece, for all the winners from different parts of the country were here matched against each other to see who should be the champion of all Greece.

The time when the games were held was a great national holiday, for the games were in honor of the head god, Zeus, as the Greeks called him. People came from far and wide to see the games, much as they do now when a World's Fair is held or a modern Olympics.

Only Greeks could enter this contest, and only those who had never committed a crime or broken any laws—as a boy or girl nowadays must have a clean record in order to be allowed to play on a college or school team. In ancient Greece, only men and boys competed in the Olympics.

---

[1] Olympia, Olympiad [ə lim· pē ə, ə lim· pē ad]

If there happened to be a war going on at the time, and there usually was, so important was this holiday that a truce was declared, and everybody went off to the games. Nothing could be allowed to interfere with the games, and even war was not as important. "Business before pleasure!" When the games were finished, they started fighting again!

The Greek boys and young men would train for four years getting ready for this big event, and then nine months before the great day they would go to Olympia to train at an openair gymnasium near the field.

The games lasted five days and began and ended with a parade and prayers and sacrifices to the Greek gods, beautiful statues to whom were placed all about the field, for this was not only sport, but a religious service in honor of Zeus and the other gods.

There were all sorts of matches—in running, jumping, wrestling, boxing, chariot-racing, and throwing the discus.

Anyone who cheated would have been put out and never again allowed to take part. The Greeks believed in what we call being a good sport. A Greek didn't brag if he won. He didn't make excuses if he lost; he didn't cry out that the decision was unfair.

The athlete who won one or more of these games was the hero of all Greece, and in particular of the town from which he came. The winner received no money prize but was crowned with a wreath made of laurel leaves. This he valued much more than an athlete nowadays does the silver cup or gold medal he may win. Besides receiving the laurel wreath, the winner had songs written to him by poets, and often statues were made of him by sculptors.

There were not only athletic matches but contests between poets and musicians to see who could write the best poetry or compose and play the sweetest music on a kind of small harp called the lyre. The winners of these contests did not receive a laurel wreath, but they were carried in triumph on the shoulders of the throng, as you may have seen the captain of a winning team picked up and raised aloft by his fellow-players after he has won.

Now, in Greek history the first event that we can be absolutely sure is true is the record of the winner of a footrace in these Olympic Games 776 years before Christ was born. From this event the Greeks began to count their history dates, as we do now from the birth of Christ. It was their Year 1.

Greek runner

The four years' time between the Olympic Games was called an Olympiad. Up to this time, they had no calendar that gave the year or date, so 776 is the date of the first Olympiad. Greek history before that time may have been partly true, but we know much of it was mythical. Beginning with 776, however, Greek history is pretty much all true.

After a long while they stopped having the games, but in 1896 it was thought it would be a good thing to start them again. For the first time in over two thousand years, new Olympic Games were again held in 1896 A.D., not in Olympia, however, but in Athens. The games used to be held only in Greece. Now they are held each time in a different country. Only Greeks used to be allowed to take part. Now, however, athletes from almost all the countries of the world are invited to compete. Only men used to take part. Now women from all over the world compete also. War used to be stopped when the time for the games arrived. Now the games are stopped when war is on.

From what we have learned of the Spartans' training, we might guess that they used to win most of the athletic prizes, and they did.

Do the Spartans still continue to win most of the prizes in the New Olympic Games?

No. Not even the Greeks now carry off the chief prizes, because Greece is just one small nation among many.

16

A Bad Beginning

HAVE you ever heard of the Seven-League Boots, the boots in which one could take many miles at a single step?

Well, there is a still bigger boot; it is over five hundred miles long, and it is in the Mediterranean Sea.

No, it's not a real boot, but it would look like one if you were miles high in an airplane and looking down upon it.

It is called Italy.

Something very important happened in Italy, not long after the First Olympiad in Greece. It was so important that it was called the Year 1, and for a thousand years people counted from it as the Greeks did from the First Olympiad and as we do now from the birth of Christ. This thing that happened was not the birth of a man, however. It was the birth of a city, and this city was called Rome.

The history of Rome starts with stories that we know are fairy tales or myths in the same way that the history of Greece does. Homer told about the wanderings of the Greek, Odysseus. A great many years later a poet named Virgil told about the wanderings of a Trojan named Æneas.[1]

Æneas fled from Troy when that city was burning down and started off to find a new home. Finally after several years, he came to Italy and the

---

[1] Æneas [i nē′ əs]

mouth of a river called the Tiber. There Æneas met the daughter of the man who was ruling over that country, a girl by the name of Lavinia, and married her, and they lived happily ever after. The children of Æneas and Lavinia ruled over the land, and they had children, and their children had children, and their children had children, until at last boy twins were born. These twins were named Romulus[2] and Remus.[3] Here endeth the first part of the story and the trouble begins, for they did not live happily ever after.

At the time the twins were born, a man had stolen the kingdom, and he feared that these two boys might grow up and take his stolen kingdom away from him. So he put the twins in a basket and set them afloat on the river Tiber, hoping that they might be carried out to sea or upset and be drowned. This, he thought, was nearly all right, so long as he didn't kill them with his own hands. But the basket drifted ashore instead of going out to sea or upsetting, and a mother wolf found the twins and nursed them as if they were her own babies. A woodpecker also helped and fed them berries. At last a shepherd found them and brought them up as if they were his own sons until they grew up and became men. This sounds a good deal like the story of Paris who was left out to die and was found and brought up by a shepherd also.

Each of the twins then wished to build a city. But they could not agree which one was to do it, and in quarreling over the matter, Romulus killed his own twin brother Remus. Romulus then built the city by the Tiber River, on the spot where he and his brother had been saved and nursed by the mother wolf. Here there were seven hills. This was in 753 B.C., and he named the city Roma after his own name, and the people who lived there were called Romans. That is why, ever afterward, the Roman kings always said they were descended from the Trojan hero Æneas, the great-great-great-grandfather of Romulus.

Don't you believe this story? Neither do I. But it is such an old, old story everyone is supposed to have heard it even though it is only a legend.

---

[2] Romulus [rom′ yə ləs]   [3] Remus [rē′ məs]

A Bad Beginning

In order to get people for the city which he had started, it is said that Romulus invited all the thieves and bad men who had escaped from jail to come and live in Rome, promising them that they would be safe there.

Then as none of the men had wives, and there were no women in

Romulus and Remus with the wolf

his new city, Romulus thought up a scheme to get the men wives. He invited some people called Sabines,[4] who lived nearby, both men and women, to come to Rome to a big party.

They accepted, and a great feast was spread. In the middle of the feast, when everyone was eating and drinking, a signal was given, and each of the Romans seized a Sabine woman for his wife and ran off with her.

The Sabine husbands immediately prepared themselves for war against the Romans, who had stolen their wives. When the battle had begun between the two armies, the Sabine women ran out in the midst of the fighting between their new and old husbands and begged them both to stop. They said they had come to love their new husbands and would not return to their old homes.

What do you think of that?

It sounds like a pretty bad beginning for a new city, doesn't it? and you may well wonder how Rome turned out—a city that started with Romulus killing his brother and that was settled by escaped prisoners who stole the wives of their neighbors. We'll see if the Romans continued to do such wicked things as their city grew older.

---

[4] Sabines [sā′ bĭnz]

17

Kings with Corkscrew Curls

AFTER Rome's bad start she had one king after another, and some of these kings were pretty good and some were pretty bad....

The most important city in the world at this time was far away from Rome on the Tigris River. This city was called Nineveh,[1] and here lived the kings of the country called Assyria, which I told you about some time ago.

As usual, the chief thing we hear about Assyria and the Assyrians is that they were fighting with their neighbors. This, however, was not the fault of their neighbors.

The Assyrian kings who lived in Nineveh wanted more land and power, and so they fought their neighbors in order to take their land away from them. These kings had long corkscrew curls. They were such vicious fighters that they were feared far and near. They treated their prisoners terribly; they skinned them alive, cut off their ears, pulled out their tongues, bored sticks into their eyes, then bragged about it. They made the people whom they conquered pay them huge sums of money and promise to fight along with them whenever they went to war.

Assyria became so strong and powerful that it owned a lot of the world, the land between the rivers called Mesopotamia, and the land to the east, north, and south, and Phoenicia, and even Egypt.

---

[1] Nineveh [nin′ ə və]

This big, big country of Assyria was ruled by the kings at Nineveh, who lived in great magnificence. They built wonderful palaces for themselves, and on each side of the way that led to the palace, they placed rows of huge statues of bulls and lions with wings and men's heads. These winged animals are what are called *cherubs* in the Bible.

Perhaps you have heard a pretty little baby angel called a cherub. Isn't it strange that these Assyrian monsters should be called cherubs also?

When the Assyrian kings were not fighting men, they were fighting wild animals, for they were very fond of hunting with bow and arrow, and they had pictures and statues made of themselves on horseback or in chariots fighting lions. Often they would capture the animals they hunted alive and put them in cages so that the people could come and see them. This was something like a zoo such as we have nowadays.

An Assyrian cherub

The rulers of Assyria had very strange names. Sennacherib[2] was one of the most famous. Sennacherib lived about 700 B.C. Once upon a time Sennacherib was fighting Jerusalem. His whole army was camped one night when as they lay asleep something happened, for when the morning came, none woke up; all were dead, both men and horses. An English poet named Byron has written a poem called *The Destruction of Sennacherib* describing this event. Perhaps they were poisoned; what do you think?

Ashurbanipal[3] was another king who ruled later—about 650 B.C. He was a great fighter too, but he was also very fond of books and reading; so Ashurbanipal started the first public library. The books in that first public library were, however, very peculiar. Of course they were not printed books, and they were not even made of paper. They were made of mud with the words pressed into the clay before it dried. This writing was cuneiform, which I have already told you about. The books were not arranged in bookcases either, but were placed in piles on the floor. They were, however, kept in careful order and numbered so that a person who wanted to see a book in the library could call for it by its number.

Assyria reached the height of her power during the reign of Sennacherib and Ashurbanipal, and everything in Nineveh was so lovely for the Ninevites that the time when Ashurbanipal reigned was called the Golden Age.

Although everything in Nineveh was so lovely for the Ninevites, everywhere else the Assyrians were hated and feared, for their armies brought death and destruction wherever they went.

It came to pass that not long after Ashurbanipal died, two of the neighbors of Nineveh could stand it no longer. These two neighbors were the king of Babylon, who lived south, and a people called the Medes, who lived to the east. The kings of Babylon and the Medes got together

---

[2] Sennacherib [sə nak′ ər ib]   [3] Ashurbanipal [ä sho͝or bä′ nē päl]

and attacked Nineveh, and together they wiped that city off the face of the earth. This was in 612 B.C.—Six-One-Two—and the power of Nineveh and Assyria was killed dead. This, therefore is called the Fall of Nineveh, the end of Nineveh. We might put up a tombstone:

18

A City of Wonders and Wickedness

THE king of Babylon had beaten Nineveh. But he didn't stop with that. He wanted his Babylon to be as great as Nineveh had been. He went on conquering other lands to the left and right until Babylon, in its turn, became the leader and ruler of other countries. Was Babylon, also, in its turn, to fall, as Nineveh had fallen?

When at last the king of Babylon died, he left his vast empire to his son. Now, the king's son was not called John or James or Charles or anything simple like that. It was—Nebuchadnezzar,[1] and I wonder if his father called him by that long name or shortened it to a nickname like *Neb*, for instance, or *Chad*, or perhaps *Nezzar*. This is the way Nebuchadnezzar wrote his name, for he used cuneiform writing. How would you like to write your name in such an unusual way?

𒀭𒀝𒆕𒌋𒌍𒋀

Name of Nebuchadnezzar in cuneiform writing

Nebuchadnezzar set to work and made the city of Babylon the largest, the most magnificent, and the most wonderful city in the world. He made the city in the shape of a square and surrounded it with a wall fifty times

---

[1] Nebuchadnezzar [neb ə kəd nez′ ər]

as high as a man—fifty times—whew!—and so broad that a chariot could be driven along the top, and in this wall he made one hundred huge brass gates. The Euphrates River flowed under the wall, across the city, and out under the wall at the other side.

Nebuchadnezzar could not find anyone in Babylon who was beautiful to be his queen. The Babylonian women must have felt pretty bad—or mad—about that. He went to Media,[2] the country that had helped his father conquer Nineveh. There he found a lovely princess, and so he married her and brought her home to Babylon.

Now, Media was a land of hills and mountains, whilst Babylon was on level ground and without even a hill in sight. Nebuchadnezzar's queen found Babylonia so flat and uninteresting that she became homesick, and she longed for her own country with its wild mountain scenery. Just to please her and keep her contented, Nebuchadnezzar set to work and *built* a hill for her, but the strange thing was he built it on top of the roof of his palace! On the sides of this hill he made beautiful gardens, and these gardens he planted not only with flowers but also with trees, so that his queen might sit in the shade and enjoy herself. These were called Hanging Gardens. The Hanging Gardens and the tremendous walls were known far and wide as one of the Seven Wonders of the World.

Would you like to know what the other Wonders were?

Well, the pyramids in Egypt were one; the magnificent statue of Zeus at Olympia, where the Olympic Games were held, was another—so those two plus the Hanging Gardens make three.

Nebuchadnezzar believed in many gods, like the ones the Phoenicians worshiped. The Jews away off in Jerusalem believed in one God. Nebuchadnezzar wanted the Jews to worship his gods, but they would not. He also wanted them to pay him taxes, and they would not. So he sent his armies to Jerusalem, destroyed the city, burnt the beautiful

---

[2] Media [mē′ dē ə]

Temple that Solomon had built, and brought the Jews and all their belongings to Babylon. There in Babylon Nebuchadnezzar kept the Jews prisoners, and there in Babylon the Jews remained prisoners for seventy years.

Babylon had become not only the most magnificent city in the world; it had become also the most wicked. The people of Babylon gave themselves up to the wildest pleasures. Their only thought seemed to be, "Let's eat, drink, and be merry"; they thought nothing of the morrow; the more wicked the pleasure the more they liked it.

But although Nebuchadnezzar seemed able to do and able to have everything in the world he wanted, he finally went crazy. He thought he was a bull, and he used to get down on his hands and knees and eat grass, imagining he was a beast of the field.

And Babylon, in spite of its tremendous walls and brass gates, was doomed. Babylon was to be conquered. It didn't seem possible. How could it be conquered, and who was to do the conquering? You would probably never guess.

19

A Surprise Party

WHEN I was a boy I was always told, and you have probably been told the same thing:

"You can have no dessert until you have eaten your dinner."

No matter whether I was hungry or not, "No dinner, no dessert." This was a rule that my father said was "like the laws of the Medes and Persians."

I didn't know then who the Medes and Persians were, but I know now that they were two Indo-European peoples living next to Babylon—you remember Nebuchadnezzar had married a Median woman—and that they were governed by laws, which were fixed so hard and fast and were so unchangeable, that we still speak of any such thing that does not change as like "the laws of the Medes and Persians."

The Medes and the Persians had a religion, which was neither like that of the Jews nor like that of the Babylonians. It had been started by a Persian named Zoroaster,[1] who was a wise man like Solomon. Zoroaster went about among the people, teaching them wise sayings and hymns. These wise sayings have been gathered into a book. Zoroaster taught that there were two great spirits in the world, the Good Spirit and the Bad Spirit.

The Good Spirit, he said was Light, and the Bad Spirit Darkness. The Good or Light he called Mazda. The Persians kept a fire constantly

---

[1] Zoroaster [zôr′ ō as tər]

burning on their altar. They thought the Good Spirit burned in the fire, and they had men watch over the flame to see that it never went out. These men who watched the flame were called Magi,[2] and they were supposed to be able to do all sorts of wonderful things, so that we call such wonderful things *magic*, and the people who are able to do them we call *magicians*. At the time of this story which I'm telling you, the ruler of the Medes and the Persians was a great king named Cyrus.

But before I go on with this story, I must tell you about a little country not far from Troy. This little country was called Lydia. Perhaps you may know a girl named Lydia. I do. Lydia was ruled over by a king named Croesus,[3] who was the richest man in the world. When we want to describe a man as very wealthy, we still say he is "as rich as Croesus."

Croesus owned nearly all the gold mines, of which there were a great many in that country, and besides this he collected money in the form of taxes from all the cities near him.

Before the time of Croesus, people did not have money such as we have now. When they wished to buy anything, they simply traded something they had for something they wanted—so many eggs for a pound of meat or so much wine for a pair of sandals. To buy anything expensive, such as a horse, they paid with a lump of gold or silver, which was weighed in the scales to see just how heavy it was. It is hard for us to think how people could get along without cents and nickels, dimes, quarters and dollars—with no money at all—and yet they did.

Croesus, in order to make things simpler, cut up his gold into small bits. Now, it was not easy for everyone to weigh each piece each time it was traded, for he might not have any scales handy. So Croesus had each piece weighed and stamped with its weight and with his name or initials to show that he guaranteed the weight. These pieces of gold and silver were only lumps with Croesus's seal pressed into them, but they were probably the

---

[2] Magi [māˈ jī]   [3] Croesus [krēˈ səs]

first real money even though they were not round and beautifully engraved like our coins.

Now, Cyrus, the great Persian king, thought he would like to own this rich country of Lydia with all its gold mines, so he set out to conquer it.

When Cyrus was on the way, Croesus sent in a hurry to the oracle in Greece to ask what was going to happen and who was going to win. You will remember what I said about the oracle at Delphi and how people used to ask the

Delphic oracle

oracle questions—to have their fortunes told, as some people still do today.

The oracle replied to Croesus's question:

"A great kingdom shall fall."

Croesus was delighted, for he thought the oracle meant that Cyrus's kingdom would fall. The oracle *was* right, but not in the way Croesus had thought.

A great kingdom did fall, but it was his own kingdom of Lydia and not Cyrus's that fell.

But Cyrus was still not satisfied with the capture of Lydia, and so at last he attacked Babylon.

Now, the people in Babylon who thought of nothing but pleasure were busy feasting and drinking and having a good time. Why should they worry about Cyrus? Their city had walls that were so high and thick and was protected by such strong gates of brass that it seemed as if no one could possibly have captured it.

But you remember that the Euphrates River ran beneath the walls and crossed right through the city. Well, one night when the young prince of Babylon named Belshazzar[4] was having a party and enjoying himself, feeling quite certain that no one could enter the city, Cyrus made a dam and turned the waters of the river to one side. Then Cyrus's army marched into the city through the dry riverbed and captured the surprised Babylonians without even a fight. It is supposed that some of the Babylonian priests helped him to do this and even opened the gates, for Babylon had become so wicked that they thought it time for it to be destroyed.

Old Lycurgus would have said, "I told you so. People who think of nothing but pleasure never come to a good end."

This surprise party was in 538—5 and 3 are 8.

Two years later Cyrus let the Jews, who had been carried away fifty years before from Jerusalem, return to the home of their fathers, thus ending the Babylonian Captivity.

Today the only thing left of this great city of Babylon—Babylon the Wicked, Babylon the Magnificent, Babylon with all its great walls and brass gates and Hanging Gardens—is a mound of earth.

---

[4] Belshazzar [bel shaz′ ər]

20

The Other Side of the World: India

INDIA is a country east of Persia. The people who live there are called Indians. The Indians, of course, are entirely different from Native Americans who were called *Indians* when early explorers believed they had reached India or the East Indies.

You may remember that India was one of the very early civilizations that grew up along a river valley. Do you remember the name of the river—Here's a hint. It sounds like India. Did you remember? It's the Indus River.

India is a very old country. Its modern neighbor, Pakistan, used to be part of India, too. Long, long ago—about 2500 B.C.—the people living along the Indus River, in what is now India and Pakistan, sailed up and down the river to trade with each other. They invented a system of writing to keep their records. They built large cities with wide, straight streets. Their houses even had bathrooms with drains that were connected to a city sewer system. Did you think that modern people were the only ones to have sewer systems? If you did, you were wrong. You can see that ancient Indians thought up this healthy system long before we did.

About a thousand years after the ancient Indians built their first cities along the Indus River, people from the west invaded their land. These people were Indo-Europeans who came from somewhere near Persia. When they first arrived, these newcomers did not know how to write. They were strong warriors though and gradually conquered more and more of India. The original Indians and the newcomers learned from each other and adopted some of each others' customs.

In the course of time there came to be four chief *castes*, or classes, of people in India. No one in one caste would have anything to do with a person in another caste. A boy or girl in one caste would never play with a boy or girl in another caste. A man from one class would never marry a woman from another. No one from one class would eat with someone from another class.

The top caste was made up of the priests and scholars. In the next caste were people like rulers and warriors. Then, in the third caste, came farmers and merchants. Fourth, and last, were laborers, men who chopped wood, or dug the soil, or carried water.

But they weren't the lowest! There were other people so low that they didn't even belong to a caste, and so they were outcasts and *untouchables*. Even today, though India is trying to make changes and caste distinctions have been made illegal, these people are the ones who sweep the streets, clean the gutters, collect the garbage, and do the dirty work that no one else will do.

India today is terribly crowded with people. It is about one-third the size of the United States but has more than three times as many people. Think what that means!

Most Indians today follow the Hindu religion, but from about 300 B.C. to 400 A.D.—seven hundred years—Buddhism was very popular. It happened this way.

About 500 B.C. there was born a prince in India by the name of Gautama[1]. Gautama saw so much suffering and trouble in the world that

---

[1] Guatama Buddha [gô′ tə mə boõd′ ə]

he felt it was not right that he himself, just because he by chance had been born rich, should be happy while others were miserable and unhappy. He gave up the life to which he had been born, a life of ease and luxury with all its good things, and spent his entire time trying to make things better for his people.

Gautama taught the people to be good; he taught them to be honest; and he taught them to help the poor and the unfortunate. After a while people began to call him Buddha, and he was considered so holy and pure that at last they came to think that he must be a god himself, and so they worshiped him as a god.

These people who believed in Buddha were called Buddhists, and many others quickly became Buddhists, too. Buddhism seemed so good that we do not wonder that great numbers of people became Buddhists.

Buddhists thought their religion was so good that they wanted everybody else to become Buddhists. They sent missionaries across land and sea all the way to the island of Japan, and this new religion spread far and wide. Today there are more Buddhists in the world than there are people in the United States.

You can see that India is a very important place. It is the home of one of the world's oldest civilizations and two of the world's important religions.

21

All the Way Around the World in China

ABOUT the same time that Gautama was starting Buddhism in India, a man in China, a great wise man named Confucius,[1] was teaching the people of China what they ought to do and what they ought not to do. His teachings filled several books and formed what came to be a way of life for the Chinese and many other people in Asia.

Confucius taught that people should be loyal and obey their kings and also that rulers had a duty to take care of their people. He believed that this would bring peace and harmony in China. He taught people to obey their parents and teachers and to honor their ancestors. This sounds something like one of the Ten Commandments: "Honor thy father and thy mother."

Confucius also taught the Golden Rule, the same Golden Rule that you are taught today, only instead of saying, "Do unto others as you would have others do unto you" he said, "Do not do to others what you would not want others to do to you."

China had one of the earliest civilizations in the world. Maybe you remember the name of the river that was the cradle of Chinese civilization. It was the Huang River, or Yellow River, that overflowed with thick yellow mud. This mud fertilized the soil where people grew

---

[1] Confucius [kon fyōō′ shəs]

their crops. People settled first along the Huang and then also along the Yangtze[2] River, also called the Long River.

China is very far away from all the other places we have been talking about. It was isolated from the rest of the ancient world. The Himalaya[3] Mountains lie to the west and the Gobi[4] Desert to the north. On the south are more mountains and seas. On the east lies the great Pacific Ocean that stretches all the way to the west coast of the United States. In the days before large sailing ships and way before airplanes, the Chinese had very little contact with any other people. So Chinese culture developed all by itself.

We know the Chinese had a written language as early as 1500 B.C. at a time when the Shang dynasty ruled northern China. You can see that Chinese writing is still very different from the writing in any other country. The Chinese never switched to an alphabet but continue to use characters—a different character for each word. It must be very hard to learn to read and write Chinese.

Huang River

Yangtze River

We have to learn only twenty-six letters. Boys and girls in China have to memorize about six hundred characters before they can do even basic reading and writing.

Many inventions were made and used in China before the rest of the world ever heard of them. Around the time of Christ, the Chinese were making silk, porcelain, and paper. By this time, the Chinese did trade with some of the other people we have read about. Chinese silk was in great demand by Romans and their neighbors around the Mediterranean.

By 600 A.D. the Chinese had invented printing and used printing presses. A few centuries later, they were making the magnetic compass,

---

[2] Yangtze [yang′ sē]
[3] Himalaya [him ə lā′ ə]

[4] Gobi [gō′ bē]

which was such a great help to the sailors. Do you know what a compass is? It's a little gadget with a needle that always points to the north. Knowing which way was north made it possible for sailors to know which way they were sailing—even when they were way out in the ocean, too far from land to be able to see the shore. Maybe someone in your class or neighborhood has a compass and can share it for everybody to see.

The Chinese also figured out how to immunize against the dread disease smallpox. They also were first to discover how to make explosive powder, the kind that we use both for gunpowder and for fireworks.

From all this, you can see that the Chinese may have been relatively isolated, but they were very busy making things that the rest of the world found really exciting when people learned about them.

22

Rich Man, Poor Man

WHENEVER I pass a group of children playing ball, I almost always hear someone shout, "That's no fair!"

There always seem to be some players who think the others are not playing fair. Sides are always quarreling.

They need an umpire.

When Athens was young there were two sides among the people—the rich and the poor, the aristocrats and the common people—and they were always quarreling. Each side was trying to get more power, and each side said the other wasn't playing fair.

They needed an umpire.

Athens had had kings, but the kings took the side of the rich, and so finally the Athenians had kicked out the last king, and after that they would have no more kings.

About the year 600 B.C. things became so very bad that a man named Draco[1] was chosen to make a set of rules for the Athenians to obey. These rules he made were called the Code of Draco.

Draco's Code made terrible punishments for anyone who broke the rules. If a man stole anything even as small a thing as a loaf of bread, he was not just fined or sent to jail; he was put to death! No matter how

---

[1] Draco [drā· kō]

small the wrong a man had done, he was put to death for it. Draco explained the reason for such a severe law by saying that a thief deserved to be put to death and should be. A man who killed another deserved *more* than to be put to death, but unfortunately there was no worse punishment to give him.

You can understand how much trouble the laws of Draco caused. They were so hard that a little later another man was called upon to make a new set of laws. This man was named Solon,[2] and his laws were very just and good. We now call senators and other people who make our laws *solons* after this man Solon who lived so long ago, even though their laws are not always just and good.

Still the people were not satisfied with Solons laws. The upper classes thought the laws gave too much to the lower classes, and the lower classes thought they gave too much to the upper. Both classes, however, obeyed the laws for a while, although both classes complained against them.

But about 560 B.C. a man named Pisistratus[3] stepped in and took charge of things himself. He was not elected nor chosen by the people. He simply made himself ruler, and he was so powerful that no one could stop him. It was as if a boy made himself captain or umpire without being chosen by those on the team.

There were others from time to time in Greece who did the same thing, and they were called *tyrants*. So Pisistratus was a tyrant. Nowadays only a ruler who is cruel and unjust is called a tyrant. Pisistratus, however, settled the difficulties of both sides, and though a tyrant in the Greek sense, he was neither cruel nor unjust. In fact, Pisistratus ruled according to the laws of Solon, and he did a great deal to improve Athens and the life of the people. Among other things he did, he had Homer's poems written down, so that people could read them, for before this time people knew them only from hearing them recited. It is remarkable how

---

[2] Solon [sō′ lən]   [3] Pisistratus [pī sis′ trə təs]

histories can be passed down orally—just by telling the story. In cultures without writing, people had to have very good memories.

The people put up with Pisistratus and also with his son for a while. Finally the Athenians got tired of the son's rule and drove all the Pisistratus family out of Athens in 510 B.C.

The next man to try to settle the quarrels of the two sides was named Cleisthenes.[4] It is hard, sometimes, to learn the name of a stranger to whom we have just been introduced unless we hear his name several times. I will say over his name so that you can get used to hearing it:

CLEISTHENES;

CLEISTHENES;

CLEISTHENES.

Your parents may be poor or they may be rich.

If they are poor each has one vote when there is an election.

If they are rich each has one vote but only one vote and no more.

If people break the laws, whether they are rich or whether they are poor, they must go to jail.

It was not always so; it is not always so even now. But long ago it was much worse.

Cleisthenes gave every man a vote—rich and poor alike—but he did not give women a vote. In ancient times, women often were kept out of politics. Still, the people of Athens believed that Cleisthenes ruled wisely and well. Cleisthenes started something called ostracism.[5] If for any reason the people wanted to get rid of a man, all they had to do was to scratch his name on any piece of a broken pot or jar they might find and drop it in a voting-box on a certain day. If there were enough such votes, the man would have to leave the city and stay away for ten years.

---

[4] Cleisthenes [klĭs´ the nēz]   [5] ostracism [os´ trə siz əm]

This was called *ostracism*, from the Greek name for such a broken piece of pottery, on which the name was written. Even today we use this same word to speak of a person whom no one will have anything to do with, whom no one wants around, saying he had been ostracized.

Ostracism

Have you ever been sent away from the table to the kitchen or to your room for misbehaving?

Then you, too, have been ostracized.

23

Rome Kicks Out Her Kings

IN 509 B.C. something happened in Rome. There were two classes of people in Rome, just as there were in Athens: the wealthy people who were called patricians, and the poor people who were called plebeians. We use the same words now and call people who are rich and aristocratic *patricians*, and the people who are poor and uneducated *plebeians*. The patricians were allowed to vote, but the plebeians were not allowed to vote.

At last, however, the plebeians had been given the right to vote. But in B.C. Rome had a king named Tarquin.[1] He didn't think the plebeians; should be allowed to vote, and so he said they should not. The plebeians would not stand this, and therefore they got together and drove Tarquin out of the city, as the Athenians had driven out their king. This was in 509 B.C., and Tarquin was the last king Rome ever had.

After King Tarquin had been driven out, the Romans started what is called a republic, something like our own country, but they were afraid to have only one man as president for fear he might make himself king, and they had had enough of kings.

So the Romans elected *two men* each year to be rulers over them, and these two men they called consuls. Each consul had a bodyguard of twelve men. These men were given the name *lictors*, and each lictor carried an ax

---

[1] Tarquin [tär' kwin]

tied up in a bundle of sticks. This bundle of sticks with the ax-head sticking out in the middle or at the end was known as *fasces* and signified that the consuls had power to punish by whipping with the sticks or by chopping off one's head with the ax. Some modern coins and postage stamps have fasces pictured on them.

Perhaps you have seen fasces used as ornaments or decoration around monuments or public buildings.

One of the first two consuls was named Brutus[2] the Elder, and he had two sons. The king, Tarquin, who had been driven out of the city, plotted to get back to Rome and become king once more. He was able to persuade some Romans to help him. Among those whom he persuaded were, strange to say, the two sons of Brutus—the new consul of Rome.

Lictor carrying fasces

Brutus found out this plot and learned that his own children had helped Tarquin. Then Brutus had his sons tried. They were found guilty, and in spite of the fact that they were his own children, he had the lictors put both of them to death as well as the other traitors to Rome.

Tarquin did not succeed in getting back the rule of Rome in this way. The next year he tried again. This time he got together an army of his neighbors, the Etruscans, and with this army he attacked Rome.

Now, there was a wooden bridge across the Tiber River, which separated the Etruscans from the city of Rome. In order to keep the Etruscans from crossing into the city, a Roman named Horatius,[3] who had already lost one eye in fighting for Rome, gave orders to have this bridge broken down.

---

[2] Brutus [broo′ təs]   [3] Horatius [hə rā′ shəs]

While the bridge was being chopped down, Horatius, with two of his friends, stood on the far side of the bridge and fought back the whole Etruscan army. When the bridge was cracking under the blows of the Roman soldiers, Horatius ordered his two friends to run quickly to the other side before the bridge fell.

Then Horatius, all by himself, kept the enemy back until at last the bridge crashed into the river. Horatius then jumped into the water with all his armor on and swam toward the Roman shore. Though arrows the Etruscans shot were falling all around him, and though his armor weighed him down, he reached the other side safely. Even the Etruscans were thrilled at his bravery, and, enemies though they were, they cheered him loudly.

There is a very famous poem called *Horatius at the Bridge*, which describes this brave deed.

A few years after Horatius, there lived another Roman named Cincinnatus.[4] He was only a simple farmer with a little farm on the bank of the Tiber, but he was very wise and good, and the people of Rome honored and trusted him.

One day when an enemy was about to attack the city—for in those days there always seemed to be enemies everywhere ready to attack Rome on any excuse—the people had to have a leader and a general. They thought of Cincinnatus and went and asked him to be dictator.

Now, a dictator was the name they gave to a man who in a case of sudden danger was called upon to command the army and in fact all the people during the time of the danger. Cincinnatus left his plow, went with the people to the city, got together an army, went out and defeated the enemy, and returned to Rome, all in twenty-four hours!

The people were so much pleased with the quick and decisive way in which Cincinnatus had saved Rome that they wanted him to keep right

---

[4] Cincinnatus [sin sə nā′ təs]

on being their general in time of peace. Even though they hated kings so much, they would have made him king if he would have accepted.

But Cincinnatus did not want any such thing. His duty done, he wanted to return to his wife and humble home and his little farm. In spite of what many would have thought a wonderful chance, he did go back to his plow, choosing to be just a simple farmer instead of being king.

The city of Cincinnati in Ohio is named after a society which was founded in honor of this old Roman, who lived nearly five hundred years before Christ.

24

Greece vs. Persia

Do you know what those two little letters *vs.* mean between Greece and Persia in the name of this story?

Perhaps you have seen them used on football tickets when there was to be a match between two teams as, for example, Harvard vs. Yale.

They stand for *versus*, which means *against*.

Well, there was to be a great match between Greece and Persia, but it wasn't a game; it was a fight for life and death, a fight between little Greece and great big Persia.

Cyrus,[1] the great Persian king, had conquered Babylon and other countries, as well, and he had kept on conquering until Persia ruled most of the world, all except Greece and Italy.

About the year 500 B.C. the new ruler of this vast Persian Empire was a man named Darius.[2] Darius looked at the map, as you might do, and saw that he owned and ruled over a large part of it. What a pity, thought he, that there should be a little country like Greece that did not belong to him!

Darius said to himself, "I must have this piece of land called Greece to complete my empire." Besides, the Greeks had given him some trouble. They had helped some of his subjects to rebel against him. Darius said,

---

[1] Cyrus [si′ rəs]   [2] Darius [də ri′ əs]

"I must punish these Greeks for what they have done and then just add their country to mine."

He called his son-in-law and told him to go over to Greece and conquer it.

His son-in-law did as he was told and started out with a fleet and an army to do the punishing. But before his fleet could reach Greece it was destroyed by a storm, and he had to go back home without having done anything.

Darius was very angry at this, mad with his son-in-law and mad with the gods who he thought had wrecked his ships, and he made up his mind that he himself would go and do the punishing and conquering the next time.

First, however, he sent his messengers to all the Greek cities and ordered each of them to send him some earth and some water as a sign that they would give him their land and become his subjects peaceably without a fight.

Many Greek cities were so frightened by the threat of Darius and by his mighty power that they gave in at once and sent earth and water as they were told to do.

But little Athens and little Sparta both hotly refused to do so, in spite of the fact that they were only two small cities against the vast empire of Darius.

Athens took Darius's messenger and threw him into a well, saying, "There is earth and water for you; help yourself"; and Sparta did likewise. Then these two cities joined their forces and called on all their neighbors to join with them to fight for their native land against Darius and Persia.

Darius made ready to conquer Athens and then Sparta.

In order to reach Athens his army had to be carried across the sea in boats. Of course, in those days there were no steamboats. Steamboats were invented nearly two thousand years later.

The only way to make a boat go was with sails or with oars. To make a large boat move with oars, it was necessary to have a great many rowers—three rows one above the other on each side of the boat.

Such a boat was called a *trireme*, which means three rows of oars. It took about 600 of these boats to carry Darius's army over to Greece. Each of these 600 boats carried, besides the rowers or crew, about 200 soldiers. You can see for yourself how many soldiers Darius had in this army, if there were 600 shiploads of them and 200 soldiers on each ship. Yes, that is an example in multiplication—120,000 soldiers—that's right.

A trireme

The Persians sailed across the sea; and this time there was no storm, and they reached the shore of Greece safely. They landed on a spot called the plain of Marathon, which was only about twenty-six miles away from Athens. You will see presently why I have told you just the number of miles—twenty-six.

When the Athenians heard that the Persians were coming, they wanted to get Sparta to help in a hurry, as she had promised to do.

Now, there were no telegraphs or telephones or railroads, of course, in those days. There was no way in which they could send a message to Sparta except to have it carried by hand.

They called on a famous runner named Pheidippides[3] to carry the message. Pheidippides started out and ran the whole way from Athens to Sparta, about one hundred and fifty miles, to carry the message. He ran night and day, hardly stopping at all to rest or to eat, and on the second day he was in Sparta.

The Spartans, however, sent back word that they couldn't start just then; the moon wasn't full, and it was bad luck to start when the moon wasn't

---

[3] Pheidippides [fī dip′ i dēz]

full, as nowadays some superstitious people think it bad luck to start on a trip on Friday. They said they would come after a while, when the moon was full.

The Athenians couldn't wait for the moon. They knew the Persians would be in Athens before then, and they didn't want them to get as far as that.

So all the fighting men in Athens left their city and went forth to meet the Persians on the plain of Marathon—twenty-six miles away.

The Athenians were led by a man named Miltiades,[4] and there were only ten thousand soldiers. Besides these, there were one thousand more from a little nearby town, which was friendly with Athens and wished to stand by her— eleven thousand in all. If you figure it out, you will see that there were perhaps ten times as many Persians as there were Greeks, ten Persian soldiers to one Greek soldier.

The Greeks, however, were trained athletes, as we know, and their whole manner of life made them physically fit. The Persians were no match for them. In spite of the small number of Greeks, the large number of Persians were beaten, and beaten badly. Of course the Greeks were far better soldiers than the Persians, for all their training made them so, but more than all this, they were fighting for themselves to save their homes and their families.

Perhaps you have heard the fable of the hound who was chasing a hare. The hare escaped. The hound was made fun of for not catching the little hare. To which the hound replied, "I was only running for my supper; the hare was running for his life."

The Persian soldiers were not fighting for their homes or families, which were away back across the sea; and it made little difference to them who won, anyway, for most were merely hirelings or slaves; they were fighting for a king because he ordered them to.

---

[4]Miltiades [mil tī′ ə dēz]

The first marathon race

Naturally the Greeks were overjoyed at this victory.

Pheidippides, the famous runner, who was now at Marathon, started off at once to carry the joyful news back to Athens, twenty-six miles away. He ran the whole distance without stopping for breath. He had not had time to rest up from his long run to Sparta, which he had taken only a few days before, and so fast did he run this long distance that as soon as he had reached Athens and gasped the news to the Athenians in the marketplace he dropped down dead!

In honor of this famous run, they have nowadays in the new Olympic Games, what is called a Marathon race, in which the athletes run this same distance: twenty-six miles. This battle of Marathon took place in 490 B.C. and is one of the most famous battles in all history, for the great

Persian army was beaten by one little city and its neighbor, and the Persians had to go back to their homes in disgrace.

A little handful of people, who governed themselves, had defeated a great king with a large army of only hired soldiers or slaves.

But this was not the last the Greeks were to see of the Persians.

25

Fighting Mad

DARIUS was now angrier than ever, and still more determined to whip those stubborn Greeks, who dared to defy him and his enormous power; and he began to get ready for one more attempt. This time, however, he made up his mind that he would get together such an army and navy that there would be no chance in the world against it, and he made a solemn oath to destroy the Greeks. So for several years he gathered troops and supplies, but something happened, and in spite of his oath he did not carry out his plan. Why? You guessed it. He died.

But Darius had a son named Xerxes[1]—pronounced as if it began with a Z.

When I was a boy, there was an alphabet rhyme that began, "A is for Apple," and went on down to "X is for Xerxes, a great Persian king." I learned the rhyme, though I did not know at that time anything about either Xerxes or Persia.

Xerxes was just as determined as his father had been that the Greeks must be beaten, so he went on getting ready.

However, the Greeks also were just as determined that they must *not* be beaten, so they, too, went on getting ready, for they knew the Persians would sooner or later come back and try again.

---

[1] Xerxes [zurk′ sēz]

At this time there were two chief men in Athens, and each was trying to be leader. One was named Themistocles—pronounced *The MIS to kleez*—and the other Aristides—pronounced *Ar is TI deez*. Notice how many Greek names seem to end in the letters *es*.

Themistocles urged the Athenians to get ready for what he knew was coming, the next war with Persia. Especially did he urge the Athenians to build a fleet of boats, for they had no boats and the Persians had a great many.

Aristides, on the other hand, didn't believe in Themistocles's scheme to build boats. He thought it a foolish expense and talked against it.

Aristides had always been so wise and fair that people called him Aristides the Just. Even so, some people wanted to get rid of him, because they thought he was wrong about building a fleet of boats and Themistocles was right. They waited till the time came to vote, when they could ostracize anyone they wanted to get rid of. Do you remember who started this custom? Cleisthenes—about 500 B.C.

When the day for voting came, a man who could not write and did not know Aristides by sight happened to ask his help in voting. Aristides inquired what name he should write, and the man replied, "Aristides."

Aristides did not tell who he was, but merely said:

"Why do you want to get rid of this man? Has he done anything wrong?"

"Oh, no," the voter replied. "He hasn't done anything wrong," but with a long sigh he said, "I'm so tired of hearing him always called *The Just*."

Aristides must have been surprised by this unreasonable answer, but nevertheless he wrote his own name for the voter, and when the votes were counted, there were so many that he was ostracized.

Though it did not seem quite fair that Aristides should be ostracized, it was fortunate, as it turned out, that Themistocles had his way, and it was fortunate the Athenians went on preparing for war.

They built a fleet of triremes. Then they got all the cities and towns in Greece to agree to join forces in case of war. Sparta, on account of its fame as a city of soldiers, was made the leader of all the others in case war should come.

And then, just ten years after the battle of Marathon in 490 B.C. the great Persian army was again ready to attack Greece. It had been brought together from all parts of the vast Persian Empire and was far bigger than the former army with its 120,000 men, although that was a large army for those days.

This time the army is supposed to have consisted of over two million soldiers—two million; just think of that! The question then was how to get so many soldiers over to Greece. Such a multitude could not be carried across to Greece in boats, for even the largest triremes only held a few hundred men, and it would have taken—well, can you tell how many boats, to carry over two million? Probably many more triremes than there were in the whole world at that time. Xerxes decided to have his army march to Greece, the long way but the only way round. So they started.

Now, there is a strip of water called a *strait*, something like a wide river, right across the path the Persian army had to take. This strait was then called the Hellespont.[2] It is, of course still there, but if you look on the map you will find it is now called the Dardanelles.[3] There was no bridge across the Hellespont, for it was almost a mile wide, and they didn't have bridges as long as that in those days. Xerxes fastened boats together in a line that stretched from one shore to the other shore, and over these boats he built a floor to form a bridge so that his army could cross upon it.

Hardly had he finished building the bridge, however, when a storm arose and destroyed it. Xerxes, in anger at the waves, ordered that the water of the Hellespont be whipped as if it were an enemy or a slave he

---

[2] Hellespont [hel′ ə spont]   [3] Dardanelles [där dn elz′]

were punishing. Then he built another bridge, and this time the water behaved itself, and his soldiers were able to cross over safely.

So vast was Xerxes's army that it is said to have taken it seven days and seven nights marching continuously all the time in two long unbroken lines to get over to the opposite shore. Xerxes's fleet followed the army as closely as they could along the shore, and at last they reached the top of Greece. Down through the north of Greece the army came, overrunning everything before it, and it seemed as though nothing on earth could stop such numbers of men.

26

One Against a Thousand

THERE is a little narrow passageway with the mountains on one side and the water on the other through which the Persians had to go to reach Athens. This pass is called Thermopylae,[1] and you might guess what Thermopylae means if you notice that the first part is like Thermos bottle, which means *hot* bottle. As a matter of fact, Thermopylae meant Hot Gateway and was so named because this natural gateway to Greece had hot springs near by.

The Greeks decided that it was best to stop the Persians at this gate—to go to meet them there first before they reached Athens. In such a place a few Greek soldiers could fight better against a much larger number.

It also seemed wise to send picked Greek troops to meet the Persians, the very best soldiers in Greece with the very bravest general to lead them.

The Spartan king, who was named Leonidas[2]—which in Greek means *like a lion*—was chosen to go to Thermopylae, and with him seven thousand soldiers—seven thousand soldiers to block the way of two million Persians! Three hundred of these were Spartans, and a Spartan was taught that he must never surrender, never give up. A Spartan mother used to say to her son:

"Come back *with* your shield or *on* it."

---

[1] Thermopylae [thər mop′ ə lē]   [2] Leonidas [lē on′ i dəs]

When Xerxes found his way blocked by this ridiculously small band of soldiers, he sent his messengers ordering them to surrender, to give themselves up.

What do you suppose Leonidas replied?

It was what we should expect a Spartan to answer, brief and to the point; that is, *laconic*. He said simply:

"Come and take us."

As there was nothing left for Xerxes to do but fight, he started his army forward.

For two days the Persians fought the Greeks, but Leonidas still held the pass, and the Persians were unable to get through.

Then a Greek traitor and coward, who thought he might save his own life and be given a rich prize by Xerxes, told that king of a secret path over the mountains by which he and his army might slip through and get around Leonidas and his soldiers who blocked the way.

The next morning Leonidas learned that the Persians had found the secret path and were already on the way to pen him in from behind. There was still a chance, however, for his men to escape, and Leonidas told all those who wanted to do so to leave. Those who remained knew that the fight was absolutely hopeless and that it meant certain death for all of them. In spite of this, however, one thousand men, including all the three hundred Spartans stood by their leader, for, said they:

"We have been ordered to hold the pass, and a Spartan obeys orders, and never surrenders, no matter what happens."

There Leonidas and his thousand men fought to the bitter end until all except one of their number was killed.

The gateway to the city of Athens was now open, and things looked very bleak for the Greeks, for there was nothing to prevent the Persians from marching over the dead bodies of Leonidas and his men straight on to Athens.

The Athenians, wondering what was to happen to them, hurriedly went to the oracle at Delphi and asked what they should do.

The oracle replied that the city of Athens itself was doomed, that it would be destroyed, there was no hope for it, but that the Athenians themselves would be saved by wooden walls.

This answer, as was usually the case in whatever the oracle said, was a riddle, the meaning of which seemed hard to solve. Themistocles, however, said that he knew the answer. You remember that it was he who had been working so hard to have a fleet of ships built. Themistocles said that the oracle meant these ships when it spoke of the wooden walls.

The Athenians, following the supposed advice of the oracle, left their city as Themistocles told them and went on board the ships, which were not far away, in a bay called Salamis.[3]

The Persian army reached Athens and found it deserted. They burned and destroyed the city as the oracle said. Then they marched on to the Bay of Salamis, where the Athenians were on board the ships. There, on a hill overlooking the bay, Xerxes had a throne built for himself so that he could sit, as if in a box at the theater looking at a play, and watch his own large fleet destroy the much smaller one of the Greeks with all the Athenians on board.

The Greek fleet was commanded, of course, by Themistocles. His ships were in this narrow bay or strait of water, somewhat in the same way that the soldiers of Leonidas had been in the narrow valley at Thermopylae.

Themistocles, seeing that the Bay of Salamis looked somewhat like the Pass of Thermopylae, had an idea. He made believe he was a traitor like the traitor at Thermopylae and sent word to Xerxes that if the Persian fleet divided and one half stayed at one end of the strait and the other half closed off the other end of the strait, the Greeks would be penned in between and caught as in a trap.

---

[3] Salamis [sal· ə mis]

Xerxes on his throne watching Battle of Salamis

Xerxes thought this a good idea, so he gave orders to have his ships do as Themistocles had suggested. But Xerxes, sitting smiling on his throne, had the surprise of his life. The result was just the opposite of what he had expected. With the Persian fleet separated in two parts, the Greeks in between could fight both halves of the divided fleet separately, and the space was so narrow that the Persians' ships got in the way of each other and rammed and sank their own boats.

The Persian fleet was completely beaten, and the proud and boastful Xerxes, with most of his army and all the navy that was left, made a hasty retreat back to Persia the way they had come.

This was the last time the Persians ever tried to conquer little Greece.

If Themistocles had not had his way and built such a strong fleet, what do you think would have become of Athens and Greece!

27

The Golden Age

When we were talking about the Stone Age and the Bronze Age, I told you that later we should also hear of a Golden Age.

Well, we have come to the Golden Age now. This doesn't mean that people at this time used things made of gold, nor that they had a great deal of gold money. It means—well, let us see what sort of a time it was, and then you can tell what it means.

After the wars with Persia, Athens seemed to have been cheered up by her victory to do wonderful things, and the next fifty years after the Persians were driven out of Greece—that is, 480 to 430 B.C.—were the most wonderful years in the history of Greece, and perhaps the most wonderful years in the history of Europe.

Athens had been burned down by Xerxes. At the time it happened this seemed like a terrible misfortune. But it wasn't. The people set to work and built a much finer and much more beautiful city than the old one had been.

Now, the chief person in Athens at this time was a man named Pericles.[1] He was not a king nor a ruler, but he was so very wise and such a wonderful speaker and such a popular leader that he was able to make the Athenians do as he thought best. He was like the popular captain of a football or soccer team who is a fine player himself and makes fine players of all the others on

---

[1] Pericles [per′ i klēz]

his team. Athens was his team, and he trained it so well that all the players were tops in their positions. Some people became great artists. Some people became great writers. Others still became great *philosophers*. Do you know what philosophers are? They are wise men and women who know a great deal and love knowledge.

The artists built many beautiful buildings, theaters, and temples. They made wonderful statues of the Greek gods and goddesses and placed them on the buildings and about the city.

The philosophers taught the people how to be wise and good.

The writers composed fine poems and plays. The plays were not like those we have nowadays but were all about the doings of the gods and goddesses.

The theaters were not like those we have nowadays, either. They were always out of doors, usually on the side of a hill, where a grandstand could be built facing the stage. There was little or no scenery, and instead of an orchestra of musicians, there was a chorus of singers to accompany the actors. The actors wore false faces or masks to show what their feelings were, a *comic* mask with a grinning face when they wanted to be funny and a *tragic* mask with a sorrowful face when they wanted to seem sad.

Tragic and comic masks

Perhaps you have seen pictures of these masks, for in the decorations of our own theaters these same comic and tragic masks are sometimes used.

Athens had been named after the goddess Athena, who was supposed to watch out for and look after the city. The Athenians thought she should have a special temple. Accordingly, they built one to her on the top of a hill called the Acropolis.[2] This temple they called in her honor the Parthenon,[3] meaning the *maiden*, one of the names by which she was known.

---

[2] Acropolis [ə krop′ ə lis]   [3] Parthenon [pär′ thə non]

The Parthenon

The Parthenon is considered by some people to be the most beautiful building in the world, although as you see by the picture, as it is today, it is now in ruins. In the center of this temple was a huge statue of Athena made of gold and ivory by a sculptor named Phidias.[4] We are told that it was the most beautiful statue in the world as the Parthenon was the most beautiful building, but it has completely disappeared, and no one knows what became of it. One might guess, however, that the gold and ivory tempted thieves, who may have stolen it piece by piece.

Phidias made many other statues on the outside of the Parthenon, but most of these have been carried away and put in museums or have been lost or destroyed.

This statue of Athena and the other sculptures on the Parthenon made Phidias so famous that he was asked to make a statue of Zeus to be placed at Olympia, where the Olympic Games were held. The statue of Zeus was finer even than the one he had made of Athena and was so splendid that it was called one of the Seven Wonders of the World. You remember the pyramids of Egypt and the Hanging Gardens of Babylon were two others of the Seven Wonders. It is interesting that each of these

[4] Phidias [fid ⋅ ē əs]

three Wonders was located in a different continent. Can you tell which was in Africa, which in Asia, and which in Europe?

Phidias has been called the greatest sculptor who ever lived, but he did a thing which the Greeks considered a crime and would not forgive. We do not see anything so terribly wrong in what he did, but the Greeks' idea of right and wrong was different from ours. This is what he did. On the shield of the statue of Athena that he had made, Phidias carved a picture of himself and also one of his friend Pericles. It was merely a part of the decoration of the shield, and hardly anyone would have noticed it. But according to the Greek notion, it was a sacrilege to make a picture of a human being on a statue of a goddess. When the Athenians found out what Phidias had done, they threw him into prison, and there he died.

The Greeks used different kinds of columns on their buildings, and these columns are used in many public and in some private buildings today. I'll tell you what each kind is like; then see how many you can find.

The Parthenon was built in a style called *Doric*.[5]

The top of the column is called the capital, and the capital of the Doric column is shaped like a saucer with a square cover on top of it. There was no base or block at the bottom of the column. It rested directly on the floor. As the Doric column is so plain and strong-looking, it was called the man's style.

The second style is called *Ionic*.[6]

The capital of the Ionic column has a base, and the capital has ornaments like curls underneath the square top, and the column has a base.

As this column is more slender and more ornamental than the Doric, it was called the woman's style.

The third style is called *Corinthian*.[7]

---

[5] Doric [dôr´ ik]
[6] Ionic [ī on´ ik]
[7] Corinthian [kə rin´ thē ən]

The capital of the Corinthian column is higher than either of the other two and still more ornamental. It is said that the architect who first made this column got his idea for its capital from seeing a basketful of toys that had been placed on a child's grave as was the custom instead of flowers. The basket had been covered with a slab, and the leaves of the thistle called the acanthus had grown up around the basket. It looked so pretty that the architect thought it would make a beautiful capital for a column, and so he copied it.

1. Doric 2. Ionic 3. Corinthian

I asked some boys which one could find the most columns. The next day one boy said he had seen two Ionic columns, one on each side of the door of his house. The second had seen ten Doric columns on the savings bank. But the third said he had seen 138 Corinthian columns.

"Where on earth did you see so many?" I asked.

"I counted the lampposts from my house to the school," he said. "They were kind of Corinthian columns."

One of the friends of Pericles was a man named Herodotus.[8] He wrote in Greek the first history of the world. For this reason Herodotus is called the Father of History, and someday if you study Greek you may read what he wrote in his own language. Of course, at that time there was very little history to write. What has happened since *hadn't* happened then. He wrote about Egypt and other parts of the ancient world. He wrote about places so far away that most Greeks had never visited them. One was Kush,[9] in Africa way south of Egypt. Mostly Herodotus's history was a story of the wars with Persia, which I have just told you about.

In those days every once in a while a terrible contagious disease, called

---

[8] Herodotus [hə rod′ ə təs]   [9] Kush [k ŏŏsh]

a *plague*, would break out, and people would be taken sick and die by the thousands, for the doctors knew very little about the plague or how to cure it. Such a plague came upon Athens, and the Athenians died like poisoned flies. Pericles himself nursed the sick and did all he could for them, but finally he, too, was taken sick with plague and died. This happened at the very end of the Golden Age, which has been called in honor of its greatest man, the Age of Pericles.

28

When Greek Meets Greek

THE Golden Age, when Athens was so wonderful, lasted for only fifty years.

Why, do you suppose, did it stop at all?

It stopped chiefly because of a fight.

This time, however, the fight was not between Greece and someone outside, as in the Persian Wars. The fight was between two cities that had before this been more or less friendly—mostly less—between Sparta and Athens. It was a family quarrel between Greeks. The fight was all because one of these cities—Sparta—was jealous of the other—Athens.

The Spartans, as you know, were fine soldiers. The Athenians were fine soldiers, too. But ever since Themistocles had beaten the Persians at Salamis with the ships he had built, Athens had had a fine fleet as well, and Sparta had no fleet. Furthermore, Athens had become the most beautiful and most cultured city in the whole world.

Sparta did not care much about Athens's beautiful buildings and her education and culture and that sort of thing; that did not interest Sparta. What did make Sparta jealous was Athen's fleet. Sparta was inland, not on nor near the seashore as Athens was; so Sparta could not have a fleet at all. That city did not intend, however, to let Athens get ahead;

therefore, on one excuse or another, Sparta with all of *its* neighbors started a war against Athens with all of *its* neighbors.

Sparta was in a part of Greece that was called by the hard name, the Peloponnesus. In those days, people did not think this a hard name, for they were as familiar with it as you are with such a name as Massachusetts, for instance, which would seem just as hard to a Greek as Peloponnesus does to you. This war between Athens and Sparta was, therefore, called the Peloponnesian[1] War from the fact that it was not only Sparta but all of the Peloponnesus that fought against Athens.

We think a war lasts entirely too long if it lasts four or five years, but the Peloponnesian War lasted twenty-seven years! There is a saying, "When Greek meets Greek then comes a tug of war!" which means to say, "When two equal fighters such as Athens and Sparta, both Greek, meet each other in battle, who knows how it will end?"

I am not going to tell you about all the battles that took place during these twenty-seven years, but at the end of this long and bloody war, both cities were tired and worn out, and the glory of Athens was gone. Although Sparta was ahead, neither city ever amounted to much afterward. The Peloponnesian War ruined them both. That's the way war does!

All during the Peloponnesian War there was a man in Athens by the name of Socrates[2] who, many think, was one of the wisest and best men who ever lived. He was called a philosopher and went about the city teaching the people what was right and what they ought to do. But instead of actually *telling* the people what he thought was right, he asked them questions which made them see what was right. In this way, chiefly by asking questions, he led people to find out for themselves what he wanted them to know. This kind of teaching, simply by asking questions, has ever since been called Socratic.

---

[1] Peloponnesian [pel ə pə nē′ zhən]   [2] Socrates [sok′ r ə tēz]

Socrates had a snub nose and was bald and quite ugly, and yet he was very popular with the Athenians, which may seem strange, for the Athenians loved beautiful faces and beautiful figures and beautiful things, and Socrates was anything but beautiful. It must have been the beauty of Socrates's character that made them forget his ugliness, as I know some boys and girls who think their teacher is perfectly beautiful and just because she is so good and kind they love her, although she is really not pretty at all.

Socrates had a wife named Xantippe.[3] She had a bad temper and was the worst kind of a grouch. She thought Socrates was wasting his time, that he was a loafer, as he did no work that brought in any money. One day she scolded him so loudly that he left the house, whereupon she threw a bucket of water on him. Socrates, who never answered back, merely remarked to himself:

"After thunder, rain may be expected."

Socrates didn't believe in all the Greek gods, Zeus, Aphrodite, and the rest, but he was careful not to say so himself, for the Greeks were very particular that no one should say or do anything against their gods. Phidias, you remember, was thrown into prison for merely putting his picture on the shield of the goddess Athena, and one would have been put to death for teaching young men not to believe in the gods.

At last, however, Socrates, as he had feared he would be, was charged with not believing in the Greek gods and with teaching others not to believe in them. For this he was condemned to death. He was ordered to drink a cup of hemlock, which was a deadly poison. Socrates's pupils, or disciples, as they were then called, tried to have him refuse to drink the cup, but he would not disobey the order; and so, when he was nearly seventy years old, with all his disciples around him, he drank the cup of hemlock and died.

---

[3] Xantippe [zan tip′ ē]

Although Socrates lived many hundreds of years ago, he believed and taught some things that people today also believe.

One of these things he believed was that each of us has inside a *conscience*, which tells us what is right and what is wrong; we don't have to read from a book or be told by another what is right or what is wrong.

Another thing he taught was that there is a life after death and that when we die our souls live on.

No wonder he was not afraid himself to die!

29

Wise Men and Otherwise

HAVE you ever been playing in your yard when a strange boy who had been watching from the other side of the fence asked to be let into the game, saying he would show you how to play? You didn't want him around, and you didn't want him in, but somehow or other he got in and was soon bossing everybody else.

Well, there was a man named Philip who lived north of Greece, and he had been watching Sparta and Athens—not playing but fighting—and he wanted to get into the game. Philip was king of a little country called Macedonia,[1] but he thought he would like to be king of Greece also, and it seemed to him a good time, when Sparta and Athens were down and out after the Peloponnesian War, to step in and make himself king of that country. Philip was a great fighter, but he didn't want to fight Greece unless he had to. He wanted to be made king peaceably, and he wanted Greece to do it willingly. He thought up a scheme to bring this about, and this was his scheme.

He knew, as you do, how the Greeks hated the Persians, whom they had driven out of their country over a hundred years before. Although the Persian Wars had taken place so long ago, the Greeks had never forgotten the bravery of their forefathers and the tales of their victories over the Persians. These stories had been told them over and over by their parents and

---

[1] Macedonia [mas i dō′ nē ə]

grandparents, and they loved to read and reread them in Herodotus's history of the world.

So Philip said to the Greeks, "Your ancestors drove the Persians out of Greece, to be sure, but the Persians went back to their country, and you didn't go after them and punish them as you should have done. You didn't try to get even with them. Why don't you go over to Persia and conquer it now, and make the Persians pay for what they did to you?"

Then he slyly added, "Let me help you. I'll lead you against them."

No one seemed to see through Philip's scheme—nobody except one man. This man was an Athenian named Demosthenes.[2]

Demosthenes, when he was a boy, had decided that he would someday be a great speaker or orator, just as you might say you are going to be a doctor, or an aviator, or a teacher when you grow up.

Demosthenes had picked the one profession which by nature he was worst fitted for. In the first place, he had such a very soft, weak voice that one could hardly hear him. Besides, this, he stammered very badly and could not recite even a short poem without hesitating and stumbling so that people laughed at him. It seemed absurd, therefore, that he should aim to be a great speaker.

But Demosthenes practiced and *practiced* and *practiced* by himself. He went down on the seashore and put pebbles in his mouth to make it more difficult to speak clearly. Then he spoke to the roaring waves, making believe that he was addressing an angry crowd, who were trying to drown the sound of his voice, so that he would have to speak very loud indeed.

At last, by keeping constantly at it, Demosthenes did become a very great speaker. He spoke so wonderfully that he could make his audience laugh or make them cry whenever he wanted to, and he could persuade them to do almost anything he wished.

---

[2] Demosthenes [di mos′ thə nēz]

Now, Demosthenes was the man who saw through Philip's scheme for conquering Persia. He knew that Philip's real aim was to become king of Greece. So he made twelve speeches against him. These speeches were known as Philippics,[3] as they were against Philip. So famous were they that even today we call a speech that bitterly attacks anyone a *Philippic*.

The Greeks who heard Demosthenes were red-hot against Philip while they listened to him. But as soon as they got away from the sound of Demosthenes's words, the same Greeks became lukewarm and did nothing to stop Philip.

At last, in spite of everything that Demosthenes had said, Philip had his way and became king over all Greece.

Before, however, he could start out, as he had promised, to conquer Persia, he was killed by one of his own men, so that he was unable to carry out his plan.

Philip had a son named Alexander. Alexander was only twenty years old, but when his father died he became king of Macedonia and also of Greece.

When Alexander was a mere child, he saw some men trying without success to tame a young and very wild horse that shied and reared in the air so that no one was able to ride it. Alexander asked to be allowed to try to ride the animal. Alexander's father made fun of his son for wanting to attempt what those older than he had been unable to do, but at last gave his consent.

Now, Alexander had noticed what the others, although much older, had not noticed. The horse seemed to be afraid of its own shadow, for young colts are easily frightened by anything dark and moving, as some children are afraid of the dark at night.

Alexander turned the horse around facing the sun, so that its shadow would be behind, out of sight. He then mounted the animal and, to the amazement of all, rode off without any further trouble.

---

[3] Philippics [fi lip′ iks]

His father was delighted at his son's cleverness and gave him the horse as a reward. Alexander named the horse Bucephalus[4] and became so fond of him that when the horse died Alexander built a monument to him and named several cities after him.

Now, Alexander was a wonderful boy, but he had such a wonderful teacher named Aristotle[5] that some people think part, at least, of his greatness was due to the teacher.

Aristotle was probably the greatest teacher who ever lived. If there were more great teachers like Aristotle, it seems likely there would have been more great pupils like Alexander.

Aristotle wrote books about all sorts of things—books about the stars called astronomy, books about animals called zoology, and books on other subjects that you probably have never even heard of, such as psychology and politics.

For hundreds of years these books that Aristotle wrote were the schoolbooks that boys and girls studied, and for many years they were the *only* schoolbooks. Nowadays, schoolbooks usually change every few years after they are written. See how remarkable it was that Aristotle's schoolbooks should have been used for so long a time.

Aristotle had been taught by a man named Plato, who was also a great teacher and philosopher. Plato had been a pupil of Socrates, so that Aristotle was a kind of *grand-pupil* of Socrates. You have heard of the Wise Men of the East. These were the three Wise Men of Greece.

SOCRATES,

PLATO,

ARISTOTLE.

Some day you may read what they wrote or said over two thousand years ago.

30

A Boy King

WHEN you are twenty years old, what do you think you will be doing?

Will you be attending college?

Will you be working, or what?

When Alexander was twenty, he was king of both Macedonia and Greece. But Macedonia and Greece were entirely too small for this wonderful young man. He wanted to rule a much bigger country; in fact, he thought he would like to rule the whole world; that was all—nothing more.

So Alexander went right ahead with his father's plan to conquer Persia. The time had come to pay back Persia for that last invasion one hundred and fifty years before.

He got together an army and crossed the Hellespont into Asia and won battle after battle against the first Persian armies that went out to stop him.

He kept moving on, for Persia was a vast empire.

Soon he came to a town where in a temple there was kept a rope tied into a very farfamed and puzzling knot. It was called the Gordian[1] Knot, and it was very famous because the oracle had said that whoever should undo this knot would conquer Persia. No one had ever been able to untie it.

When Alexander heard the story, he went to the temple and took a look at the knot. He saw at once that it would be impossible to untie it, so,

---

[1] Gordian [gôr′ dē ən]

instead of even trying, as others had done, he drew his sword and with one stroke cut the knot in two.

Now when a person settles something difficult, not by fussing with it as one untangles a snarl, but at a single stroke, cutting through all difficulties, we say he "cuts the Gordian Knot."'

From that time on, Alexander conquered one city after another and never lost any battle of importance until he had conquered the whole of Persia.

He then went into Egypt, which belonged to Persia at that time, and conquered that country, too. To celebrate this victory, he founded a town near the mouth of the Nile and named it after himself, Alexandria. He started there a great library that later grew to be so big that there were said to be five hundred thousand books in it—that is, half a million—and was the largest library of ancient times. The books were not like those in the library of Ashurbanipal nor the kind we have now, of course, because printing had not been invented. They were every one of them written by hand, and not on pages, but on long sheets which were rolled up on sticks to form a scroll.

A scroll, pens, and ink

In the harbor of Alexandria was a little island called Pharos,[2] and on this island some years later was built a remarkable lighthouse named for the island, the Pharos. It was really a building more like a modern skyscraper with a tower. It was over thirty stories high, which seemed most remarkable at that time when most buildings were only one or two stories high, and its light could be seen for many miles. The Pharos of Alexandria was called one of the Seven Wonders of the World. You have already heard of three others, so this makes the fourth.

Alexandria grew, in the course of time, to be the largest and most important

---

[2] Pharos [fār′ os]

seaport of the ancient world. Now, however, the Pharos and the library and all the old buildings have long since disappeared.

Alexander did not stay very long in any one place. He was restless. He wanted to keep on the move. He wanted to see new places and to conquer new people. He almost forgot his own little country of Macedonia and Greece. Instead of being homesick, however, as almost any one would have been, he kept going farther and farther away from home all the time. We should call such a man an adventurer or an explorer, as well as a great general. Alexander kept on conquering and didn't stop conquering until he had reached far-off India.

There in India his army, which had stayed on with him all the way, became homesick and wanted to go back. They had been away from home for more than ten years and were so far off that they were afraid they would never get back.

Alexander was now only thirty years old, but he was called Alexander the Great, for he was ruler of the whole world—at least, most of it that was then known to most Greeks, except Italy, which was still only a collection of little, unimportant towns at that time. When Alexander found there were no more countries left for him to conquer, he was so disappointed that he wept!

At last, when there was nothing more to conquer, he agreed to do what his army begged him and started slowly back toward Greece.

He got as far as Babylon, the city once so large and so magnificent. There he celebrated with a feast, but while feasting and drinking he suddenly died. He never reached Greece.

This was in 323 b.c. when he was but 33 years old. You can remember these figures easily, for they are all 3's except the middle figure in the date, which is one less than 3.

Alexander the Great had conquered the largest country that had ever been under the rule of one man, and yet this was not the only reason we call him *the Great.*

He was not only a great ruler and a great general, but—this may surprise you—he was also a great teacher. Aristotle had taught him to be that.

Alexander taught the Greek language to the people he conquered so that they could read Greek books. He taught them about Greek sculpture and painting. He taught them the wise sayings of the Greek philosophers, Socrates and Plato and his own teacher, Aristotle. He trained the people in athletics as the Greeks did for their Olympic Games.

Alexander had married a beautiful Persian woman named Roxana,[3] but their only child was still a baby, not born until after his father's death; so when the great king died there was no one to rule after him. He had told his generals before he died that the strongest one of them should be the next ruler; they must fight it out among themselves.

His generals did fight to see who should win, and finally four of them who were victorious decided to divide up this great empire and each have a share.

One of his generals was named Ptolemy I,[4] and he took Egypt as his share and ruled well; but the others did not amount to much, and after a while their shares became unimportant and went to pieces. Like a toy balloon which stretches and stretches as you blow it up, Alexander's empire grew bigger and bigger until—all of a sudden—*pop*—nothing was left but the pieces.

---

[3] Roxana [rok san′ ə]   [4] Ptolemy [tol′ ə mē]

31

Picking a Fight

EVERY dog has his day.

A tennis or track champion wins over the one who was champion before and then has a few years during which he or she is unbeaten. Sooner or later, however, some younger and better athlete wins and in turn takes the championship.

It seems almost the same way with countries as with people. One country wins the championship from another, holds it for a few years, and then, when older, finally loses it to some new-comer.

We have seen that

Nineveh was champion for a while; then

Babylon had a turn; then

Persia had a turn; then

Greece; and, lastly,

Macedonia.

You may wonder who was to be the next champion after Alexander's empire went to pieces—who was to have the next turn.

When Alexander was conquering the world, he went east toward the rising sun, and south. He paid little attention to the country to the west toward the setting sun. Rome, which we have not heard of for some time, was then only a small town with narrow streets and frame houses. It was not nearly important enough for Alexander to think much about. Rome itself was not thinking of anything then except keeping the neighboring soldiers out.

In the course of time, however, Rome began to grow up and was not only able to take care of itself but could put up a very stiff fight. Rome fought and won battles with most of the other towns in Italy, until at last Rome became champion of the whole of the *boot*. Then the Romans began to look around to see what other countries there were outside of Italy that they might conquer.

Perhaps you have noticed that Italy, the *boot*, seems about to kick a little island as if it were a football. This island is Sicily,[1] and just opposite Sicily across the Mediterranean in North Africa was a city called Carthage.

Carthage had been founded by the Phoenicians many years before and had become a very rich and powerful city. Over the years, Phoenicians mixed with the local North Africans called Berbers and formed a unique culture.

They planted big farms with fruit trees and olive trees. They owned herds of cattle and sheep and horses. Wealthy families owned large country estates.

As Carthage was by the sea, it had built many ships and traded with all the other seaports along the Mediterranean, just as the old Phoenician cities of Tyre and Sidon had done. By now, Carthage controlled the whole western end of the Mediterranean Sea.

Carthage did not like to see Rome getting so strong and growing so big and becoming so powerful. In other words, Carthage felt challenged by Rome.

Rome, on her side, was jealous of the wealth and trade of Carthage. So Romans anxiously looked around for some excuse to get into a fight with their rival across the sea.

---

[1] Sicily [sis′ ə lē]

Map of Mediterranean showing Carthage, Spain, etc.

Now, you know how easy it is to pick a quarrel and start a fight when you are looking for trouble. One boy sticks out his tongue, the other gives him a kick, and the fight is on.

Well, two countries are at times just like little boys; they start a fight with just as little excuse, and though they call the fight *war* it is nothing but a *scrap*. Only there are no parents to come along and make them both go home.

It didn't take long for Rome and Carthage to find an excuse, and a war was started between them. The Romans called this fight a Punic[2] War, for *Punic* was their name for Phoenician, and the Carthaginians originally were Phoenicians.

As Carthage was across the water, the Romans could not get there except in boats. But Rome had no boats. Rome was not on the seashore and knew nothing about making boats, nor about sailing them.

The Carthaginians, on the other hand, had many, many boats, and were old and experienced sailors.

Romans happened to find the wreck of a Carthaginian ship that had been cast ashore, and they at once set to work to make a copy of it. In a remarkably short time they had built one ship, then another and another, until they had a great many ships. Then, though the Romans were new at the game, they attacked the Carthaginian fleet.

It would seem that the Carthaginians could easily have won, for the Romans knew so little about boats. In sea battles, before this, the fighting had been done by running into the enemy and ramming and sinking their ships.

The Romans knew they were no match for the Carthaginians in this sort of fighting. So they thought up a way in which they could fight them as on land.

To do this they invented a kind of big hook which they called a *crow*. The idea was for a ship to run close alongside a Carthaginian ship and, instead of trying to sink her, to throw out this big hook or *crow*, catch hold of the other ship, and pull both boats close together. The Roman soldiers would then scramble over the sides into the enemy's boat and fight them the same way they would on land.

The scheme worked.

This new kind of fighting took the Carthaginians by surprise, and they were no match for the Romans at first.

---

[2] Punic [pyo͞o ′ nik]

Rome did not have things all her own way by any means. The Carthaginians soon learned how to fight in this fashion, too. So Rome lost, as well as won, battles both on land and on sea. At last Rome did win, and the Carthaginians were beaten. Thus ended the first Punic War.

32

The Boot Kicks and Stamps

THE Carthaginians were not beaten for good. They were only waiting for another chance to get even. As, however, they had been unsuccessful in attacking Italy from in front as they had been doing, they made up their minds to attack from the back. Their scheme was to go the long way round through Spain and down into Italy from the north.

In order to do this, first of all they had to conquer Spain so that they could get through. They did this, however, rather easily, for the Carthaginians had a very great general named Hannibal. Then came the great difficulty, to get into Italy by this back way.

Across the top of the *boot*, at the north of Italy, there are the great mountains called the Alps. They are miles high and covered even in summer with ice and snow. There are crags and steep cliffs along which anyone passing who made a single misstep would be dashed to death thousands of feet below.

It was the Alps, therefore, that formed a bigger and better wall than any city or country could possibly build. Of course the Romans thought it impossible for any army to climb over such a terribly high and dangerous wall.

Time and again there have been things that people call impossible to do, and then someone has come along and done them.

People said it was impossible to fly.

Then someone did it.

People said it was impossible to cross the Alps with an army.

Then Hannibal came along, and before the Romans knew what had happened, he had done it. He had crossed the Alps with his army and was in at the back door! Hannibal brought with him elephants from Africa. These were the *tanks* of ancient warfare and were highly valued. Can you imagine the long columns of soldiers and elephants crossing those high mountains?

The Romans were unable to keep him from marching on toward their city, winning battle after battle as he came along. They were unable to prevent his marching up and down Italy, conquering other towns in Italy and doing pretty much as he pleased. It seemed as if Rome were beaten and would lose all of Italy.

Now, in some games, if you can't defend your own goal, it may be a good plan to try attacking your opponent's goal.

Romans thought they would try this plan. While Hannibal was attacking, Rome would attack Carthage while its general was away and there was no strong goalkeeper to defend that city.

The Romans sent a young man named Scipio[1] with an army to do this.

First, however, Scipio went to Spain to cut Hannibal off from the way he had come.

Scipio then went over to Africa to attack Carthage itself.

The Carthaginians, frightened at being attacked with their general and his army far off in Italy, sent as fast as they could for Hannibal to come home. When at last he arrived, it was too late. Scipio fought a famous battle at Zama[2] near Carthage, and the Carthaginians were beaten, beaten a second time by the Romans. Thus ended the second Punic War in 202 B.C. This is another easy name and easy date:

ZAMA—202 B.C.

---

[1] Scipio [sip′ ē ō]   [2] Zama [zä′ mä]

The Romans had won two wars against Carthage; you would think that they would now have been satisfied. But they weren't. They thought they had not beaten Carthage badly enough. They were afraid Carthage was not quite dead or that it might come to life. They thought there might be a little spark left that might start a fire if it weren't trampled out.

Now, it is bad sport to pummel your opponent after he is beaten, and Carthage was beaten—beaten, black and blue. Yet a few years later the Romans attacked again for the third and last time.

Carthage was unable to defend itself, and the Romans destroyed the city. Later, though, the Roman general Julius Caesar rebuilt the city. Still later, the Romans built other cities nearby, with fine roads connecting them and with great aqueducts bringing them water. Today we can visit the Roman ruins in what is now Tunisia.

33

The New Champion of the World

You can well imagine how proud all the Romans now were that they *were* Romans, for Rome was the champion fighter of the world. If a man could toss his head and say, "I am a Roman citizen," people were always ready to do something for him, afraid to do him any harm, afraid what might happen to them if they did. Rome was ruler not only of Italy but of Spain and North Africa. Like other earlier nations, once Rome had started conquering, it kept on conquering, until by 100 B.C. Rome was ruler of almost all the countries bordering the Mediterranean Sea—all except Egypt.

The New Champion of the World, who was to be champion for a great many years, was very businesslike and practical.

The Greeks loved beautiful things, beautiful buildings, beautiful sculpture, beautiful poems. The Romans copied the Greeks and learned from them how to make many beautiful things, but the Romans were most interested in practical and useful things. For example, now that the Romans ruled the world, they had to be able to send messengers and armies easily and quickly in every direction to the end of the empire and back again. It was necessary to have roads, for of course there were no railroads then. Now, an ordinary road made by simply clearing away the ground gets full of deep ruts and in rainy weather becomes so muddy that it can hardly be used at all.

Rome set to work and built roads. These roads were like paved streets. Large rocks were placed at the bottom for a foundation, smaller stones placed on top, and large, flat paving-stones laid over all. Thousands of miles of such roads were built to all parts of the empire. One could go from almost anywhere all the way to Rome on paved roads. We still have an expression, "All roads lead to Rome." So well were these roads made that many of them still exist today, two thousand years after they were built.

The Romans also showed their practical minds by making two very important city improvements. If you live in a city, you turn on a spigot and you get plenty of pure water whenever you want it. The people in cities at that time, however, usually had to get their water both for drinking and for washing from wells or springs nearby. These springs and wells often became dirty and made the people very sick. Every once in a while because of such dirty water there were those terrible plagues, those terribly contagious diseases like the one I told you about in Athens when people died faster than they could be buried.

The Romans wanted pure water, so they set to work to find lakes from which they could get pure water. As oftentimes these lakes were many miles away from the city, they then built big pipes to carry the water all the way to the city. Such a pipe was not made of iron or terra-cotta as nowadays, but of stone and concrete, and was called an *aqueduct*, which in Latin means *water-carrier*. If this aqueduct had to cross a river or a valley, they built a bridge to hold it up. Many of these Roman aqueducts are still standing and in use today.

Now, up to this time waste water, after it had been used, and also every other kind of dirt and refuse, was simply dumped into the street. This

Roman aqueduct

naturally made the city or town filthy and unhealthy and was another cause of plagues.

The Romans, however, built great underground sewers to carry off this dirt and waste water and empty it into the river or into some other place where they thought it would do no harm and cause no sickness. Now we know that it's not good to dump sewage into rivers because they can become polluted. Then if people drink that water, they'll get sick. The Romans knew that they had to get the sewage off the city streets, but they didn't know how to avoid polluting their rivers. Nowadays, every large city has aqueducts and sewers as a matter of course, but the Romans were the first Europeans to build them on a large scale.

One of the most important things that Rome did was to make rules that everyone had to obey; laws, we call them. Many of these laws were so fair and just that some of our own laws today are copied from them.

All the cities and towns of the Roman Empire had to pay money or taxes to Rome. Rome therefore became a very wealthy city. Millions of this money, which was brought to her, was spent in putting up beautiful buildings in the city, temples to the gods, splendid palaces for the rulers, public baths, and huge open-air places called *amphitheaters* where the people could be amused.

The amphitheaters were something like our football and baseball fields or stadiums. They did not have football or baseball, however. They had chariot races, and deadly fights between men, or between men and animals. Chariots were small carts with large wheels drawn by two or by four horses and driven by a man standing up. Perhaps you have seen chariot races in the circus.

The sport that the Romans enjoyed most of all was a fight of gladiators. Gladiators were very strong and powerful men who had been captured in battle by the Romans. They were made to fight with one another or with wild animals for the amusement of the crowds. These gladiatorial fights were very cruel, but the Romans enjoyed seeing blood shed. They liked to see one man kill another or a wild animal. It was so amusing. The movies would not have interested them half as much. Usually the gladiators fought until one or the other was killed, for the people were not, as a rule, satisfied until this was done.

Sometimes, however, if a gladiator, who had been knocked out, had shown himself particularly brave and a good fighter or a good sport, the people seated all around the amphitheater would turn their thumbs *up* as a sign that his life was to be spared by the other gladiator. The winning gladiator, before killing his opponent whom he had down, would wait to see what the people wished. If they turned their thumbs *down*, it meant he was to finish the fight by killing his man.

Although Rome had become such a fine and beautiful and healthy city in which to live, the rich people were getting most of the money that came there from all over the empire. They were getting richer and richer all the time, while the poor people, who got nothing, were getting poorer and poorer all the time. The Romans brought the people they conquered in battle to Rome and made them work for them without pay. These were slaves and they did all the work. It is said that there were more than twice as many slaves as Romans—two slaves for every Roman citizen.

Now, Scipio, who had conquered Hannibal in the Punic War, had a daughter named Cornelia Graccha, and she had two sons. They were very fine boys, and Cornelia was naturally very proud of them.

One day a very rich Roman woman was visiting Cornelia and showing off all her rings and necklaces and other ornaments, of which she had a great many and was very proud.

When she had shown off all she had, she asked to see Cornelia's jewels.

Cornelia called to her two boys, who were playing outside, and when they came in to their mother she put her arms around them and said:

"These are *my* jewels."

But boys who are jewels when they are young do not always turn out to be jewels when they grow up. You may wonder how Cornelia's jewels turned out.

When they grew up, the Gracchi,[1] as they were called, saw such great extravagance among the rich and such great misery among the poor that they wanted to do something about it. They saw that the poor had hardly anything to eat and no place to live. This did not seem fair. They tried to lower the price of food, so that the poor might be able to buy enough to eat. They tried to find some way to give the poor at least a small piece of land where they might raise a few vegetables. They were partly successful in bringing this about. But the rich people didn't like giving up anything to the poor, and they killed one of the Gracchus brothers, and later they killed the other one, also. These were Cornelia's jewels.

---

[1] Gracchi [grak′ ī]

34

The Noblest Roman of Them All

HERE'S a puzzle for you:

A man once found a very old piece of money that had on it the date *100* B.C.

That couldn't be so. Why not? See if you can tell without looking at the answer at the bottom of the page.[1]

In the year 100 B.C. was born in Rome a boy who was named Julius Caesar.

If you had asked him when he was born, he would have said in the Year 653.

Why do you suppose?

Because Roman boys counted time from the founding of Rome in 753 B.C. and Caesar was born 653 years after the city was founded. That makes it 100 years before Christ, doesn't it?

Pirates seemed to be everywhere in the Mediterranean Sea at that time—*Pirates*. Now that Rome was ruler of the world, there were many ships carrying gold from different parts of the empire to Rome. The pirates sailed up and down, lying in wait to capture and rob these ships laden with gold.

When Caesar grew to be a young man, he was sent off to sea to fight these pirates, and he was captured by them. The pirates kept Caesar a

---

[1] People living 100 years before Christ was born could not have known when he was to be born and so could not put such a date on the coins they made.

prisoner and sent to Rome saying they would not let him go unless Rome sent them a great deal of money. Caesar knew that he would be killed if the money was not sent. He knew, too, that he might be killed anyway. He was not only *not* afraid, but he told the pirates that if he lived to get back home he would return with a fleet and punish every one of them. When at last the money came they let him go, nevertheless. They thought Caesar would not dare to do what he said. They thought he was just *talking big*. At any rate, they did not believe he would be able to catch them. Caesar, however, kept his word, came back after them as he said he would do, and took them prisoners. Then he had them all put to death on the cross, which was the Roman way of punishing thieves.

The far-off places of the Roman Empire were always fighting against Rome, trying to get rid of the foreign rule, and they had to be kept in order by a general with an army. As Caesar had shown such bravery in fighting the pirates he was given an army and sent to fight two of these far-off places—Spain and a country north of Spain then known as Gaul, which is now France.

Caesar conquered these countries, and then he wrote a history of his battles in Latin, which of course was his own language. Nowadays this book, called *Caesar's Commentaries*, is usually the first book read by those who study Latin.

In 55 B.C. Caesar crossed over in ships to the island of Britain, conquered a large part of it, and went back again next year, in 54 B.C.

Caesar was becoming famous for the way he conquered and ruled over the western part of the Roman Empire. Besides this, he was very popular with his soldiers.

Now there was in Rome at this time another general named Pompey.[2] Pompey had been successfully fighting in the eastern part of the

---

[2] Pompey [pom′ pē]

Roman Empire while Caesar had been fighting in the west. Pompey had been a great friend of Caesar, but when he saw how much land Caesar had conquered and how popular he was with his soldiers, he became very jealous of him. Notice how many quarrels and wars are caused simply by jealousy. You have heard of at least two already.

While Caesar was away with his army, Pompey went to the Roman Senate and persuaded the senators to order Caesar to give up the command of his army and return to Rome.

When Caesar received the order from the Senate to give up his command and return to Rome, he thought over the matter for some time. Then at last he made up his mind that he would return to Rome, but he would *not* give up his command. Instead, he decided that he and his army would take command of Rome itself.

Now, there was a little stream called the *Rubicon,*[3] which separated the part of the country over which Caesar was given charge from that of Rome. The Roman law forbade any general to cross this stream with an army ready to fight—this was the line beyond which he must not pass, for the Romans were afraid that if a general with an army got too close to Rome he might make himself king.

When Caesar decided not to obey the Senate, he crossed this stream— the Rubicon—with his army and marched on to Rome.

People now speak of any dividing line from danger as "the Rubicon" and say that a person "crosses the Rubicon" when he takes a step from which there is no turning back, when he starts something difficult or dangerous which he must finish.

When Pompey heard that Caesar was coming, he took to his heels and fled to Greece. In a few days Caesar had made himself head not only of

[3] Rubicon [roō′ bi kon]

Rome but of all Italy. Caesar then went after Pompey in Greece and in a battle with his army beat him badly.

Now that Pompey was out of the way, Caesar was the chief ruler of the whole of the Roman Empire.

Egypt did not yet belong to Rome. Caesar next went there and conquered that country. Now, in Egypt there was ruling a beautiful queen named Cleopatra.[4] Cleopatra was so charming that she seemed able to make everyone fall in love with her. Cleopatra flirted with Caesar and so fascinated him that he almost forgot everything else. Although he had won Egypt, he allowed Cleopatra to remain queen over that country.

Just at this time some people in the far eastern part of the empire started a war to get rid of the rule of Rome. Caesar left Egypt, traveled rapidly to the place where the enemy were, made quick work of conquering them, then sent back the news of his victory to Rome in the most laconic (do you remember what that means?) description ever given of a battle. There were only three words in the message. Although the messenger could have carried three thousand as easily as three words, Caesar sent a message that would have been short even for a telegram. He wrote, "Veni, vidi, vici," which means, "I came, I saw, I conquered."

When Caesar at last got back to Rome, the people wanted to make him king, or said they did. Caesar was already more than king, for he was head of the whole Roman Empire. But he wasn't called king, for there had been no kings since 509 B.C., when Tarquin was driven out. The Romans had been afraid of kings and hated them, or were supposed to hate them.

A few of the people thought that Caesar was getting too much power and believed it would be a terrible thing to make him a king. They

---

[4] Cleopatra [klē ə pa′ trə]

therefore decided on a plot to prevent such a thing happening. One of these plotters was a man named Brutus, who had been Caesar's very best friend.

One day when Caesar was expected to visit the Roman Senate, they lay in wait for him until he should appear—in the same way I have seen boys hide around the corner for some schoolmate, against whom they had a grudge, until he should come out of school.

Caesar came along, and just as he was about to enter the Senate the plotters crowded around him, and one after another they stabbed him.

Caesar, taken by surprise, tried to defend himself; but all he had was his stylus, which was a kind of pen he used for writing, and he could not do much with that, in spite of a famous saying, "The pen is mightier than the sword."

When at last Caesar saw Brutus—his best friend—strike at him, his heart seemed broken and he gave up. Then, exclaiming in Latin, "Et tu, Brute!" which means, "And thou, O Brutus!" he fell down dead. This was in 44 B.C.

Antony,[5] one of Caesar's true friends, made a speech over Caesar's dead body, and his words so stirred the crowd of people that gathered round that they would have torn the murderers to pieces if they could have caught them.

Shakespeare has written a play called *Julius Caesar*, and the month of July is named after him.

Now whom do you suppose Antony called "The Noblest Roman of Them All"?

"Julius Caesar"?

No, you're wrong. Brutus, the friend who stabbed Caesar, was called, "The Noblest Roman of Them All."

Why, do you suppose?

---

[5] Antony [an´ tə nē]

You'll have to read Antony's speech at the end of the play to find out. Caesar was pronounced in Latin *kaiser;*[6] and in later years the rulers of Germany were called this, and those of Russia by the shortened form, *czar.*[7]

35
An Emperor Who Was Made a God

A person is famous who has a town or a street named after him or her. Will you ever do anything great enough to have even an alley named after you?

Just suppose a month, one of the twelve months of the year, was given your name!

Millions upon millions of people would then write and speak your name forever!

I'm going to tell you about a man who not only had a month named after him but who was made a god!

After Caesar had been killed, three men ruled the Roman Empire. One of these three men was Antony, the friend of Caesar, who made the famous speech over his dead body. The second was Caesar's adopted son, who was named Octavius.[1] The name of the third you don't need to know, for Antony and Octavius soon got rid of him. Then no sooner had they forced him out than each of these two began to plot to get the share of the other.

Antony's share, over which he ruled, was the eastern part of the empire. The capital of this part was Alexandria in Egypt, hence Antony went there to live.

---

[1] Octavius [ok tā′ vē əs]

In Egypt Antony fell in love with Cleopatra, as Caesar before him had done, and he finally married her.

Octavius, in the west, which was his share, then made war on Antony and Cleopatra together, and in the end beat them both. Antony felt so bad at being beaten by Octavius that he committed suicide.

His widow, Cleopatra, thereupon, flirted with Octavius as she had with Julius Caesar and Antony, hoping to make him also fall in love with her and so win him in that way.

It was no use. Octavius was a different kind of man from both Julius Caesar and Antony. He was cold-blooded and businesslike. He had no heart for love-making. He would not let a woman charm him or turn him aside from his plan, which was to be the greatest man in the world!

Cleopatra saw that it was no use trying to fool him. Then she heard that she was going to be taken back to Rome and paraded through the streets, as was done with any other prisoners taken in battle. She could not stand such a shame as that, and so she made up her mind she would not be taken back to Rome.

Now, in Egypt there is a kind of snake called an asp, which is deadly poisonous. Taking one of these asps in her hand, she uncovered her breast and let it bite her, and so she died.

Octavius was now ruler over all the countries that belonged to Rome, and when he returned home to that city, the people hailed him *Emperor*. He then gave up the name Octavius and had himself called *Augustus Caesar*,[2] which is like saying, *His Majesty, Caesar*. This was in 27 B.C. The Romans had got rid of their kings in 509. From now on Rome had emperors, who were more than kings, for they ruled over many countries.

Octavius, now with his name changed to Augustus Caesar, was only thirty-six years old when he became sole master of the Roman world. Rome was the great capital of this vast empire.

---

[2] Augustus Caesar [ə gus′ təs sē′ zər]

Augustus set to work to make Rome a beautiful city. He tore down a great many of the old buildings made of brick and put up in their place a remarkable number of new and handsome buildings of marble. Augustus always bragged that he found Rome brick and left it marble.

One of the finest buildings in Rome, the Pantheon[3] was built. Pantheon means the temple of all the gods. Do not mix this with the Parthenon in Athens, for the two buildings are quite different, and though the names look something alike and sound something alike, they mean quite different things. Parthenon is from the goddess Athena Parthenos[4]; Pantheon is from the two words *Pan theon*, which means *all gods*.

The Pantheon has a great dome made of brick and mortar. This dome is shaped like a bowl turned upside down, and in the very center of the top of the dome is a round opening called an eye. This open eye is the only "window" in the building, but through it, even on a cloudy day, enough light comes so that you can clearly see the whole handsome interior.

So magnificent did the city become with all these wonderful buildings, and so permanently did it seem to be built, that it was known as The

Roman Pantheon

---

[3] Pantheon [pan′ thē on]   [4] Athena Parthenos [ə thē′ nə pär′ thə nōs]

Eternal City and is still so spoken of.

There was a public square in Rome called the Forum. Here markets were held and the people came together for all sorts of things. Around the Forum were erected temples to the gods, courthouses, and other public buildings. The courthouses were something like the temples that the Greeks built, only the columns were put on the inside of the building instead of on the outside.

Triumphal arches also were erected to celebrate great victories. When a conquering hero returned from the war, he and his army passed through such an arch in a triumphal parade.

There had been in Rome a great amphitheater that is supposed to have held more people than any structure that has ever been built—two hundred thousand, it is said, or more than all the people who live in some good-sized cities. This was called the Circus Maximus.[5] It was at last torn down to make room for other buildings.

Another amphitheater was the Colosseum,[6] but this was not built until some time after Augustus had died. It held about the same number as the largest stadium in this country does today. Here were held those fights between men, called gladiators, and wild animals that I have already told you about. It is still standing, and, though it is in ruins, you can sit in the same seats where the old Roman emperors did, see the dens where the wild animals were kept, the doors where they were let into the arena, and even bloody marks that are said to be the stains made by the slain men and beasts.

So many famous writers lived at the time of Augustus that this has been called the Augustan[7] Age. Two of the best known Latin poets lived at this time. These poets were Virgil and Horace.[8] Virgil wrote the *Æneid*,[9] which told of the wanderings of Æneas, the Trojan, who settled in Italy,

---

[5] Circus Maximus [sür′ kəs mak′ sə məs]
[6] Colosseum [kol ə sē′ əm]
[7] Augustan [ô gus′ tən]

[8] Horace [hôr′ is]
[9] Æneid [i nē′ id]

and was the great-great-great-grandfather of Romulus and Remus. Horace wrote many short poems called odes. They were long songs of shepherds and shepherdesses and songs of the farm and country life. People liked his songs, and many still name their sons after him.

When Augustus Caesar died, he was made a god because he had done so much for Rome; temples were built in which he was worshiped, and the month of August was named after him.

36

"Thine Is the Kingdom, the Power, and the Glory"

AUGUSTUS Caesar had been Ruler of the World.

He had found Rome brick and left it marble.

He had had a month named after him, and

He had been made a god!

Surely no one could ever be greater than he! Yet a greater man than he was living at the very same time—although Augustus himself knew nothing about Him and lived and died without ever having heard of Him. This man was born in the eastern part of Augustus's empire in a tiny little village called Bethlehem, and His name was Jesus.

For many, many years after Jesus was born no one except His family and friends knew or cared anything about His birth or paid the slightest attention to it.

Jesus was a Jew, the son of a carpenter. As a boy and young man He led a very simple and quiet life working in His father's shop. He did not begin to preach until He was more than thirty years old. Then He went about teaching the people what we learn today as the Christian religion.

He taught that there was one God over all.

He taught brotherly love, that one should love one's neighbor as oneself.

He taught the Golden Rule; that is, "Do unto others as you would have them do unto you."

He taught that there was a life after death for which this short life on earth was only a preparation; that therefore you should "lay up your treasures in heaven" by doing good works here.

Some of the Jews listened to Jesus and believed what He taught them. They thought He was going to set them free from the rule of the Romans, which they hated. Some of the temple priests, however, were afraid of what Jesus taught. Because so many people listened to Him and believed in Him, the priests were afraid they would lose their influence to a man whose ideas they believed were wrong. So they plotted to have Him put to death.

Now the men who were plotting Jesus's death could not have Him put to death without the permission of the Roman ruler of that part of the empire where Jesus lived. This ruler was named Pilate.[1] So they went to Pilate and told him that Jesus was trying to make Himself king. Jesus of course meant and always said that He was a heavenly ruler and not an earthly king. These men knew that Pilate would not care at all what religion Jesus taught. There were all sorts of religions in the Roman Empire—those that believed in idols and those that believed in the sun, moon, and so on. One more new religion made little difference to the Romans, and Jesus would not be put to death simply for teaching another. But the priests knew if they could make Pilate believe that Jesus was trying to make Himself a king, that was a thing for which He could be crucified. Pilate did not believe much in what they said against Jesus. It was a small matter to him. But he wanted to please them and keep his government in order, so he told them he would have Jesus put to death because they wanted it. So He was crucified.

Jesus had chosen twelve of his fellow Jews to teach what he told them. These twelve men were called apostles. After Jesus was crucified, the apostles went through the land teaching the people what He had taught them.

---

[1] Pilate [pī' lət]

Those who believed in and followed His teachings were called disciples of Christ (the Greek word for "messiah")[2] or Christians. The apostles were teachers; the disciples were pupils.

One thing that no Christian, or Jew either, could do was worship the Roman emperor. Most people in the empire found it easy to add one new god, but Christians, of course, could not do that. The Romans thought that these disciples of Christ were trying to start a new world empire and that they were against Rome and the emperor and should be arrested and put in prison. The Christians, therefore, held their meetings in secret places, sometimes even underground, so that they would not be found and arrested.

After a while the leaders of the Christians became bolder. They came out of their secret places and taught and preached openly, although they knew they might sooner or later be thrown into prison and perhaps killed. Indeed, so strongly did they believe in the teachings of Christ that they seemed even glad to die for His sake, as He had died on the cross for them.

In the first hundred years after Christ, there were a great many Christians put to death because they were thought traitors. Christians who died for Christ's sake were called *martyrs*. The first martyr was named Stephen. He was stoned to death about 33 A.D.

One of the men who helped in putting Stephen to death was a man named Saul. Saul was a Roman citizen and, like other Roman citizens, was proud of that fact. He thought the Christians were enemies of his country, and he did everything he could to have the Christians punished. Then, all of a sudden, Saul had a change of heart and came to believe in the religion of the very people whom he had been fighting. Whatever Saul did or whatever he believed, he did or believed with his whole soul. Though he had never seen Christ, he became one of the chief Christians and then was made an apostle and was called by his Roman name, Paul.

[2] Messiah [me sī′ ə]

Paul preached the new religion far and wide just as earnestly as he had fought against it at first. Then he, too, was condemned to death. Paul, however, was, as I have said, a Roman citizen, and a Roman citizen could not be put to death by the ordinary judges who were not Roman citizens nor in the ordinary way by crucifying. So Paul appealed to the emperor, but he was put in prison in Rome and afterward beheaded. He is now known as St. Paul.

Peter was another of the chief apostles. Christ had said to him, "I will give unto thee the keys of the kingdom of heaven."[3] Peter, too, was thrown into prison, and was sentenced to be crucified. He asked to be crucified with his head downward. He thought it too great an honor to die in just the same way as his Lord. On this spot in Rome where Peter was put to death was built long afterward the largest church in the world, the Cathedral of St. Peter.

As everything before Christ's birth is called B.C. and everything since his birth is called A.D., you would naturally suppose that 0 would be the date of His birth.

It was not until some five hundred years later that people began to date from Christ's birth. And then, when they did begin to date from this event, they made a mistake. It was found out that Christ was really born four years before He was supposed to have been born—that is, in 4 B.C.—but when the mistake was found out, it was then too late to change.

---

[3] Matthew 16:19

37

Blood and Thunder

I once had a big Newfoundland dog, and he was one of the best friends a boy ever had. I don't know who it was that named him; he was named before I got him; but whoever it was must either have been ignorant of history or a bad chooser of names. He was called Nero,[1] and even a dog would have hated such a name, had he known whose it once was.

Every good story usually has a villain to make it interesting. The story of Rome has plenty of villains, but one of the worst was Nero. He was a Roman emperor who lived not long after Christ, and he is considered one of the cruelest and wickedest rulers that ever lived.

He killed his mother. He killed his wife. He killed his teacher, who was named Seneca.[2] Seneca was a very good teacher, too.

We think that Nero ordered both Peter and Paul put to death, for they were executed at the time of Nero's rule.

Nero seemed to take great pleasure in making others suffer. He loved to see men torn to pieces by wild beasts; it amused him greatly. I have seen boys who liked to throw stones at dogs just to hear them yelp, or tear the wings off butterflies. Such boys must have some Nero in them; don't you think?

---

[1] Nero [nēr′ ō]   [2] Seneca [sen′ i kə]

If a man was a Christian, that gave Nero an excuse to torture him horribly. Nero had some of the Christians wrapped in tar and pitch, then placed around the garden of his palace and set fire to, as if they were torches. It is even said that Nero set Rome on fire just for the fun of seeing the city burn. Then he sat in a tower and, while he watched the blaze spreading played on a stringed instrument. The saying is that *"Nero fiddled while Rome burned."* The fire burned day and night for a whole week and destroyed more than half the city. Nero then laid the blame on the Christians, who, he said, started the fire. Did you ever blame someone else for something you had done?

Some think Nero really was crazy, and we hope he was, for it is hard to think any human being who was not crazy could act as he did.

Nero built himself an immense palace and overlaid it extravagantly with gold and mother-of-pearl. It was known as Nero's House of Gold. At its front door he put up a colossal statue of himself in bronze fifty feet high. Both the House of Gold and the statue were later destroyed, but the Colosseum, which was built a few years afterward, was named Colosseum from this *coloss-al* statue of Nero that was once there.

Nero was very conceited. He thought he could write poetry and sing beautifully. Although he did both very badly, he liked to show off, and no one dared to laugh at him. Had anyone been so bold as to make fun of him or even to smile, he would have had that person put to death instantly.

Even Roman people who were not Christians feared and hated Nero. The military rebelled against him. Before they had a chance to do anything, Nero heard what they were planning, and in order to save himself the disgrace of being put to death by his own people he decided to kill himself. He was such a coward, however, that he couldn't quite bring himself to plunge the sword into his breast. Finally, his slave, impatient to finish the job, shoved the blade in. Thus was Rome rid of one of its worst rulers.

So much for the first part of this *blood and thunder* story. Here is the second part:

The Jews in Jerusalem didn't like to have Rome rule over them. They never had. Like the Christians, the Jews could not worship the emperor as a god. But they were afraid to do much about it. In the Year 70 A.D. they rebelled; that is, they said they would no longer obey Rome or pay money to the government. The emperor sent his son, who was named Titus,[3] with an army to put an end to the rebellion, to punish them as if they were disobedient children.

The Jews crowded into their city of Jerusalem to make a last stand against the Romans. But Titus destroyed that city completely and the Jews in it, a million of them, it is supposed. Then he robbed the great temple of all its valuable ornaments and brought them back to Rome. The great temple was then destroyed.

To celebrate this victory over Jerusalem an arch was built in the Forum at Rome, and through this arch Titus and his army marched in triumph. On this arch was carved a procession, showing Titus leaving the city of Jerusalem with the temple ornaments. Chief among these ornaments was a golden seven-branched candlestick he had taken from the temple. Today we see many copies in brass of this famous seven-branched candlestick. It is called a *menorah*, which is the Hebrew word for candlestick.

The city was rebuilt later, but most of the Jews who survived have ever since been living in many other countries of the world. When people leave their homeland and spread, it is called a *diaspora*.

The third part of this story is the *thunder*.

In Italy there is a volcano named Vesuvius.[4] You remember that *volcano* came from the name Vulcan, the blacksmith god, and people

---

[3] Titus [tī′ təs]   [4] Vesuvius [ve sōō′ vē ə s]

Vesuvius erupting, Pompeii in foreground

imagined that his forge in the heart of a volcano made the smoke and flame and ashes. From time to time this volcano, Vesuvius, thunders and quakes and spouts forth fire and throws up stones and gas and boils over with red-hot melted rock called lava. It is the hot inside of the earth exploding. Yet people build houses and towns nearby and live even on the sides of the volcano. Every once in a while their homes are destroyed when the volcano quakes or pours forth fire. Yet the same people go right back and build again in the same place!

There was at the time of Titus a little town named Pompeii[5] near the base of Vesuvius. Wealthy Romans used to go there to spend the summer. Suddenly, one day in the year 79 A.D., just after Titus had become emperor, Vesuvius began to spout forth fire. The people living in Pompeii rushed for their lives, but they didn't have time to get away. They were smothered with the gases from the volcano before they had time to move and, falling down dead, were buried deep in a boiling rain of fire and ashes, just where they happened to be when the eruption, as it is called, took place.

The people and their houses lay buried beneath the ashes for nearly two thousand years, and in the course of time everyone had forgotten there ever had been such a place. People came back as they had before and built houses over the spot where everyone had forgotten there once was a city. Then one day a man was digging a well over the spot where

---

[5] Pompeii [pom pā´]

Pompeii had once been. He dug up a man's hand—no, not a real hand, but the hand of a statue. He told others, and they set to work and dug and dug to see what else they could find until the whole town was dug out. And now one can go to Pompeii and see it very much as it was in 79 A.D. before it was destroyed.

There are houses of the Romans who went there to spend their vacations. There are shops and temples and palaces and public baths and the theater and the market place or forum. The streets were paved with blocks of lava, once melted stone. They still show ruts which were worn into them by the wheels of the chariots that the Romans used to drive. Stepping stones were placed at some crossings, so that in case of heavy rains, when the streets were full of water, one could cross on them from curb to curb. These stepping stones are still there. The floors of the houses were made of bits of colored stone to form pictures. These are called *mosaics*. They are still there. In the vestibule of one house, there is in the floor a mosaic picture of a dog. Under it are the Latin words, *Cave canem*. What does that mean? Can you guess? It means, *Look out for the dog!*

The bones of the people who were caught and buried alive in the ashes were also found. There were also found bronze ornaments worn by the women, vases that decorated the home, pots and pans and dishes, and lamps which they used to light the houses. Beds and chairs were found just as they had been buried. Still more remarkable, cakes were found on the table, a loaf of bread half eaten, meat ready to be cooked, a kettle on the fire with the ashes still underneath it—beans and peas and *one egg* unbroken—probably the oldest egg in the world!

38

A Good Emperor and a Bad Son

ROME'S wicked emperor, Nero, had been dead a hundred years when there came to the throne a new emperor named Marcus Aurelius.[1] He was just as good as Nero was bad. Many people think he was one of the noblest and greatest men who ever lived.

At this time most of the Romans had very little religion of any sort. They were not Christians, but neither did they put much faith in their own gods—Jupiter and Juno and the rest. They honored them because they had been brought up to honor them and because they thought that if they didn't honor them, they might have bad luck. So they took no chances.

But instead of believing in such gods, many other Romans followed the teachings of some wise man, or philosopher, and tried to obey the rules that he had made.

About 300 B.C. a Greek philosopher named Zeno[2] had taught a philosophy called Stoicism. His ideas became popular, and a century later they spread to Rome. Many Romans liked Stoicism because it taught good behavior, wisdom, and strength to suffer hardship and pain. Seneca, the teacher whom Nero killed, became a Stoic[3] and wrote about Stoicism.

A hundred years later, along came the emperor Marcus Aurelius. He was a Stoic, too, and he needed to be, for he had a hard and difficult life.

---

[1] Marcus Aurelius [mär′ kəs ô rē′ lē əs]
[2] Zeno [zē′ nō]
[3] Stoic [stō′ ik]

He wrote down his thoughts, now called his *Meditations*. He didn't intend to have his thoughts published; he just wrote them down to remind himself how he ought to think and behave.

Here are some of the ideas that Marcus Aurelius believed in:

- I must calmly endure pain and suffering.
- I must put up with everything that happens, no matter how bad it may seem. Whatever happens has been caused by God, and God is good. Therefore everything that happens is good.
- I must always do my duty.
- I must not seek pleasure.
- Good behavior is the best thing in life.
- I must obey the laws of God.
- All men are brothers, and I must treat everyone as well as if he were my brother.

Marcus Aurelius was a good Stoic. He followed his own rules, and he always did what he thought was his duty. He was kind to people, was good to the poor, and managed to get rid of much of the cruelty and brutality in the gladiators' shows.

Even today, people—thousands of them—read Marcus Aurelius's *Meditations*. Some of his sayings sound almost as though they come from the Bible. Even today, too, people who bear pain and hardship without a murmur are described as stoic.

One of Marcus Aurelius's rules was "Forgive your enemies." Though Marcus Aurelius was not a Christian, nevertheless he was more moral in the way he acted than some of the later emperors who *were* Christians!

Like many people who are very good themselves, Marcus Aurelius was unable to bring up his son to be good. Commodus,[4] his son, was just as bad as his father was good. When the son grew up and was able to choose for himself and do as he pleased, he forgot all about doing his duty and behaving well and obeying the laws of God. Instead, Commodus's one thought was pleasure, and the worst kind of pleasure at that. Commodus forgot his father's ideas about being kind to others and treating them like brothers. He thought only of giving himself a good time.

Commodus was an athlete and had beautiful muscles and a handsome figure, of which he was so proud that he had a statue made of himself. The statue showed him as the strong and muscular god Hercules. Commodus made the people worship him as if he were this god. Just to show off his muscles and his muscular ability, he himself took part in prizefights. He poisoned or killed anyone who found fault with or criticized him. He led a wild and dissipated life, but at last he met the end that he deserved. Many attempts to kill him failed, but finally he was strangled to death by a wrestler.

Pleasure! For Commodus, pleasure meant feasting too much and drinking too much and going to wild all-night parties. But there are other kinds of pleasure, good kinds, and Commodus had nothing to do with them.

About the same time as Zeno, there lived another Greek wise man, or philosopher, named Epicurus.[5] His ideas, too, became popular in Rome, and thousands followed his teachings. The Epicureans[6]—the followers of Epicurus —thought that the highest good was pleasure, but the pleasure must be of *the right kind*.

Here are a few of the pleasures that the Epicureans considered good:

---

[4] Commodus [kom′ ə dəs]
[5] Epicurus [ep i kyoor′ əs]

[6] Epicureans [ep i kyoo rē′ ənz]

- Being honest and truthful
- Being just to others
- Friendship with good people
- Simple, clean living
- Freedom from superstition
- Freedom from fear
- Quiet study
- Calmness

Any pleasure that causes pain, thought the Epicureans, is not really a pleasure—not at all. How much happier Commodus would have been if he had followed the ideas of Epicurus instead of his own wild, selfish ideas!

39
I_ H_ _ S_ _ _ _ V_ _ _ _ _

THE name of this story I'm going to put at the end, for you wouldn't know what it means, anyway, until you have heard the story, and so it's no use looking ahead.

All through the years since Christ was crucified, some people who said they believed in Christ had been terribly treated—*persecuted*, we call it—because they were Christians. They had been flogged; they had been stoned; they had been torn with iron hooks. They had been roasted and burned to death. Yet, strange as it may seem, in spite of this terrible treatment, more and more people were becoming Christians every day. They believed so strongly in life after death, and they believed that they would be so much happier after death if they died for Christ's sake, that they seemed even glad to suffer and to be killed. At last the emperor himself put a stop to all these persecutions. This is how it happened.

About the year 300 A.D. Rome had an emperor by the name of Constantine. Constantine was not a Christian. His gods were the old Roman gods. He probably did not put much faith in them, however.

Well, once upon a time Constantine was fighting with an enemy when he dreamed one night that he saw in the sky a flaming cross. Beneath this cross were written the Latin words, *In hoc signo vinces*. In English this is, "In this sign thou shalt conquer." Constantine thought this meant that if he carried the Christian cross into battle, he would conquer. He thought it would at least be worthwhile to give the Christian god a trial. So he marked the sign of the cross on the shields carried by his soldiers, and he did win the battle. To celebrate his victory, the Roman Senate built the Arch of Constantine, a triumphal arch with three openings, in the Forum of Rome. After this, Constantine made Christianity a legal religion in the Roman Empire. It is believed that he was baptized just before he died. From that time on, all the Roman emperors who came after Constantine—all except one—were Christians.

Constantine's mother was named Helena.[1] She became a Christian. Then she gave up her life to Christian works and built churches at Bethlehem and on the Mount of Olives. It is said that she went to Palestine[2] and found the actual cross on which Christ had been crucified three hundred years before and sent part of it to Rome. When she died she was made a saint. She is now called St. Helena.

Constantine built a church over the spot where St. Peter was supposed to have been crucified. Many years later, this church was torn down so that a much larger and grander church in honor of St. Peter might be built there.

Constantine did not care for Rome. He preferred to live in another city in the Eastern part of the Roman Empire. This city was called Byzantium.[3] So he moved from Rome to Byzantium and made that city his capital. Byzantium was called New Rome, and then the name was changed to Constantine's city. In Greek, the word for *city* is *polis*. We see the word used in Anna*polis* and Indiana*polis*. Constantine's City became Constantinepolis, and then shortened to Constantinople.

Hardly had the Roman Empire become Christian before a quarrel arose between those Christians who believed one thing and those who believed

---

[1] Helena [hel′ ən ə]
[2] Palestine [pal′ ə stīn]

[3] Byzantium [bi zan′ shē əm]

another. The chief thing they quarreled about was whether Christ was equal to God the Father or not equal to Him. Constantine called the two disagreeing sides together at a place called Nicaea to settle the question. There the leaders of each side argued the matter hotly. Finally, it was decided that the Christian Church should believe that God the Son and God the Father were equal. Then they agreed to put what they believed in words. This was called a creed, which means *believe,* and because it was made at Nicaea[4] it was known as the Nicene[5] Creed, which many Christians still say every Sunday.

Before the time of Constantine, there were no weekly holidays in the Roman Empire. Sunday was no different from any other day. People worked or did just the same things on Sunday as they did on other days. Constantine thought Christians should have one day a week for the worship of God—a *holy day*, or holiday, as we call it—so he made Sunday the Christian day of rest, a *holy day* such as Saturday is for Jews and Friday is for Muslims.

Although Constantine was head of the Roman Empire, there was another man whom all Christians throughout the world looked to as their spiritual head. This man was the Bishop of Rome. In Latin he was called *Papa*, which means the same thing in Latin that it does in English, *father.* So the bishop of Rome was called *Papa*, and this became *pope.* St. Peter was supposed to have been the first bishop of Rome. For many centuries the pope was the spiritual ruler of all Christians everywhere, no matter in what country they lived.

As now you know what the name of this story means, I'm putting it here:

In Hoc Signo Vinces

---

[4] Nicaea [nī sē′ ə] [5] Nicene [nī sēn′]

40

Barbarian Invaders

BUT Rome with the Roman Empire had had its day. The empire had risen as high as it could. It was Rome's turn to fall. It was Rome's turn to be conquered. But you cannot guess what people were to do the conquering and to be next in power.

For centuries there had been Germanic tribes living on the northern borders of the Roman Empire. Every now and then they tried to cross over the border into Roman lands, and the Romans had to be constantly fighting them to keep them back where they belonged. Julius Caesar had fought with them. So had Marcus Aurelius and so had Constantine. The Romans called these people *barbarians*, which is what they called all people who were not Romans. The Romans believed that all barbarians were fierce and warlike.

Many of these Germanic people had light hair and blue eyes; that is, they were what we call blonds. The Greeks and Romans and other people who lived around the Mediterranean Sea had dark hair and dark eyes. They were what we call brunettes.

Although some of the Germanic peoples had moved into the Roman Empire, many lived in sparsely populated areas, not in cities. They lived in huts made of wood, sometimes of branches woven together—like a

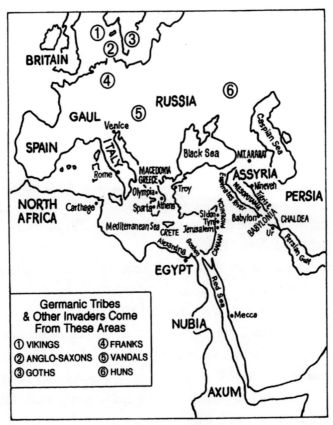

Invasions from the north

large basket. The women raised vegetables and took care of the cows and horses. The men did the hunting and fighting and blacksmithing. Blacksmithing was very important, for the blacksmith made the swords and spears with which they fought and the tools with which they worked. That is why the name *Smith* was so honored among them.

When the men went to battle they wore the heads of animals they had killed, an ox's head, horns and all, or the head of a wolf or bear or fox. This was to make themselves look fierce and to frighten the enemy.

Bravery was the chief thing the men thought good. A man might lie, he might steal, he might even commit murder, but if he was a brave warrior, he was called a good man. The Germanic tribes did not have a king. They elected their chiefs, and of course they always chose the man who was the bravest and strongest. But he could not make his son ruler after him. He was more like a president than a king.

These northern people had an entirely different set of gods from those of Greece and Rome. Their chief god, as you might guess, was the god of war, and they called him Woden.[1] Woden was also the god of the sky. He was like the two Greek gods, Zeus and Ares, put together. Woden was supposed to live in a wonderful palace in the sky called Valhalla, and many tales are told of the wonderful things he did and of the adventures he had. Wednesday, which was once Wodensday, is named after him. That is why there is a letter *d* in this word, although we don't pronounce it.

After Woden, Thor was the next most important god. He was the god of thunder and lightning. He carried a hammer with which he fought great giants who lived in the far-off cold lands and were called *ice-giants*. Thursday, which was once Thorsday, is named after him.

Another god was named Tiu, and from his name we get Tuesday, and another Freya,[2] from whom we get Friday, so that four out of seven of our days are named after Germanic gods, in spite of the fact that none of us believe in these gods.

Germanic warrior

---

[1] Woden [wōd n]   [2] Freya [frā′ ə]

Of the other three days of the week, Sunday and Monday of course are named after the sun and moon, and Saturday is named after a Roman god, Saturn.

About the year 400 A.D. these northern neighbors were becoming particularly troublesome to the Romans. They began to push their way down into the northern part of the Roman Empire, and after a few years the Romans could hold them back no longer. Two of these Germanic tribes went over into Britain, and the Romans who were living there found it wisest to get out, go back to Rome, and leave the country and its native people to the invaders.

These tribes who settled in Britain were known as Angles and Saxons. So the country came to be called the land of the Angles, or, for short, *Angle-land*. After the words *Angle-land* were said over for many years, they became *England*, which is what we call the country today. The people of England are still known by the full name *Anglo-Saxons*, and this is the name by which we call anyone descended from these tribes of Angles and Saxons who settled in Britain about 400 A.D.

Another tribe called the Vandals went into Gaul. Gaul is where France is now. Then they kept on down into Spain, stealing, smashing, burning, and destroying. They crossed over by boats into North Africa. They damaged or destroyed everything they came upon. So today when anyone damages or destroys property wickedly, we call him a *vandal*. If you cut up your desk, tear your books, or scratch names on walls or fences, you, too, are a vandal.

A tribe called the Franks followed the Vandals into Gaul, and there they stayed, giving the name *France* to that country.

The people north of Italy were the Goths. They had a leader by the name of Alaric.[3] Alaric and his Goths crossed over the mountains into Italy and robbed or destroyed everything of value they could lay their

---

[3] Alaric [al ′ ər ik]

hands on. They then entered Rome and carried away whatever they wanted, and the Romans could not stop them. But the worst was yet to come.

41

Barbarians Meet the Champions of the World

FARTHER north and to the east was a tribe of people who were considered by both the Romans and the Germanic tribes to be very fierce. They were called Huns. They lived far off in the eastern forests, in a part of the world that no one then knew much about.

Even the Germans themselves, fierce fighters though they were, feared the Huns, and it was chiefly because they were afraid of them and wanted to get away from them as far as they could that the Germans went over the borders into the Roman Empire. It was much easier to fight the Romans than it was to fight the Huns.

The leader of the Huns, named Attila,[1] boasted that nothing ever grew again where his horse had trod. He and his Huns had conquered and laid waste the country all the way from the East almost to Paris. At last a Roman-Germanic army made a stand against them and fought a great battle at a place not so very far from Paris, a place called Châlons.[2]

The Germans fought desperately; they fought madly; and the Huns were beaten. It was lucky they were beaten, for if they had won, these wild barbarians might have conquered and ruled the world. So the battle of Châlons, 451 A.D., is written in history in capital letters and large figures—CHÂLONS, 451.

---

[1] Attila [ə til′ ə]   [2] Châlons [sha lôn′]

After Attila and his Huns had been beaten at Châlons, they then went after the Romans. Turning back they went down into Italy, where there was no one able to stop them. They destroyed everything as they moved on. The people of the country didn't even attempt to fight. They thought the Huns were monsters and simply fled before them. On to Rome the Huns went.

Now, there was in Rome at this time a pope named Leo I which means Lion. Leo, of course, was neither a soldier nor a fighting man, but he and his cardinals and bishops went out from Rome to meet Attila. They were not clad in armor, and none of them carried any weapons with which to fight. The pope and those with him were dressed in gorgeous robes and richly colored garments. It seemed as if they must be slaughtered by Attila and his Huns like lambs before wolves.

Something strange happened when Attila and the pope met; exactly what no one knows. Perhaps Attila was awed by the pomp and splendor of those Christians. Perhaps he feared what heaven might do to him if he destroyed those holy beings who had come out to meet him as if from heaven. At any rate, he did not destroy them, nor did he enter Rome, but turned about and left Italy, left it for good and all, and he and his Huns returned to the unknown land to the north from which they had come.

Now that the dreaded Attila was out of the way, the Vandals in Africa saw their chance to attack Rome. Attila had barely left Italy before the Vandals crossed over from Africa and sailed up the Tiber to Rome. They captured the city without any difficulty, helped themselves to everything they wanted, and carried away all Rome's treasures.

Poor old Rome! The *Eternal City* was at last beaten, beaten for good! It had been the champion for a great many years. But now all Rome's strength was gone. The city was no longer able to defend itself. Rome's last emperor had the high-sounding name *Romulus Augustulus,*[3] the

---

[3] Romulus Augustulus [rom′ yə ləs ô gus′ tyə lus]

same name as the first king, Romulus, with the addition of Augustulus, which means the little Augustus. But in spite of his high-sounding name, Romulus Augustulus could do nothing.

It was in the year 476 that Rome was beaten. The western half of the empire, of which Rome had been the capital, broke up into pieces, and the pieces were ruled over by various Germanic rulers. Like Humpty Dumpty, Rome had had a great fall, and all the king's horses and all the king's men couldn't put it together again. Only the eastern part, of which Constantinople was the capital, still went on. This eastern half was not conquered by the barbarians, and it still kept going for nearly a thousand years longer until—but wait till we come to that time in history.

People speak of this date, 476, as the end of Ancient History. A date like 476 is very convenient and definite, and people like definite dates, but of course Ancient History didn't come to a sudden end the way one year comes to an end on December 31 and another year begins at once. You might say that Ancient History began to fade away long before 476 and that a new era began to fade in over a long period of time both before and after 476. Still, 476 is a good date to remember.

This new era, called the Middle Ages or the medieval period, began, then, in 476 and lasted until 1453. What happened in 1453? You will learn that later.

During the early part of the Middle Ages, till, about the year 1000, the Germanic peoples were the chief people in Europe. They were quick to learn many things from the Romans whom they had conquered. Even before they had conquered Rome, most of them had already become Christians. They also learned Latin.

Without the unity of the Roman Empire, people no longer traveled very much or very far. This meant that people from places like Spain and Italy and Gaul didn't talk to each other very often. Over the years they began to use different expressions and to pronounce words differently. As centuries passed, the common people no longer spoke the old classical Latin but spoke what were really the new languages of Spanish, Italian, and French. These were different from Latin and different from each other, too. However, because they all grew out of Latin, they have a lot of words that are very much alike.

In Britain, the Anglo-Saxons would have nothing to do with the Romans and would not use the Roman language but kept their own language. After a while this language of the Anglo-Saxons was called English. The Anglo-Saxons also kept their own religion until about one hundred years later, or about 600 A.D.

At that time some English slaves were being sold in the slave-market in Rome. They were very handsome. The pope saw them and asked who they were.

"They are Angles," he was told.

"Angles!" exclaimed he. "They are handsome enough to be 'angels,' and they should certainly be Christians."

Rome sent some missionaries to England to convert the English: to change Angles to angels. So at last the English, too, became Christians.

42

New Places—New Heroes

GERMANIC kings were ruling over pieces of the Western Empire, but in Constantinople a Roman was still ruling over the Eastern Empire. This Roman was named Justinian.[1] Now, up to this time there had been a great many rules or laws by which the people were governed. There were so many of these rules and they were so mixed up that one law would tell you you could do one thing and another would tell you you couldn't. It was as if your mother said you could stay up till nine o'clock tonight and your father said you must go to bed at eight. It was hard for people to tell, therefore, what one must do and what one must not do.

In order to untangle this snarl, Justinian had a set of laws made for the government of his people, and many of these were so good and so just that they are still the law today. If you notice that Justinian begins with *Just*, this will help you to remember that he was the one who made *just* laws.

Another thing Justinian did that has lasted to the present time was to build in Constantinople a very beautiful church called Santa Sophia. Though it is no longer a church, it is still standing after all these years and is a beautiful sight to see. Still another thing he did that you could never guess. It had nothing to do with war or law or buildings.

---

[1] Justinian [ju stin′ ē ən]

Travelers from the Far East, where China now is, had brought back tales of a wonderful caterpillar that wound itself up with a fine, thin thread over a mile long, and they told stories of how the Chinese unwound this thread and wove it into cloth of the finest and smoothest kind. This thread, as you might guess, was called silk, and the caterpillar that made it was called the silkworm. People in Europe had seen this beautiful silk cloth, but how it was made had been a mystery—a secret. They thought it so wonderfully beautiful that it was supposed to have been made by fairies or elves or even sent down from heaven. Justinian found out about these caterpillars and had men bring these silkworms into Europe so that his people also might make silk cloth and have silk ribbons and fine silk garments, and therefore we give him the honor of starting the manufacturing of silk in Europe.

About the same time that Justinian lived, there was a king in France named Clovis.[2] Clovis belonged to the Germanic tribe called the Franks, which gave the name *France* to that country. Clovis believed in Thor and Woden as all of his people did. Clovis had a wife named Clotilda,[3] whom he loved very dearly. Clotilda thought all the fighting and cruelty, which her people seemed to like, was wrong. She had heard about the religion of Christ, which did not believe in quarreling and fighting, and she thought she would like to be a Christian. So she was baptized. She then tried to persuade her husband, Clovis, to become a Christian, also.

Clovis was just then going to war—the very thing the Christians preached against. However, just to please his wife, he promised her, if he won the battle, he would become a Christian. He did win, and he kept his word and was baptized and had his soldiers baptized also. Clovis made Paris his capital, and Paris is still the capital of France.

It was about this same time, also, that a king named Arthur was ruling in England. Many stories and poems have been written about him, most of which are mythical. Although we know these stories are not

---

[2] Clovis [klō′ vis]   [3] Clotilda [klō til′ də]

historically true, they are, nevertheless, important and interesting—like those tales that are told about the heroes of the Trojan War.

It was said that there was a sword called Excalibur[4] stuck so fast in a stone that no one could draw it out except the man who should be king of England. All the nobles had tried without success to draw the sword, when one day a young boy named Arthur pulled it out with the greatest ease, and he was accordingly proclaimed king.

King Arthur chose a company of the nobles to rule with him, and as they sat with him at a round table they were known as the Knights of the Round Table. Tennyson, a great English poet, has written in verse an account of the doings of King Arthur and his knights in a long poem called *The Idylls of the King*, which you will have to read yourself, for we must go on to the next story.

---

[4] Excalibur [ek skal′ ə bər]

43

Being Good

WHAT do you mean by *being good*?

The Germans thought being good was being brave.

The Athenians thought that whatever was beautiful was good.

The Stoics thought that doing one's duty and suffering hardship calmly was being good.

The Epicureans thought the right kinds of pleasure were good.

The martyrs thought being good meant suffering and dying for Christ's sake.

Ever since the time of the martyrs, some Christians who wanted to be very, very good indeed, went off into the wilderness and lived by themselves. They wished to be far away from other people, so that they could spend all their time praying and thinking holy thoughts. This, they believed was being good.

One of the strangest of these men who wanted to get away from others was named St. Simeon Stylites.[1] He built for himself a pillar or column fifty feet high, and on the top of it he lived with room only to sit but not to lie down. There on the top he lived for many years, day and night, winter and summer, while the sun shone on him and the rain rained on him, and he never came down at all. He could be reached only by a ladder, which his friends used to take him food. High up out of the world, he thought he could best lead a holy

---

[1] Simeon Stylites [sim′ ē ən stì′ lĭ′ tēz]

life. That was his idea of being good although we should think such a person simply crazy.

In the course of time, however, men and women who wanted to lead holy lives, instead of living alone as they had done at first, gathered in groups and built themselves homes. The men were called monks, the women nuns or virgins, and the houses where they lived were known as monasteries or abbeys. The head monk of an abbey was called an abbot, from the Aramaic word *abba*, which means *father* in the language that Jesus spoke. The abbot ruled over the other monks like a father over his children, giving them orders and punishing them when he thought they needed it. Abbesses were in charge of their nuns in the same way.

In the five hundreds there lived an Italian monk named Benedict. He believed very strongly that one must work if he was to be holy, that work was a necessary part of being holy. He thought, also, that monks should have no money of their own, for Christ had said in the Bible, "If thou wilt be perfect, go and sell that which thou hast, and give to the poor." (Matthew 19:21) Benedict started an order for those people who would agree to three things:

The first thing they were to agree to was to have no money.

The second thing was not to marry.

The third thing was to obey the abbot or abbess.

Men and women who joined this order were called Benedictines.

Now, you might think there would have been hardly anyone who would promise for life three such things as to have no money, to obey the abbot—no matter what he told them to do—and never to marry. Nevertheless, there were a great many in every country of Europe who did become Benedictines.

Usually monks or nuns lived in little bare rooms like prison cells, and ate their very simple meals together at a single table in a room called the refectory. They sang praise at sunrise and sunset, and four times during the day besides; they even woke up at midnight to sing prayers. Singing praise was their main job, but not all they had to do. Work of every kind they were obliged to do, and they did it joyfully, whether the work was scrubbing floors or digging in the garden. People who had been rich and people who had been poor all followed the same rules.

Sometimes a monastery was situated in a barren or swampy spot on land that had been given the monks because it was not good or, even worse than no good, dangerously unhealthy. But the monks set to work and drained off the water, tilled the soil, and made the waste places bloom like the rose. They then raised vegetables for their table, fodder for their horses and cattle and sheep. Everything they ate or used or needed, they raised or made.

They did not only the rougher handwork; they did fine handwork, too. Movable type had not been invented, and printing was not known in Europe at this time. Books had to be written by hand, and the monks and nuns who had reading and writing skills were the ones to do this job. They copied the old books in Latin and Greek. Sometimes one monk would slowly read the book to be copied, and several other monks at one time would copy what he dictated. In this way a number of copies would be made.

The pages of the books were not made of paper but of calfskin or sheepskin, called vellum, and this vellum was much stronger and lasted much longer than paper.

These old books which the monks wrote were called *manuscripts*, which means *handwritten*. Many of these may now be seen in museums and libraries. Some of these manuscripts have been beautifully handpainted with loving care and the initial letters and borders ornamented with designs of flowers and vines and birds and pictures in red and gold and other colors. If monks and nuns hadn't done this copying, many of the old books would have been lost and unknown to us.

The monks also kept diaries, writing down from day to day and year to year an account of the important things that happened. These old diaries, or chronicles, as they were called, tell us the history of the times. As there were then no newspapers, if these chronicles had not been written we should not know what went on at that time.

Monk copying a manuscript

The monks were the best educated people of those days, and they taught others—both young and old—the things they themselves knew. The monasteries were also inns for travelers, for anyone who came and asked for lodging was received and given food and a place to sleep whether he had any money to pay or not.

Monks and nuns helped the poor and needy. The sick, too, came to monasteries to be treated and taken care of, so that a monastery was often something like a hospital, too. Many people who had received such help or attention made rich gifts to the monasteries, so they became very wealthy, although neither monks nor nuns could own so much as a spoon for themselves.

So you see monks and nuns were not merely holy; they were lights in an age when the world had grown dull and dangerous. Yes, they were lights, and there were other lights too shining in those years. You will read about them a little later in this book.

44

A Christian Kingdom in Africa

BY the time of the Roman Emperor Constantine, Christianity had been taught all around the Roman Empire; in countries like Italy and Greece in southern Europe; in the countries like Syria and Turkey in the Middle East; and in countries like Egypt and Libya in North Africa. One of the most important early Christians, St. Augustine,[1] was bishop of the North African city of Hippo. He was a famous teacher and writer. The very first monks lived in Egypt, usually out in the desert. The Egyptian city of Alexandria, which Alexander the Great had built so long ago, became important in the Christian world. The bishops of Alexandria were leaders in the early church.

Missionaries traveled beyond the Roman Empire, not only north into Europe but also south into Africa. Some of these missionaries went south of Egypt into Nubia and Axum.[2] Nubia lay directly south of Egypt and today is called Sudan. Axum is southeast and is part of the modern nation of Ethiopia. You already know that Nubia has a history going back as far as Egypt's history. Axum also has a long history that I will tell you now.

Axum was located on the shore of the Red Sea. It is just a short distance across the water from Arabia. A thousand years before Christ, some people from Saba[3] on the tip of Arabia migrated to Axum, settled,

---

[1] Augustine [ô gus´ tin]
[2] Axum [ăk soom´]

[3] Saba [sä´ bə]

and mixed with the people there. Later, the kings of Axum conquered and ruled Saba. You can see these two peoples had a lot to do with each other over the years.

One Queen of Sheba (a place also known as Saba) is said to have gone to Jerusalem at the invitation of the Hebrew King Solomon. Perhaps she was one of his wives. In any case, there is a legend that has been told for many years in Ethiopia that the kings there are descended from King Solomon and the Queen of Sheba. Even the last king of Ethiopia, Haile Selassie,[4] who ruled until 1974, claimed that the famous Biblical king and queen were his great great great, great . . . grandparents.

Because of its long seacoast, Axum became a trading center. Ships from Axum sailed north along the Red Sea to Egypt, south in the Indian Ocean along the east coast of Africa, and across that ocean all the way to India. The ships carried valuable goods like gold and ivory and spices. Axum also sent caravans across the desert to trade with places that could not be reached by water. Axumite merchants traded with the Roman Empire. Merchants from Rome and Greece came to live in Axum to conduct business there. Axum became a very rich kingdom. The kings wore luxurious robes and rode in chariots pulled by elephants. One king of Axum is particularly famous. This is King Ezana,[5] who came to the throne around 330 A.D., just around the time of the Roman Emperor Constantine.

Like most ancient rulers, King Ezana was a military leader. He extended his empire by conquering his neighbors. But he is best known because he converted to Christianity. He was converted by two young Christians from Syria who were brought as slaves to Axum. Legend has it that these young men either were shipwrecked or were captured by pirates in the Red Sea. Since they knew how to write, they were brought to the king's court to work as scribes. One worked particularly hard to convert King Ezana. When he succeeded, Ezana made Christianity the

---

[4] Haile Selassie [hī′ lē sə las′ ē]   [5] Ezana [ə zä′ nə]

Northeastern Africa

official religion of his nation. The Christians of Axum were in close
contact with the Christians of Alexandria, Egypt. At first, Christians in
both Egypt and Axum held their services in Greek. Later they began to
worship in their own languages, Coptic in Egypt and Ge'ez[6] in Axum.
The king of Axum had the Bible translated into Ge'ez.

---

[6] Ge'ez [gēz]

Axum remained a Christian kingdom through the centuries. In the Middle Ages, when the Christian countries in Europe were building the great cathedrals that you will read about in later chapters, the kings of Axum were also building great churches. Some of these are unlike any other churches that you will ever see. One king, a man named Lalibela,[7] sent stone carvers into a remote mountain area. First the carvers cut deep down into underground rock and made trenches. Then the workers were lowered into the trenches to carve the actual churches out of the solid rock. One has the shape of a cross. The largest is more than one hundred feet long. Inside, beautiful paintings with bright colors and gold leaf decorate the walls and altars. If you travel to Ethiopia, you can still visit these churches today.

Several centuries after the time of King Ezana, Axum was cut off from most of the Christian world. Arabs, whom you will read about in the next chapter, conquered all of North Africa and established a new religion called Islam.[8] Some people in Egypt continued to be Christians, but most Egyptians and also many Nubians were converted to Islam. Axum was cut off from many of its old trade routes, so Axum's wealth declined. The country did manage to preserve its independence and its religion. Because they were so far away, Europeans lost track of the Ethiopian Christians. But they were still there. And now we have rediscovered their history.

---

[7] Lalibela, King [lä li bel′ ə]   [8] Islam [is′ läm]

45

Muhammad and the Early Years of Islam

WE have already heard about two religions that began in the part of the world we now call the Middle East. These are Judaism and Christianity. In this story, I'll tell you about a third religion that began in the same area. This religion is called Islam.

Every hundred years is called a century, but a thing that seems a little strange is this—the hundred years from 500 to 600 is called the sixth century, not the fifth; the hundred years from 600 to 700 is called the seventh century, not the sixth, and so on. Well, we have now reached the seventh century, the six hundreds, and we are to learn of a man who was to make a change in the whole world.

There lived in Arabia a man named Muhammad.[1] He was born into humble circumstances. Because his parents died when he was young, he was raised by an uncle. His uncle operated camel caravans, which transported passengers and goods much as trains or trucks do today. The Arabian city of Mecca,[2] where Muhammad lived, was the center of the caravan trade. These camel caravans traveled across the Arabian Desert to North Africa and to the lands along the eastern end of the Mediterranean Sea. Although Muhammad had little formal education, he traveled to many wonderful places with the caravans and met many

---

[1] Muhammad [mōō ham′ əd]   [2] Mecca [mek′ ə]

World of Islam

different kinds of people. While working for his uncle, he met a wealthy Arabian woman named Khadija. They were soon married and lived happily together. Muhammad and Khadija had four daughters.

A remarkable thing happened to Muhammad when he was around forty years old. According to Muslim tradition, the story is told that he was visiting a mountain in the desert, where he often went to study and think. One day the angel Gabriel appeared and delivered a message from God. Muhammad listened to this message and set out to teach it to others. But Muhammad did not intend to start a whole new religion.

He believed in the same God that the Jews and Christians worshiped. In Arabia there were Jews and Christians, as well as others who still worshiped idols. These groups often fought over their religious differences. Muhammad hoped that his teachings would make them more understanding of one another.

Muhammad saw a lot of unjust and bad behavior around him. He taught that people should change their selfish ways of living and be more concerned for those less fortunate. But, of course, it is impossible to get everyone to agree to change. A new religion began, instead, among those people who believed in Muhammad's teachings. His followers became known as Muslims, and their religion is called Islam. Islam means "submission" to God.

Khadija was the first to follow her husband's teachings. Soon others in Mecca followed, but there were some who wanted to stop Muhammad's teachings. In 622 A.D. Muhammad and his followers moved from Mecca to the city of Medina. This first migration is called the Hegira.³ Some years later, they returned to Mecca, but Muslims today still teach the story of the angel Gabriel appearing before Muhammad and of the Hegira.

In 622 A.D. Muhammad and his followers moved from Mecca to the city of Medina.

The Muslims began their calendar with the year of the Hegira, calling 622 A.D. the Year 1, just as Christians began their calendar from the year of Jesus's birth and the Romans from the year of the founding of their city. Have you noticed that the Christians, the Romans, and the Muslims each have a different Year 1?

Muhammad lived only ten years after the Hegira; that is, until 632 A.D. The new Muslim leaders were called caliphs. The caliphs continued to spread Muhammad's teachings. The first caliph was Abu Bakr; the second was named Omar.⁴ These teachings from God were written down and became the Qur'an (sometimes spelled as Koran), the Muslim holy book. "Qur'an" comes from a word that means "to recite" because Muslims learn to recite the Qur'an when they are young.

³ Hegira [hi ji′ rə]   ⁴Omar [ō mär′]

"Allah"[5] is the Arabic word for God. When Muslims pray to Allah, they are praying to the same God that Christians and Jews worship. Muslims believe that Muhammad was the last of God's prophets. They also believe that Abraham, Moses, and Jesus were also God's prophets.

Muslims worship in a building called a mosque, just as Christians worship in a church, and Jews worship in a synagogue or temple. They also pray five times each day, if possible, wherever they may be. A man called a muezzin[6] goes out on the balcony of a minaret, or tower, of a mosque and calls aloud, "Come to prayer. Come to prayer. There is but one God, and He is Allah."

*Muezzin on minaret
calling to prayer*

When Muslims pray, they face toward the city of Mecca because the holiest shrine of Muslims, called the Ka'ba, is located there. At least once in their lifetime, Muslims try to make the pilgrimage to the holy city of Mecca.

During the early years of Islam, its leaders were building an empire, much of it in the lands that had once been a part of the Roman Empire. Muslim armies traveled around the Mediterranean, through the Middle East, all the way to Constantinople.

At Constantinople, the gateway from Asia to Europe, they were turned back by Christians, who poured hot tar and burning oil from the walls of the city. The Muslims tried many times to capture Constantinople but without success. Muslim armies also went westward through North Africa, across the Strait of Gibraltar into Spain and across the Pyrenees Mountains into southern France. In 732 A.D., just one hundred years after the death of Muhammad, they met their match near the town of Tours[7] in France.

When Muslims pray, they face toward the city of Mecca . . . .
the holiest shrine of Muslims called the Ka'ba is located there.

The king of France had a right-hand man named Charles, who had been nicknamed Charles the Hammer because he could strike such terrific blows. Charles was also called Mayor of the Palace, which meant that he was the chief servant of the king. Charles the Hammer and his French soldiers defeated the Muslims and kept them from moving farther into Europe.

In just a century, Islam had spread far and wide. People in countries bordering the Mediterranean, from Constantinople, all the way around North Africa on the southern edge, and north through Spain into France, lived under Muslim rulers. Many ordinary people had become Muslim. Even today, Islam is the main religion in the Middle East and North Africa.

46

PERHAPS you have read the *Arabian Nights*.
This is the story of

Arabian Days

In the one hundred years after Muhammad died, the Muslims conquered the Middle East and North Africa. Soon after that, they conquered Persia and lands farther east. Before long, their empire was larger than the Roman Empire had been. For the Middle East and North Africa, the centuries that followed were indeed Arabian Days. Although they failed to conquer most of Europe, over the years people there learned many things from the Muslims.

The Phoenicians invented our alphabet, but the Arabs invented the figures which we use today in arithmetic. 1, 2, 3, 4, and so on are called Arabic figures. The Romans used letters instead of figures: V stood for 5, X for 10, C for 100, M for 1000, and so on. Think how difficult it must have been for a Roman boy to add such numbers as

$$
\begin{array}{r}
IV \\
XII \\
+ \ MC \\
XCII \\
\underline{VII} \\
\end{array}
$$

They could not be added up in columns as we do. When you think of multiplying and dividing with Roman numbers, it seems almost impossible, for example:

$$
\begin{aligned}
MCVII \\
\times\ \underline{XIX}
\end{aligned}
$$

Occasionally you may see Roman figures still used—on clock faces, for instance—but all the figures that you use every day in your arithmetic are Arabic figures.

Another thing:

The Arabs built many beautiful buildings; these buildings look quite different from those that the Greeks and Romans and Christians built. The doors and window openings, instead of being square or round, were usually horseshoe-shaped. On the top of their mosques they liked to put domes shaped something like an onion, and at the corners they put tall spires or minarets from which the muezzin could call aloud the hour for prayer. They covered the walls of their buildings with beautiful mosaics and designs. The Muslims, however, were very careful that these designs were not copies of anything in nature, for they had a commandment in the Qur'an something like the Christian commandment, "Thou shalt not make . . . any likeness of anything that is in heaven above, or that is in the earth beneath, or that is in the water under the earth." Because of this commandment, most Muslims never made drawings or pictures of any living thing, neither of plants nor animals. They thought they would be breaking the commandment if they did. So they made designs out of lines and curves without copying anything from nature. These designs were called *arabesques*,[1] and although they were not like anything in nature, they were often very beautiful.

---

[1] arabesques [ar ə besks ']

Still another thing:

In Arabia there grew a little bush on which were small berries with seeds inside. The sheep seemed to like these berries and, when they ate them, became very lively. The Arabs themselves tried eating the seeds of these berries with the same effect. Then they made a drink out of these seeds by roasting and grinding them and boiling them in water. This was coffee—which the Arabs had discovered and which is now drunk all over the world.

Another drink made from berries, often from grapes, is alcohol. The Muslims did not like what alcohol does to people who drink it, and so they forbade every Muslim from drinking anything containing alcohol, such as wine, beer, or whiskey.

Still another thing:

Woolen cloth which people used for clothing was made from the hair of sheep or goats. As it took the hair of a great many such animals to make a very little cloth, woolen cloth was expensive. The Arabs found out a way of making cloth from a plant, the cotton plant, which of course was much cheaper. Then in order to decorate the cloth and make it pretty and attractive, they stamped the plain cloth with wooden blocks shaped in different forms and dipped in color. This printed cloth that the Arabs invented was called *calico*.

Still another thing:

The Arabs made swords and knives of such wonderful steel that the blades could be bent double without breaking. The blades were said to be so keen they could cut through the finest hair if floated on water, a thing that only the sharpest razor will do, and yet at the same time so strong that they could cut through a bar of steel. Such swords were made in the East at a place called Damascus,[2] which is in Syria, and in the West at a place called Toledo, which is in Spain; and so these swords and

---

[2] Damascus [də mas′ kəs]

knives were known as Damascus or Toledo blades. Unfortunately, no one now knows the Arabs' secret for making such marvelous blades. It is what is called a lost art.

Near where Babylon once was, the Arabs built a city named Baghdad.[3] You have heard of it if you have ever read any of the *Arabian Nights*, for most of these stories were told about Baghdad. It was the eastern capital of the Muslims. There in Baghdad the Arabs built a great school that was famous for many, many years. At Cordova[4] in Spain was the western capital of the Muslims, and there they built another great school. Later, after Islam spread south of the Sahara Desert to West Africa, Muslims there built another wonderful school in a city called Timbuktu.[5]

I might tell you many other things these people did—how they made clocks with pendulums to keep time—people had no real clocks before; how they started wonderful libraries of books; and so on—but this is enough for the present to show you what intelligent people they were.

The Arabs belong to the Semite family, the same family to which the Phoenicians and Jews belong. The Arabs were as clever as their cousins the Phoenicians, who, you remember, were very clever, but they were also as religious as their other cousins the Jews, who, you remember, were very religious.

The Muslims had ideas about women that are different from ours. Most thought it was immodest for a woman to show her face to men, and so every woman had to wear a thick veil which hid her face—all except her eyes—whenever she went out where there were men. With such a veil she could see but not be seen. Muslims believed their women would be protected by wearing the veil. Muslims also taught that one man might have up to four wives, if he could protect them all and care for them equally.

---

[3] Baghdad [bag′ dad]
[4] Cordova [cor′ də və]

[5] Timbuktu [tim buk tōō′]

Muslim veiled woman standing by Saracenic ornamental arch

One other thing that the Muslims did was to copy and save the writings of the Greek poets and philosophers like Aristotle. Many of these were lost in Western Europe after the fall of Rome. You will see later that Muslim scholars saved these writings and gave them back to Europeans to study centuries later.

47

Two Empires, Two Emperors

EUROPE had been *in the dark* for three hundred years. You know what I mean. There were not enough educated people to make it bright.

The Arabs were bright, but they were not in Europe.

In 800 there was a man—a king—who by his might and power was able to join the pieces of Europe together once again to form a new Roman Empire. He was not a Roman, however, but a Frank. Franks, you remember, were one of the Germanic tribes that ruled Europe after the end of the Roman Empire. This king of the Franks was named Charles. He was a grandson of the Charles the Hammer who had stopped the Muslims at Tours, and he was called by the French name Charlemagne, which means Charles the Great.

Charlemagne at first was king of France alone, but he was not satisfied to be king of that country only. He soon conquered the countries on each side of him, parts of Spain and Germany. He built his capital in a place in Germany called Aachen, or Aix-la-Chapelle[1] in French. At Aix-la-Chapelle there were warm springs which made fine baths, and Charlemagne was very fond of bathing and was a fine swimmer.

A large part of Italy was then ruled over by the pope. But the pope was having a good deal of trouble with some tribes in the north of Italy, and

---

[1] Aix-la-Chapelle [eks la sha pel´]

he asked Charlemagne if he wouldn't come down and conquer them. Charlemagne was quite ready and willing to help the pope, so he went over into Italy and easily settled those troublesome tribes. The pope was grateful to Charlemagne for this and wished to reward him.

Now, Christians everywhere used to make trips to Rome in order to pray at the great Church of St. Peter, which had been built over the spot where St. Peter had been crucified. Well, at Christmas time in the Year 800 Charlemagne paid such a visit to Rome. On Christmas day he went to the Church of St. Peter and was praying at the altar when the pope came forward and put a crown on his head. The pope then hailed him *Emperor*, and as the pope at that time could make kings and emperors, Charlemagne became emperor of Italy added to the other countries over which he already ruled. Charlemagne's empire was now like a new but smaller Roman Empire, but with this big difference: it was ruled over not by a Roman, but by a Frank.

In those days, few people had any education, and hardly anyone could read or write. Charlemagne wanted an education. He was so anxious to know everything there was to be known. He wanted to be able to do everything anyone could do, but there was no one in his own country who knew enough or was able to teach him. In England, however, there was a very learned monk named Alcuin.[2] He knew more than anyone else in Northern Europe, so Charlemagne invited Alcuin to come over from England and teach him and his people. Alcuin taught both Christian literature and also some Latin and Greek writings that had survived the years of warfare in Europe.

Charlemagne learned all these things very easily, but when it came to the simple matter of learning to write he found this very hard. He did learn to read, but he seemed unable to learn to write. It is said that he slept with his writing pad under his pillow and practiced whenever he

---

[2] Alcuin [al ꞏ kwin]

awoke. Yet he never learned to write much more than his name. He did not begin to study until he was a grown man, but he kept on studying all the rest of his life. To make sure that others would have the opportunity he missed, Charlemagne ordered every monastery in his kingdom to open a school. He also opened a school right in his own palace. Why do you suppose he did that?

In spite of the fact that Charlemagne's daughters were princesses, he had them taught how to weave and sew and make clothes and cook just as if they had to earn their own living. Although Charlemagne was such a rich and powerful monarch and could have everything he wanted, he preferred to eat plain food and dress in plain clothes. He did not like all the finery that those about him loved. One day, just to make his nobles see how ridiculously dressed they were in silks and satins, he took them out hunting in the woods while a storm was going on, so that he could laugh at them. You can imagine how their silk and satin robes looked after being soaked with rain, covered with mud, and torn by briers.

Although his tastes were simple in matters of dress, he made his home a magnificent palace. He furnished it with gold and silver tables and chairs and other gorgeous furniture. He built in it swimming pools and a wonderful library and a theater and surrounded it with beautiful gardens.

At this time and all through the Dark Ages people had a strange way of finding out whether a person had stolen or committed a murder or any other crime. The person suspected was not taken into court and tried before a judge and a jury to see whether he was telling the truth and had done the thing or not. Instead he was made to carry a redhot iron for ten steps, or to dip his arm into boiling water, or to walk over red-hot coals. If he were not guilty, it was thought no harm would come to him, or if he was burned, it was thought that the burn would heal right away. This was called *trial by ordeal*. It probably started from the story told in the

Bible of Shadrach, Meshech, and Abednego,[3] who, you remember, in the time of Nebuchadnezzar, had walked through the fiery furnace unharmed because they had done no wrong. Though Charlemagne was so intelligent, he believed in the trial by ordeal. Today we have no such cruel and unfair way of finding out whether one is guilty or not. Yet we say of a person who has a lot of trouble that seems to be a test of his character, "He is going through an ordeal."

While Charlemagne was living, there was a caliph in far-off Baghdad named Harun[4], which is the Arabic spelling of Aaron.[5] You may have heard of him if you have read any of the *Arabian Nights*, for the stories of the *Arabian Nights* were written at this time, and Harun is described in them. Although Harun was a Muslim, not a Christian, and though he was ruler of an empire that fought the Christians, nevertheless he admired Charlemagne very much. To show how much he thought of him, he sent him valuable presents—among other things, a clock which struck the hours, which you remember, was an invention of the Arabs. This was a great curiosity, for there were then no clocks in Europe. People had to tell time by the shadow the sun cast on a sundial, or else by the amount of water or sand that dripped or ran out from one jar to another. He also sent Charlemagne an elephant, which was a great curiosity at the court of the Frankish king.

Harun was a very wise and good ruler over the Muslims, and that is why he came to be called *al-Rashid*, which means *the Just*. Do you remember what Greek was also called *the Just*?[6] Harun used to disguise himself as a workman and go about among his people. He would talk with those he met along the street and in the market place, trying to find out how they felt about his government and about things in general. He found they would talk freely to him when he was dressed in old clothes, for then they did not know who he was but thought him a fellow

---

[3] Abednego [a bed′ nə gō]

[4] Harun-al-Rashid [hä roon′ äl rä shēd′]

[5] Aaron [âr′ ən]

[6] Aristides

workman. In this way, Harun learned a great deal about his people's troubles and what they liked or didn't like about his rule. He then would go back to his palace and give orders to have rules and laws made to correct anything that seemed wrong or unjust.

After Charlemagne died there was no one great enough or strong enough to hold the new Roman Empire together, and once again it broke up into small pieces; and, "All the king's horses and all the king's men could not put it together again."

48

Getting a Start

ENGLAND is just a little island.

It was quite an unimportant little island in 900 A.D. Much later, England grew rich and strong and, for a while, had an empire spread all over the world.

England is still just a little island.

But it is now an important island in the world!

About one hundred years after Charlemagne—that is, 900—there was a king of England named Alfred. When Alfred was a boy he had a hard time learning to read, for he did not like to study. In those days many of the hand-written books made by the monks had pretty drawings and letters made in bright colors and even in gold. One day Alfred's mother showed such a book to her children and promised to give it to the one who could read it first. That was a game. Alfred wanted to win the book, so, for the first time in his life, he really tried. He studied so hard that in a very short time he had learned to read before his brothers. Alfred won the book.

When Alfred grew up, England was being troubled by pirates. These pirates were cousins of the English—a Germanic tribe called Danes. The English had long ago become Christians and civilized, but the Danes were still rough and wild. They came over from their own country across the water, landed on the coast of England, robbed the towns and villages, and then sailed back to their homes, carrying off everything valuable they could lay their hands on—like bad boys who climb a farmer's fence and steal apples from his orchard. At last the Danes became so bold that they didn't even run away after robbing the country; they were like the bad boys who stick out their tongues and throw stones at the farmer who comes after them. The king's armies went out to punish these pirates, but, instead of beating, they were beaten. It began to look as if these Danes, who were able to do pretty much as they pleased, might conquer England and rule over the English.

Once when things looked pretty bad for England, King Alfred was without an army. Alone, ragged, tired out, and hungry, he came to the hut of a shepherd and asked for something to eat. The shepherd's wife was baking some cakes by the fire, and she told Alfred he should have one if he watched them while she went out to milk the cow. Alfred sat down by the fire, but in thinking about what he could do to beat the Danes he forgot all about the cakes, and when the shepherd's wife returned they were all burned. Thereupon she scolded him roundly and drove him off, not knowing that it was her king that she was treating in this way, for he never told her who he was.

Alfred decided that the best way to fight the Danes was not on land but on the water, so he set to work to build boats bigger and better than those the Danes had. After a while he had something of a fleet, and the boats he built were bigger than those of the Danes, but they were so big that they could not go into the shallow water without running aground. The Danes' boats, on account of their small size, could go safely close in to shore. In deep water, however, Alfred's fleet was very strong and powerful. This was the first navy that England ever had. England's navy became the largest in the world for a while, and Alfred the Great was the one who started it more than a thousand years ago.

After fighting with the Danes for many years, Alfred finally thought it best to make an agreement with them and give them a part of England to live in if they would promise to stop stealing and live peaceably. The Danes did agree to this, and they settled down peaceably on the land that Alfred gave them—and then became Christians. Over the years, the Danes and the English married each other and raised families. Eventually they became one nationality and no one knew any more whose ancestors were Danes and whose were English.

Alfred made very strict laws and severely punished those who did wrong. Indeed, it is said that the people of England were so careful to obey the law in his reign that one might leave gold by the roadside, and no one would steal it.

Alfred not only built a navy and made wise laws, but he, like Charlemagne, started a school at court for both children and grownups, many of whom were as ignorant as the children. He did many other useful things besides.

He invented, for instance, a way of telling time by a burning candle. You have heard how wonderful the clock, that which Harun al-Rashid sent to Charlemagne one hundred years before, was thought to be. Although striking clocks are, of course, very common nowadays, it was an extraordinary thing then when there were no clocks nor watches at all in England. Alfred found out how fast candles burned down and marked lines around them at different heights—just the distance apart that they burned in one hour. These were called *time-candles*.

Candles were also used for lighting but when they were carried outdoors, they were very likely to be blown out by the wind. So Alfred put the candle inside of a little box, and in order that the light might shine through the box, he made sides of very thin pieces of cow's-horn, as glass then was very scarce.

Such inventions may seem very small and unimportant, and they are when you think of the marvelous inventions and wonderful machines that are made by the thousands nowadays. These inventions of Alfred were no more than the household ideas for which some magazines now offer only a few dollars apiece. But I have told you about them just to show you how ignorant the English, as well as other Germanic tribes of Europe, were in those days. How much superior were the Arab thinkers with their striking clocks. The English were just getting a start.

49

The End of the World

WHAT would you do if you knew the world was coming to an end next week, or even next year?

The people who lived in the tenth century thought the Bible[1] said something that meant that the world was coming to an end in the Year 1000—which was called the millennium from the Latin word meaning a thousand years.

Some people were glad that the world was coming to an end. They were so poor and miserable and unhappy here that they were anxious to go to heaven, where everything would be fine and lovely—if they had been good here. They were particularly good and did everything they could to earn a place for themselves in heaven when this old world should end.

Others were not so anxious to have the world come to an end. But, they thought, if it were coming to an end so soon, they might as well hurry up and enjoy themselves here while they still had a chance.

Well, the Year 1000 came, and nothing happened. At first people simply thought that a mistake had been made in counting the years—that there had not really been one thousand years since Christ's birth. The years went by, and still people waited for the end. They reread their

---

[1] Book of Revelations, chapter 20

Bibles and thought perhaps it meant a thousand years after Christ's *death*, instead of his birth. As time went on, without any change, they began to think the end was delayed for some reason they could not explain. It was not for many years after the millennium that most people came at last to realize that the world was not going to stop after all.

Every once in a while someone who thinks he knows more than others says the end of the world is not far off, but we may be quite sure that the world will keep on going long after we have all grown up and died and our children have done the same.

At this time, when people were looking for the end of the world, there was in the north of Europe a people who did not become Christians until around the year 1000 and cared nothing about what the Bible said as to the end of the world. They belonged to the same family as the Danes who had come to England in the time of Alfred. They were called Norsemen or Vikings. They were bold seafaring men, as hardy and unafraid as the Phoenician sailors of old. Their boats were painted black and had prows carved with figures of sea monsters or dragons. They sailed the northern seas and went farther westward toward the setting sun than any other sailors that we know about had ever gone. They had discovered Iceland and Greenland, and at last under their chief who was named Leif[2] Ericson they reached the shores of America. About the same year that the Christians in Europe were expecting the end of the world—the Year 1000—the Vikings had gone to what some people thought was the end of the world.

The Vikings called this new place Vineland or Wineland because they found grapes, from which wine is made, growing there. They told stories called *sagas* about their voyages to Vineland, and we can still read these stories. In the sagas, Vineland is described as a beautiful country, rich with grass and timber and wild wheat, with abundant animals and fish,

---

[2] Leif [lēf]

and mild in winter. The Vikings met people living there whom we now call Native Americans.

We're not sure exactly where these adventurous people went. We know that they reached Newfoundland, Canada and they may have gone as far south as Cape Cod in Massachusetts. The Vikings did not stay for very long in America, although they continued to sail the North Atlantic. We can only wonder if Columbus knew about the Vineland sagas and their stories about the land across the Atlantic, west of Europe.

50

Real Castles

YOU may think that castles belong only in fairy tales of princes and princesses.

But about the Year 1000 there were castles almost everywhere over Europe, and they were not fairy castles but real ones with real people in them.

After the downfall of Rome in 476, the Roman Empire was broken to pieces like a cut-up puzzle-map, and people built castles on the pieces, and they kept on building castles up to the 1400's. This is why and how people built them and why they at last stopped building them.

Whenever any ruler, whether he was a king or only a prince, conquered another ruler, he gave to his generals, who had fought with him and helped him to win, pieces of the conquered land as a reward instead of paying them in money. The generals in turn gave pieces of their land to the chief men who had been under them and helped them in battle. These men who were given land were called lords or nobles, and each lord was called a vassal of him who gave the land. Each vassal had to promise to fight with his lord whenever he was needed. He could not make this promise lightly in an offhand way, however. He had to do it formally so that it would seem more binding. The vassal had to kneel in front of his lord, and make the solemn promise to fight when called upon. This was called *doing homage*. Then once a year, at least, thereafter, he had to make the same promise over again. This method of giving away land was known as the Feudal[1] System.

Each of these lords or nobles then built himself a castle on the land that was given him, and there he lived like a little king with all his workpeople about him. The castle was not only his home, but it had to be a fort as well to protect him from other lords who might try to take his castle away from him. He usually placed it on the top of a hill or a cliff, so that the enemy could not reach it easily, if at all. It had great stone walls often ten feet or more thick. Surrounding the walls there was usually a ditch called a *moat* filled with water to make it more difficult for an enemy to get into the castle.

In times of peace, when there was no fighting, the men farmed the land outside the castle; but when there was war between lords, all the people went inside the castle walls, carrying all the food and cattle and everything else they had, so that they could live there for months or even years while the fighting was going on. A castle, therefore, had to be very

large to hold so many people and animals for so long a time, and often it was really like a walled town.

Medieval women managed many of the things that went on inside the castle—cooking, spinning thread, weaving cloth, overseeing the servants, and taking care of the animals. When the men were away at war, sometimes for months or even years at a time, the women were in charge of all the farming activities and the family's

Castle, drawbridge, moat, and knights

[1] Feudal [fyōōd· əl]

money as well. Because there were so many wars, many women became widows. In that case, they took total charge of the family estates.

Inside the walls of the castle were many smaller buildings to house the people and animals and for cooking and storing the food. There might even be a church or chapel. The chief building was, of course, the house of the lord himself and this was called the *keep*.

The main room of the keep was the Great Hall, which was like a very large living room and dining room combined. Here meals were served at tables which were simply long and wide boards placed on something to hold them up. These boards were taken down and put away after the meal was over. That is where we get the names *boarding* and *boarding house*. There were no forks nor spoons nor plates nor saucers nor napkins. Everyone ate with his fingers and licked them or wiped them on his clothes. Table manners were more like *stable* manners. The bones and scraps they threw on the floor or to the dogs, who were allowed in the room. Itchy scratchy! What a mess! At the end of the meal towels and a large bowl of water were brought in so that those who wished might wash their hands. Do you suppose anybody washed the floor?

After dinner the household was entertained during the long evenings with songs and stories by men called minstrels, who played and sang and amused the company.

Shut up within the castle walls, it seemed as if the lord and his people would be absolutely safe against any attacks of his enemies. In the first place, any enemy would have had to cross the moat or ditch filled with water, which surrounded the castle. Across this moat there was a drawbridge to the entrance or gate of the castle. In the entrance itself was an iron gate called a portcullis, which was usually raised like a window to allow people to pass. In time of war the drawbridge was raised. But in case an enemy was seen approaching and there was not time to raise the drawbridge, this portcullis could be dropped at a moment's notice. When the drawbridge was raised there was no way of getting into the castle except by crossing the moat. Anyone trying to do this would have had stones or melted tar thrown down on him. Instead of windows in the wall of the castle there were only long slits through which the fighters could shoot arrows at the enemy. At the same time, it was very difficult for anyone on the outside to hit the small crack-like openings with an arrow.

Yet attacks *were* made on castles. Sometimes the enemy built a tall wooden tower on wheels. This they would roll up as close as they could get to the walls, and from its top shoot directly over into the castle.

Sometimes they built tunnels from the outside right under the ground, under the moat, and under the castle walls into the castle itself.

Sometimes they built huge machines called battering-rams, and with these they battered down the walls.

Sometimes they used machines like great sling-shots to throw stones over the walls. Of course there were no cannons nor cannonballs nor guns nor gunpowder then.

The lord and his family were the rich people; all the others were little better than slaves. In times of peace most of the common people lived outside the castle walls on the land called the *manor*. The lord gave them just as little as he could and took from them just as much as he could. He had to feed and take some care of them, so that they could fight for him and serve him, just as he had to feed and take care of his horses that carried him to battle, and the cattle that provided him with milk and meat. But he didn't treat the people who served him as well as he did his domestic animals. The common people had to give their time and labor and a large part of the crops they raised to the lord. They themselves lived in miserable huts more like cowsheds, with only one room that had a dirt floor. Above this was perhaps a loft reached by a ladder where they went to bed. Bed was usually only a bundle of straw, and they slept in the clothes they wore during the day.

These workpeople were called *serfs*. Sometimes serfs could stand this kind of life no longer, and they would run away. If a serf was not caught within a year and a day, he was a free man. But if he was caught before the year and a day were up, the lord might whip him, brand him with hot irons, or even cut off his hands. Indeed, a lord could do almost anything he wished with his serfs except kill them—or sell them.

What do you think of the Feudal System?

51
Knights and Days of Chivalry

THOSE *years* in history which I have been telling you about are known as the *days* of chivalry—which means the times of ladies and gentlemen. The lord and his family were the gentlemen and the ladies. All the other people, by far the greater number, were just common people.

There were no schools for these common people. Little was done for them. They were taught to work and nothing else. The sons of a lord of a castle, however, were very carefully taught. Even they were taught only two things, how to be gentlemen and how to fight. Reading and writing were thought of no importance; in fact, it was usually considered a waste of time to learn such things.

This is the way the son of a lord was brought up. He stayed with his mother until he was seven years old. When he reached the age of seven he was called a page; and for the next seven years—that is, until he was fourteen, he remained a page. During the time he was a page, his chief business was to wait on the ladies of the castle. He ran their errands, carried their messages, waited on tables, etc. He also learned to ride a horse and to be brave and courteous.

When he was fourteen years old, he became a squire and remained a squire for the next seven years; that is, until he was twenty-one. During the time he was a squire he waited on the men, as he had waited on the ladies when he was a page. He attended to the men's horses, went to battle with them, led an extra horse, and carried another spear or lance, in case these should be needed.

When he was twenty-one years old, if he had been a good squire and had learned the lessons that he was taught, he then became a knight. Becoming a knight was an important ceremony like graduating exercises, for the grown boy was now to take up the business of a man.

To get ready for this ceremony, first, he bathed. This may not seem worth mentioning, but in those days one very rarely took a bath, sometimes not for years. He was then dressed in new clothes. Thus washed and dressed, he prayed all night long in the church. When day came, he appeared before all the people and solemnly swore always to do and to be certain things:

> To be brave and good
> To fight for the Christian religion
> To protect the weak
> To honor women

These were his vows. A white leather belt was then put on him and gold spurs fastened on his boots. After this had been done, he knelt, and his lord struck him over the shoulders with the flat side of a sword, saying as he did so, "I dub thee knight."

A knight went into battle covered with a suit of armor made of iron rings or steel plates like fish scales, and with a helmet or hood of iron. This suit protected him from the arrows and lances of the enemy. Of course if they had had any shot or shell, armor would have been no use at all, but they had no such things then.

Knights were so completely covered by their armor that when sides became mixed up in fighting, they could not tell one another apart. It was impossible to know who were friends and who were enemies.

So the knights wore, on the outside of the coat that went over their armor, a design of an animal, such as a lion, or of a plant or a rose or a cross or some ornament, and this design was known as a coat of arms.

A knight, as I told you, was first of all taught to be a gentleman, and so we sometimes speak of one who has good manners and is courteous, especially to ladies, as knightly or chivalrous. When a knight came into the presence of a lady he took off his helmet. It meant, "You are my friend, and so I do not need my helmet." That is why gentlemen raise their hats nowadays when they meet ladies.

But the most important thing the knights had to learn was to fight. Even their games were play fights.

Each country and each age has had its own games or sports in which it has taken special delight. The Greeks had their Olympic Games. The Romans had their chariot races and gladiatorial contests. We have football and baseball. But the chief sport of the knights was a kind of sham battle called the tournament.

The tournament was held in a field known as the *lists*. Large crowds with banners flying and trumpets blowing would gather around the lists to watch the sham fight, as crowds nowadays flock to a big football game waving pennants and tooting horns. The knights on horseback took their places at opposite ends of the lists. They carried lances, the points of which were covered so that they would not make a wound. At a given signal, they rushed toward the center of the field and tried with their lances to throw each other off their horses. The winner who succeeded in throwing the other knights was presented with a ribbon or a keepsake by one of the ladies, and a knight thought as much of this trophy of victory as the winner of a cup in a tennis tournament nowadays.

Knights were very fond of hunting with dogs. But they also hunted with a trained bird called a falcon, and both lords and ladies delighted in this sport. The falcon was trained like a hunting dog to catch other birds, such as wild ducks and pigeons, and also small animals. The falcon was chained to the wrist of the lord or lady, and its head was covered with a hood as it was carried out to hunt.

Man with falcon

When a bird was seen, the hood was removed, and the falcon, which was very swift, would swoop down upon its prey and capture it. Thereupon the hunter would come up, take the captured animal, and put the hood on the falcon again. The men, however, usually preferred hunting the wild boar, which was a kind of pig with sharp tusks, for this was more dangerous and therefore supposed to be more of a man's sport.

52

A Pirate's *Great* Grandson

WHEN Alfred was king, the Danes had raided England.

At the same time their cousins the Norsemen had raided the coast of France.

King Alfred at last had to give the Danes a part of the English coast, and they then settled down and became Christians.

The French king likewise did the same thing. In order to save himself from further raids, he gave the Norsemen a part of the French coast. The Norsemen then, as the Danes had done, settled down and became Christians.

These Norsemen who raided France were led by a very bold and brave pirate named Rollo.[1] In return for this gift of land Rollo was supposed to do homage by kissing the king's foot. But Rollo thought it beneath him to kneel and kiss the king's foot, so he told one of his men to do it for him. His man did as he was told, but he didn't like to do it, either. As he kissed the king's foot he raised it so high that he tipped his Majesty over backward.

The part of France that was given the Norsemen came to be called Normandy, and it is so called today, and the people were known thereafter as Normans.

---

[1] Rollo [rol ⋅ lō]

Norman raising king's foot

In 1066 there was a very powerful duke ruling over Normandy. His name was William, and he was descended from Rollo the pirate. Perhaps your name may be William. If you have any English or French ancestors, you may even be descended from this William.

William was strong in body, strong in will, and strong in rule over his people. He could shoot an arrow farther, straighter, and with more deadly effect than any of his knights. No one else was strong enough even to bend the bow he used.

William and his people had become Christians, but according to their idea, the Christian God was more like their old god, Woden, under a new name. William believed that, "might made right," for he was descended from a pirate, and he still acted like a pirate. Whatever he wanted he went after and took, even though he was supposed to be a Christian.

Now, William was only a duke, not a king, and he wanted to be a king. In fact, he thought he would like to be king of England, which was just across the channel from his own dukedom. Besides, the English king Edward was William's cousin, so he thought that gave him a good claim to the throne.

It so happened that a young English prince named Harold was shipwrecked on the coast of Normandy and was found and brought before William. Now, it seemed likely that some day Harold would be king of England, and William thought this a good chance to get England for himself. Before he would let Harold leave, he made the young man promise that when his turn came to be king, he would give England to William just as if that country were a horse or a suit of armor that could be given away. In order that this promise should be solemnly binding, William made Harold place his hand on the altar and swear, just as people place a hand on the Bible nowadays, when they take an oath. After Harold had sworn on the altar, William had the top lifted and showed Harold that below it were the bones of some of the Christian saints. Swearing on the bones of a saint was the most solemn kind of an oath one could possibly take. It was thought one would not dare to break such an oath for fear of the wrath of God.

Harold then returned to England. But when the time came that he should be king, the people naturally would not let him give England to William. Besides that, Harold said that such an oath, which he had taken against his will, an oath which had been forced on him by a trick, was not binding. So Harold became king.

When William heard that Harold had been made king, he was very angry. He said that he had been cheated and that Harold had broken his oath. At once he got ready an army and sailed over to take the country away from Harold.

As William landed from his boat, he stumbled and fell headlong on the shore. All his soldiers were shocked and greatly worried by this, for they thought it very bad luck—a bad omen, the Greeks would have called it. But William was quick-witted, and as he fell he grabbed up some of the earth in both hands. Then, rising, he made believe he had fallen on purpose and, lifting his hands in the air, exclaimed that he had taken up the ground as a sign that he was going to have *all* the land of England. This changed the bad omen into good luck.

The battle started, and the English fought furiously to defend themselves against these foreigners who were trying to take their country away from them. Indeed, they had almost won the battle when William gave an order to his men to pretend they were running away.

The English then followed, wildly rejoicing, and running pell-mell after the Normans. Just as soon, however, as the English were scattered and in disorder, William gave another signal, and his men faced about quickly. The English were taken by surprise, and before they could get into fighting order again, they were defeated, and Harold, their king, was shot through the eye and killed. This was the Battle of Hastings, one of the most famous battles in English history.

Harold had put up a brave fight. But luck was against him. Only a few days before this, he had had to fight a battle with his own brother, who in a traitorous way had got together an army against him. We are sorry for Harold, and yet it was probably better for England that things turned out as they did—yet who can tell?

William marched on to London and had himself crowned king on Christmas day, 1066. Ever since then he has been known as William the Conqueror, and the event is called the Norman Conquest. After this England had a new line of kings—a Norman family and a pirate family—to rule over her.

William divided England up among his nobles as if it were a pie, and gave each a share in the feudal way. They had to do homage to him as his vassals and promise to fight for him and to do as he said. Each of William's nobles built a castle on the property he was given. William himself built a castle in London by the Thames[2] River. On the same spot Julius Caesar had built a fort, but it had disappeared; and Alfred the Great had built a castle there, but it, too, had disappeared. But the castle William built is still standing today. It is known as the Tower of London.

William was a splendid boss and very business-like. He set to work and had a list made of all the land in England, a list of all the people and of all the property they had. This record was called the Domesday[3] Book and was something like the *census* now taken in this country every ten years. This list gave the name of everyone in England and everything each owned, even down to the last cow and pig. If your ancestors were living in England then you can look in the Domesday Book and find their names, how much land they owned, and how many cows and pigs

---

[2] Thames [temz] [3] Domesday [doomz' dā]

they had.

In order that no mischief might take place at night, William started what was called the *curfew*. Every evening at a certain hour a bell was rung. Then all lights had to be put out, and everyone had to go indoors—supposedly to bed.

One thing, however, that William did made the English very angry. He was extremely fond of hunting, but there was no good place where he could hunt near London. In order to have a place for hunting, he destroyed a large number of village houses and farms and turned that part of the country into a forest. This was called the New Forest, and though it is now about nine hundred years *old* it is still called *New* to this day.

On the whole, William, although descended from a pirate, gave England a good government and made it a safe place to live. Since that time, no foreign country has ever conquered England. So 1066 was almost like the Year 1 for the English.

53

A Great Adventure

HAVE you ever played the game called "Going to Jerusalem" in which everyone scrambles to get a seat when the music stops playing?

Well, all during the Middle Ages, that is, the period between ancient times and modern times, "Going to Jerusalem" was not a game but a real journey which Christians everywhere in Europe wanted to take and did take if they could. They wanted to see the actual spot where Christ had been crucified, to pray at the Holy Sepulcher, and to bring back a palm leaf as a souvenir, which they could show their friends, hang on the wall, and talk about all the rest of their lives.

There were always some good Christians—and also some bad ones—going to Jerusalem. Sometimes they went all by themselves, but more often they went with others. As of course there were no such things as trains in those days, poor people had to walk nearly the whole way from France and from England, from Spain and from Germany, and so it took them many months and sometimes years to reach Jerusalem. These travelers were called *pilgrims*, and their trip was called a *pilgrimage*.

Jerusalem at that time had been conquered by the Turks, who were Muslims. The Turks did not like these Christian pilgrims who came to see Christ's tomb, and they didn't treat them very well. Indeed, some of the pilgrims on their return told frightful stories of the way they had been treated by the Turks and the way the holy places in Jerusalem were also treated.

Just before the Year 1100, there was a pope at Rome named Urban. Urban heard these tales that the pilgrims told, and he was shocked. He thought it was a terrible thing, anyway, for the Holy City, as Jerusalem was called, and the Holy Land, where Jerusalem was located, to be ruled over by Muslims instead of by Christians. So Urban made a speech and urged all good Christians everywhere to get together and go on a pilgrimage to the Holy Land, with the idea of fighting the Turks and taking the city of Jerusalem away from them. Jerusalem was a holy city for the Muslims, too, as it was for the Jews. No wonder there have been so many wars to control that city.

Now, there lived at that same time a monk whom people called Peter the Hermit. A hermit is a man who goes off and lives entirely by himself, usually in a cave or hut where no one can find him or go to see him, where he can spend all day in prayer. Peter the Hermit thought such a life was good for his soul, that it made him a better man to be hungry and cold and uncomfortable.

Peter the Hermit had made a pilgrimage to Jerusalem and was very angry at what he saw there. He, too, began to tell people everywhere he went how disgraceful it was for them to allow Christ's tomb to belong to Muslim rulers and called on everyone to start on a pilgrimage with him to save Jerusalem. He talked to people in the churches, on the streetcorners, in the marketplaces, on the roadside. He was such a wonderful orator that those who heard him wept at his descriptions and begged to go with him.

Before long, thousands upon thousands of people, old and young, men and women, and even some children had pledged themselves to join a band to go to Jerusalem and take it away from the Muslims. As Christ had died on the cross, they cut pieces of red cloth in the form of a cross and sewed them on the fronts of their coats as a sign that they were soldiers of the cross. These pilgrims were called *Crusaders*, which is the Latin word for a crossbearer. As they knew they would be gone a long time and perhaps never return, some sold all they had and left their homes. Some men left their wives in charge. Not only poor people, but lords and nobles and even princes, joined the army of the Crusaders, and there were, besides the crowds on foot, large companies of those who rode on horseback.

The plan was to start in the summer of 1096, four years before 1100, but a great many were so anxious to get started that they didn't wait for the time that had been set. With Peter the Hermit and another pious man named Walter the Penniless as their leaders, they started off before things were really ready.

They had no idea how very far off Jerusalem was. They hadn't studied geography nor maps. They had no idea how long it would take, no idea how they would get food to eat on their journey, no idea where they would sleep. They simply trusted in Peter the Hermit and believed that the Lord would provide everything and show them the way.

Onward they marched, "Onward, Christian Soldiers," thousands upon thousands, toward the east and far-off Jerusalem. Thousands upon thousands of them died from disease and from hunger on the way. Every time they came within sight of another city, they would ask, "Is this Jerusalem?" so little did they know of the long distance that still lay between them and that city.

When the Muslim army in Jerusalem heard that the Crusaders were coming, they went forth to meet the Christians in order to defend their city against the European invaders. The Muslims killed almost all of the Crusaders who had started out with Peter ahead of the rest. Those

Crusaders, who had started out later, marched on, as had been planned at the beginning.

Finally, after nearly four years, only a small band of that vast throng that had set out so long before reached the walls of the Holy City. When at last they saw Jerusalem before them, they were wild with joy. They fell on their knees and wept and prayed and sang hymns and thanked God that He had brought them to the end of their journey. Then they furiously attacked the city. The Christians fought so hard that at last they captured Jerusalem. Then they entered the gates and killed thousands, so that it is said the streets of the Holy City ran with blood. This seems strange behavior for the followers of Christ, who preached against fighting and commanded, "Put up thy sword, for he that taketh the sword shall perish by the sword."

The Crusaders then made one of their leaders named Godfrey ruler of the city. Most of the other Crusaders who were left then went back home. Some stayed, though, because they saw that they could have more land and greater riches than they had at home in Europe.

54

Tick-Tack-Toe; Three Kings in a Row

HERE are three kings:

Richard of England,

Philip of France, and

Frederick Barbarossa[1] of Germany.

If you say their names over several times, they keep ringing through your mind and you can't seem to stop thinking them whether you want to or not.

Jerusalem was captured. But it didn't stay captured very long. Muslims attacked and won it back again.

The Christians started a Second Crusade. Thereafter about once in a lifetime during the next two hundred years there was one Crusade after another—eight or nine in all. Sometimes these later Crusades won back Jerusalem for a while, but for a while only. Sometimes they did not succeed at all.

The Third Crusade took place about a hundred years after the first; that is, nearly 1200 A.D. These three kings—Richard of England, Philip of France, and Frederick Barbarossa—started on the Third Crusade. But they didn't all finish. I'll tell you about them in three-two-one-order.

Frederick's name, Barbarossa, meant Red Beard, for in those days it was the custom to give kings nicknames that described them. Frederick's

---

[1] Barbarossa [bär bə rōs′ ə]

Richard of England, Philip of France, and Frederick Barbarossa

capital was in Aix-la-Chapelle, as Charlemagne's had been, but Frederick was king only of Germany. When a young man, he had tried to make his country as large and powerful as the new Roman Empire that Charlemagne had made. But he was not a great enough man, and so was unable to do what Charlemagne had done. Frederick was quite old when he started out on the Third Crusade with the other two kings. But he never reached Jerusalem, for in crossing a stream on the way, he was drowned. So much for Frederick, the third king.

The second king, Philip of France, was jealous of the first king, Richard, because Richard was so very popular and well liked by the Crusaders. Philip finally gave up the Crusade and went back to France.

Richard of England was then the only king left on the Crusade. It would have been better if he, too, had gone back to his country instead of gallivanting off on a Crusade. But he thought going on a Crusade was much better sport than staying at home and working over the difficult business of governing his people.

Richard was kind and gentle, yet strong and brave. Richard the Lion-Hearted they called him. He was hard on wrongdoers but fair and square. People loved him, but they feared him, too, for he punished the wicked and those who misbehaved.

Even Richard's enemies admired him. The Muslim king of Jerusalem at the time of this Third Crusade was named Saladin.[2] Saladin, though being attacked by Richard, admired him very much and even became his friend. So Saladin, instead of fighting Richard, finally made a friendly agreement with him to treat the Holy Sepulcher and the pilgrims properly. As this arrangement was satisfactory to everyone, Richard left Jerusalem to Saladin and started back home.

On his way home Richard was captured and put in prison by the son of Frederick Barbarossa and held for a large ransom from England. Richard's friends did not know where he was and did not know how to find him.

Now, it so happened that Richard had a favorite minstrel named Blondel.[3] Blondel had composed a song of which Richard was very fond. When Richard was taken prisoner, Blondel wandered over the country singing everywhere this favorite song in the hope that Richard might hear it and reveal where he was. One day he happened to sing beneath the very tower where Richard was imprisoned. Richard heard him and answered by singing the refrain of the song. His friends then knew where he was, the ransom was paid, and Richard was allowed to go free.

When, at last, Richard did reach England, he still had adventures. This was the time when Robin Hood was robbing travelers. Richard planned to have himself taken prisoner by Robin Hood, so that he might capture him and bring him to justice. Richard disguised himself as a monk and

---

[2] Saladin [sal ′ ə din]　　　　　　[3] Blondel [blôn del ′]

was captured as he had planned. But he found Robin Hood such a good fellow after all that he forgave him and his men.

Richard's coat of arms was a design of three lions, one above the other; and this same design of three lions now forms part of the shield of England.

After Richard's Crusade, there was a Fourth Crusade, and then in the year 1212—which is an easy date to remember, because it is simply the number 12 repeated—one, two, one, two—there was a crusade of children only. This was known therefore as the Children's Crusade. It was led by a French boy about twelve years old named Stephen, who was named after the first Christian martyr.

Children from all over France left their homes and their mothers and fathers—it seems strange to us that their mothers and fathers let them start off on such a trip—and marched south to the Mediterranean Sea. Here they expected the waters of the sea would part and allow them to march on dry land to Jerusalem, as they had read in the Bible the waters of the Red Sea had done to allow the Israelites to leave Egypt. But the waters did not part.

Some sailors, however, offered to take the children to Jerusalem in their ships. They said they would do it for nothing, just for the love of the Lord. But it turned out that these sailors were really pirates, and as soon as they got the children on board their ships they steered them straight into the very land of their enemies, the Muslims. Here, it is said, the pirates sold the children as slaves. This is not a Grimm's fairy tale, and the pirates were not trapped by the children, so I cannot make a happy ending, for it was not.

The last or Eighth Crusade was led by a king of France called Louis. He was so pious and so devoted to the Lord that he was made a saint and ever after has been called St. Louis. Yet this Crusade failed, and ever since that time Jerusalem was ruled by Muslims until, in 1918, it was captured by the

English, who kept it until 1948 when the state of Israel was established. Now, both Israeli Jews and Palestinians—Muslim and Christian—want control of the Holy City. It's very sad that this city that is so sacred to Jews, Christians, and Muslims is always at the center of a war.

Not all the Crusaders were good Christians. Like some people nowadays, a great many were Christian only in name. In fact, though strange to say, quite a number of the Crusaders were nothing but scalawags, looking for excitement and adventure, and they went on a Crusade merely as an excuse to rob and plunder.

The Crusades did not succeed in their object, which was to keep Jerusalem for the Christians. In spite of that, the Crusades did a great deal of good. When the Crusades first started, the Crusaders were not nearly as civilized as the people they went to conquer. But travel sometimes teaches people more than books, and it taught the Crusaders. They learned the customs of the other lands through which they went. They learned languages and literature. They learned history and art.

There were then no public schools. Only a very, very few people had any education at all. The Crusades then did what schools might have done. They taught the people of Europe and opened up to them a whole new world of culture and knowledge.

55

Three Kingdoms in West Africa

AT the same time that medieval kingdoms like England and France were becoming important in Europe, three kingdoms in West Africa also grew strong and wealthy. They were called Ghana,[1] Mali,[2] and Songhay.[3] These kingdoms were south of the Sahara Desert, along the Niger[4] River. On your map each kingdom is outlined with a different kind of line.

This part of Africa was very wealthy because gold was mined there. For many centuries, the peoples of West Africa traded their gold with close neighbors and also with the Berber people north of the Sahara Desert. Some of the gold from West Africa was sold in the Roman Empire.

There are lots of good stories about the gold miners and traders. When the miners had gold to trade, they would carry their nuggets far away from the mines. They didn't want strangers to find out exactly where the gold came from. The miners would wait in a place that both sides agreed upon. The traders would come and leave what they had to trade. After the traders were out of sight, the miners would leave some gold. Then they would hide. They didn't want to meet the traders, who might force them to tell the location of the mines. The traders would then return and see how much gold had been left. If they thought it was a fair trade, they would take the gold and go home. If they thought that not enough was

---

[1] Ghana [gä′ nə]
[2] Mali [mä′ lē]
[3] Songhay [son gī′]
[4] Niger [nī′ jər]

Medieval kingdoms of West Africa

offered, they would back off once more and wait for the miners to leave more gold. When both sides were satisfied with the trade, they would all go home. It was like swapping baseball cards. Both sides had to be happy or there was no trade.

One thing that the West Africans needed to get in trade was salt. Can you guess why? West Africa is very hot. In those days with no refrigerators, salt was used to preserve food. Perhaps you've tasted beef jerky, which is meat that has been dried and preserved by salting. You can think of many other ways we keep our food from spoiling now, but in those days, salt was scarce and valuable. Even today we still use salt as a preservative, and we still say someone is "worth his salt" when he does a job well.

It just so happened that there was a lot of salt on the north side of the Sahara Desert. So, the people of the Niger River area traded with the Berbers of North Africa—gold for salt. Salt was so valuable that West Africans and Berbers traded an even weight of gold for salt—one pound of gold for one pound of salt. That's how valuable salt was. How would you like to be able to make that trade today?

All that gold made a number of the kingdoms in West Africa very wealthy. First a kingdom called Ghana grew large by conquering many of its neighbors. The king's power came from his well-trained army, a skillful cavalry, and gold. When the king of Ghana held an audience, he was surrounded by signs of his power and wealth: pages holding shields, swords with gold handles, horses covered with gold cloths, and the king's own horse tied to a sixty-pound gold nugget! Despite all this wealth, Ghana eventually declined in power, as all empires do sooner or later.

Mali was the next rich, important empire in West Africa. One king, Sundiata,[5] conquered the cities important in the trade crossing the Sahara. He also conquered rich gold fields. This king was not only rich, but he was also smart. Whenever his army conquered new land, he put the soldiers to work converting it to farm land—until it was time for the next battle. Soon Mali was one of the richest farming areas in West Africa, so this kingdom had plenty to eat as well as having gold and a powerful army.

The most famous king of Mali was Mansa Musa,[6] who ruled during the 14th century. He extended his empire westward to the Atlantic Ocean and ruled perhaps eight million people. Muslim traders, both Arabs and North Africans, came to Mali, and Mansa Musa converted to Islam. Like all devout Muslims, he made a pilgrimage to Mecca. Mansa Musa's pilgrimage made *him* famous! His route took him through Cairo, Egypt. He traveled with 500 slaves, each carrying a six-pound gold staff. There

---

[5] Sundiata [sun di a ' tə]   [6] Mansa Musa [man ' sə mo͞o ' sə]

were also one hundred elephants, each said to be carrying one hundred pounds of gold. Several hundred camels carried food, weapons, and other things that the pilgrims needed. In Egypt and in Arabia, Mansa Musa gave away a lot of gold. Muslims are expected to be generous, and Mansa Musa was. He also used his gold to buy presents for the people he met along the way. While he was traveling, someone asked Mansa Musa how big his kingdom was. He replied, "A year." What do you think he meant by this? Did you guess? He meant that it took him a year to travel from one end of his kingdom to the other.

When Mansa Musa came home, he brought with him artists and architects to build mosques in the city of Timbuktu and other cities in Mali. He also brought scholars and many books to start a library. Most of the books were written in Arabic, the language used by many Muslims. Timbuktu became a center of learning, and a large book market opened there. Astronomers, mathematicians, philosophers, and poets flocked to the city with its large library and many mosques. Doctors and lawyers worked and taught there. The king supported them all. A lot of foreigners came to visit Timbuktu. Some of these visitors wrote about their trips, so we can read what they said. One Muslim traveler who came from North Africa discovered an astonishing thing: Women were allowed to study and were treated with as much respect as the men!

After Mansa Musa died, the empire of Mali began to split apart. Soon a third important empire, Songhay, arose in the Niger River area. In Songhay, the king's wealth again was based on gold, and he commanded strong armies. The king, Sunni Ali Ber,[7] expanded Songhay until its empire was larger than Mali had ever been. He died in 1492, the year that Columbus set sail for the Americas. After this time, Songhay was weakened by foreigners, first by Moroccans from North Africa and then

---

[7] Sunni Ali Ber [soͦn' e a' li ber]

by the Portuguese who began sailing and trading along the African coast. The king of Songhay no longer had the power or wealth to hold his territory together. After a thousand years of wealthy empires, the lands along the Niger River split into small kingdoms.

56

Bibles Made of Stone and Glass

In Europe during the Middle Ages, people often went to church every day and often several times a day. They did not go only when there was a church service. They went to say their prayers by themselves; they went to tell their troubles to the priest, to get advice from him, to burn a candle to the Virgin Mary, or simply to chat with their friends.

All during the Crusades and immediately after the Crusades, the chief thing that many people thought about was their church.

Almost everyone in Europe was a Christian although many towns had Jewish residents as well. You may remember that Jews had been forced to leave the Holy Land way back in 70 A.D. by the Romans. Some had made their way to Europe.

For Christians, there was only one church in a neighborhood, and everyone went to the same church, for there were no Baptists, nor Episcopalians, nor Methodists; all were just Christians.

The church was everyone's meetinghouse, so people naturally gave as much money and time and labor as they could to make their church the best that could be built. That is why there were built in France and other parts of Europe at this time many of the finest churches and cathedrals in the world. These churches and cathedrals are still standing, and because they are so beautiful, people go long distances to see them.

Do you know what a cathedral is? A cathedral is not just a large church. It is the church of a bishop. In the chancel of this church, there is a special chair for the bishop. This bishop's chair is called in Latin a *cathedra*, and so his church is named a cathedral after this chair.

These churches and cathedrals were nothing like the old Greek and Roman temples; they were not like anything that had ever been built before.

If you have ever built a house out of blocks, you probably did it this way: first you stood two blocks upright, and then you laid another block across the top of these for a roof. This is the way the Greeks and Romans built.

But the Christians throughout Europe at that time did not build in this way at all.

When you were building toy houses, instead of laying a single block across the two standing ones, you may perhaps have tried leaning two blocks together like the sides of a letter A for a roof. If you did, you know what happened: the two leaning blocks pushed over the sides, and *crash*! everything tumbled. Well, these churches were built somewhat in this way, with stones arched across the standing stone columns. But to keep the stone arches from pushing over the standing stone columns, the builders put up props or braces. These props or braces were made of stone, too, and these props of stone were called *flying buttresses*.

The people in Italy thought this a crazy way of building. They thought such buildings must be shaky and might easily topple over—like a house of cards. The Goths who had conquered Italy in 476 were considered wild and ignorant and after that people called anything wild and ignorant *Gothic*. People called all buildings such as I have just described *Gothic*, although the Goths had nothing to do with the buildings.

Indeed, from my description you, too, may think such buildings propped up by flying buttresses must have been tottering and ugly, but they were neither. They were not rickety, for though occasionally one that was not carefully built did collapse, the largest and best are

Flying buttresses—apse of Notre Dame[1]

still standing today. Although there were old-fashioned people who thought no building was beautiful that was not built in the Roman or Greek style, we have come to admire the great beauty of these so-called Gothic buildings.

There were other ways in which the Gothic churches were different from the Greek and Roman temples. Before a Gothic church was started, a very large cross was first drawn on the ground with its head towards the east, because that is the direction of Jerusalem. On this cross-shaped plan, the church was built so that if you looked down from above on the finished building, it was shaped like a cross with the altar always toward the east.

Gothic churches had beautiful spires or *arrows*, which have been likened to fingers pointing to heaven. The doorways and windows were not square or round at the top, but pointed, like hands placed together in prayer.

---

[1] Notre Dame [nō′ trə däm′]

Nearly the whole side of a Gothic church was made of glass. These large windows were not, however, plain white glass, but beautiful pictures made of colored glass. Small pieces of different colors were joined together at their edges with lead to make what looked like wonderful paintings. These pictures were much finer than ordinary paintings, for the light shone through the stained glass and made the colors brilliant as jewels—blue like the clear sky, yellow like sunlight, red like a ruby. These pictures in glass told stories from the Bible. They were like colored illustrations in a book. The people who could not read, and very few could read, were able to know the Bible stories just by looking at these beautiful illustrations.

Statues of saints and angels and characters in the Bible were carved in the stonework of the church. The churches were like Bibles of stone and glass.

Besides these holy things, strange, grotesque beasts were also made in stone—monsters like no animal that has ever been seen in nature. These creatures were usually put on the outside edge or corner of the roof or they were used for waterspouts and called *gargoyles*.[2] They were supposed to scare away evil spirits from the holy place.

Gargoyle

No one now knows who were the architects or the builders of these Gothic churches or who were the sculptors or artists. Almost everyone did some work on the church. Instead of giving money, men and women gave time and labor. Men carved stone or made stained glass. Women sewed and embroidered vestments and altar cloths.

Some of these Gothic churches took hundreds of years to build, so that the workmen who started them never lived to see them finished. Some of the most famous cathedrals are Canterbury Cathedral in England, the

---

[2] gargoyles [gär´ goilz]

Cathedral of Notre Dame in Paris, Cologne[3] Cathedral in Germany, and Chartres[4] Cathedral in France.

Cologne Cathedral took the longest of all to build, as it was not entirely finished until about seven hundred years after it was begun! Some of the cathedrals were destroyed during the many wars fought since the Middle Ages.

Gothic churches were built, with loving care, of stone and jeweled glass. Nothing but the best was thought good enough. Today many churches are still built with spires, pointed doors, and some stained-glass windows, and often the altar is toward the east. But although they imitate the Gothic style in these things, they seldom have stone ceilings, as Gothic churches had, nor flying buttresses, nor walls of stained glass. Real Gothic was enormously expensive and difficult, and nowadays people haven't the time, the money, nor the interest to build in such a way.

That is the story of Gothic churches that the Goths had nothing to do with.

---

[3] Cologne [kə lōn']   [4] Chartres [shär' trə]

57

John, Whom Nobody Loved

RICHARD the Lion-Hearted, whom every-body loved, had a brother named John, whom nobody loved.

This brother John became king, but he turned out to be a very wicked king.

He is another one of the villains in history, whom we do not like, but like to hear about, and like to clap when he gets what he deserves.

John was afraid that his young nephew named Arthur might be made king in his place, so he had him murdered. Some say he hired others to do the killing; some say he murdered him with his own hands. This was a very bad beginning for his reign, but things got worse and worse as time went on.

John got into a quarrel with the pope in Rome. The pope at that time said what should be done and what should not be done in churches everywhere. The pope ordered John to make a certain man bishop in England, and John said he wouldn't do it. He wanted another man, a friend of his, to be bishop. The pope then said he would close up all the churches in England if John didn't do as he was told. John said he didn't care. Let the pope go ahead and close up all the churches if he wanted to. So the pope ordered all churches in England to be closed until John should give in. Nowadays this might not have made much difference, but then, as I have told you, the church was the one most important thing in everyone's life; in fact, nothing else mattered so much. The closing of the churches meant that no services could be held in any church. It meant that children could not be baptized, and so, if they died, it was believed they could not go to heaven. It meant that couples could not be married. It meant that the dead could not be given a Christian burial.

The people of England were shocked. It was as if heaven had put a curse on them. They were afraid that terrible things would happen to them. Of course the people blamed John, for he was the cause of the churches being closed. They were so angry at him that he became scared—afraid what his people might do to him. When at last the pope threatened to make another man king of England in John's place—yes, the pope had as much power as that—John, in fear and trembling, gave in and agreed to do everything that at first he had said he would not do and more besides. But John was pig-headed. He was always doing the wrong thing and sticking to it.

John had an idea that the world was made for the king and that people were put upon the earth simply so that the king might have servants to work for him, to earn money for him, to do what he wished them to do. Many of the kings of olden days felt the same way, though they did not go as far as John did. John would order people who were rich to give him whatever money he wanted. If they refused to give him all he asked, he would put them in prison, have their hands squeezed in an iron press until the bones cracked and the blood ran, or he would even put them to death.

John got worse and worse until at last his barons could not stand his actions any longer. So they made him prisoner and took him to a little island in the Thames River called Runnymede.[1] Here they forced John to agree to certain things that they had written down in Latin. This was in the Year 1215; and 1215 was a bad date for John, but a good date for the English people. This list of things which the barons made John agree to was called by the Latin name for a great agreement or charter, which is *Magna Carta*.

---

[1] Runnymede [run′ i mēd]

John did not agree to the Magna Carta willingly, however. He was as angry and furious as a spoiled child, who kicks and screams when forced to do something he does not want to do. He had to agree, nevertheless.

John was unable to write his name, and thus he could not sign the agreement as people sign contracts nowadays. But he wore a seal ring that was used by people who could not sign their names, and this seal he pressed into a piece of hot wax which was dropped on the agreement where one would have signed.

John agreed in the Magna Carta to give the barons some of the rights that we think every human being should have anyway, without an agreement. For instance, a person certainly has the right to keep the money he earns, and he has the right not to have it taken away from him unlawfully. A person also has the right not to be put in prison or be punished by the king or anyone else unless he has done something wrong and unless he has had a fair trial. These are two of the rights that John agreed to in the Magna Carta. There were quite a number of others.

John didn't keep his agreement, however. He broke it the very first time he had a good chance, as a person usually does when he is forced to agree to something against his will. But John died pretty soon; and so, as far as he was concerned, the Magna Carta didn't matter much. However, kings who came after him were made to agree to the same things. So after 1215 the king in England was supposed to be the servant of the people, and not the people servants of the king as they had been before that time.

58

A Great Story Teller

FAR away from England,
    Far off in the direction of the rising sun,
        Far beyond Italy and Jerusalem and the Tigris and Euphrates and Persia was a country called Cathay[1]—C-A-T-H-A-Y.

If you looked down at your feet, and the world were glass, you would see Cathay on the other side.

Cathay is the same place we now call China. There had been people living in Cathay, of course, all through the centuries that had passed, but Europeans knew little of this land or of its people.

In the thirteenth century or twelve hundreds, Mongols, who came from the north, were ruling China. Soon, it seemed that they might conquer all the other countries whose histories we have been hearing about. The ruler of the Mongols was a fierce fighter named Genghis Khan.[2] Genghis Khan had an army of Tartar horsemen who were terrific fighters.

Genghis usually found some excuse for making war on others, but if he couldn't find a good excuse, he made up one, for he was bent on building an enormous empire.

Genghis and his horsemen swept over the land from Cathay toward Europe. They burned and destroyed thousands upon thousands of

---

[1] Cathay [ka thā′]   [2] Genghis Khan [jeng′ gis kän]

towns and cities and everything in their way. No one was able to stop them.

Genghis Khan had conquered the whole land from the Pacific Ocean to the eastern part of Europe. At last he stopped. With this kingdom he seemed to be satisfied. He might well have been satisfied, for it was larger than the Roman Empire or that of Alexander the Great.

Even when Genghis died, things were no better, for his son was just as fierce a fighter as his father and conquered still more territory.

But the grandson of Genghis Khan was much less warlike than his grandfather had been. He was named Kublai Khan,[3] and he was quite different from his father and grandfather. He made his capital at a city in China called Peiping, now called Beijing,[4] and ruled over this vast empire that he had inherited from his father. Kublai built magnificent palaces and surrounded himself with beautiful gardens, and he made such a wonderful capital for himself that Solomon in all his glory did not live in such splendor as did Kublai Khan.

Now, far, far off from Beijing and the palace of Kublai Khan, in the north of Italy was a city built on the water. Its streets were of water, and boats were used instead of carriages. This city was called Venice. About the Year 1260 there were living in Venice two brothers named Nicolo and Maffeo Polo. The Polos got an idea in their heads that they would like to see something of the world. So these two Venetian merchants started off toward the rising sun looking for adventure, just like boys in storybooks who go off to seek their fortunes. After several years of travel, always toward the east, they at last came to the gardens and to the magnificent palace of Kublai Khan.

When Kublai Khan heard that strange white men from a far-off place and an unknown country were outside the palace, he wanted to see them. They were brought into his presence. They told Kublai Khan all about

---

[3] Kublai Khan [kōō′ blĭ kän]   [4] Beijing [bei jing′]

their own land. They were good story-tellers, and they made it interesting. They told him also about the Christian religion and many other things that he had never heard of. After several years, the Polos went home to Venice.

The emperor was so much interested in the Polos and in the stories they told about their country that he wanted to hear more. In 1271 the Polos returned to China with Nicolo's teenage son, Marco. The emperor persuaded them to stay with him and tell him more. He gave them rich presents. Then he made them his advisers and assistants in ruling his empire. The Polos stayed on for years and years and years and learned the language and came to be very important people in Cathay.

At last after they had spent about twenty years in Cathay, the Polos thought it was about time to go home and see their own people again. They begged leave to return. Kublai Khan did not want them to go. In the end though he did let them go, and they started back to what once had been their home.

When they at last arrived in Venice, they had been away so long and had been traveling so far that no one knew them. They had almost forgotten how to speak their own language, and they talked like foreigners. Their clothes had become worn out and ragged by their long trip. They looked like tramps, and not even their old friends recognized them. No one would believe that these ragged, dirty strangers were the same fine Venetian gentlemen who had disappeared almost twenty years before.

The Polos told their townspeople all about their adventures and the wonderfully rich lands and cities that they had visited. The townspeople only laughed at them, for they thought them story tellers.

The Polos then ripped open their ragged garments, and out fell piles of magnificent and costly jewels, diamonds and rubies and sapphires and pearls—enough to buy a kingdom. The people looked in wonder and amazement and began to believe.

Marco Polo told his stories to a man who wrote them down and made a book of them called *The Travels of Marco Polo*. This is an interesting book for you to read even today, although we cannot believe all the tales he told. We know that he exaggerated a great many things, for he liked to amaze people.

Marco Polo described the magnificence of Kublai Khan's palace. He told of its enormous dining hall, where thousands of guests could sit down at the table at one time. He told of a bird so huge that it could fly away with an elephant. He said that Noah's Ark was still on Mount Ararat, only the mountain was so high and so dangerous to climb on account of the ice and snow with which it was covered that no one could go to see if the ark really was there.

59

"Thing-a-ma-jigger" and

"What-cher-may-call-it" or

a Magic Needle and a Magic Powder

ABOUT this same time that Marco Polo returned from his travels, people in Europe began to hear and talk about a magic needle and a magic powder that did remarkable things, and some said that Marco brought them back from Cathay, but now we know that it was Arab sailors who carried many of the wondrous things from China to the Mediterranean, where Europeans learned of them.

One of these wonderful things was a little magic needle. The little magic needle, when floated on a straw or held up only at its middle, would always turn towards the north no matter how much you twisted it. Such a needle put in a case was called a *compass*.

Now, you may not see why such a little thing was so remarkable. But strange as it may seem, this little thing really made it possible to discover a new world.

Perhaps you have played the game in which a child is blindfolded, twisted around several times in the center of the room, and then told to go toward the door or the window or some other point in the room. You know how impossible it is for one who has been so turned round to tell which way to go, and you know how absurd one looks who goes in quite the opposite direction when he thinks he is going straight.

Well, the sailor at sea was something like such a blind-folded child. Of course, if the weather were fine, he could tell by the sun or the stars which way he should go. But when the weather was cloudy and bad, there was nothing for him to go by. He was then like the blindfolded child. He might easily become confused and sail in just the opposite direction from the way he wanted to go without knowing the difference.

This was perhaps one of the chief reasons why most sailors, before the compass was used, had not gone far out of sight of land. They were afraid they might not be able to find their way back. So most sailors traveled only to that part of the world that could be reached without going far out of sight of land.

But, with the compass, sailors could sail on and on through storms and cloudy weather and keep always in the direction they wanted to go. They simply had to follow the little magnetic needle suspended in its box. No matter how much the boat turned or twisted or tossed, the little needle always pointed to the north. Of course sailors did not always want to go north, but it was very easy to tell any other direction if they knew which was north. South was exactly opposite, east was to the right, and west was to the left. All they had to do was to steer the boat on the course in whatever direction they wished.

It was a long while, however, before sailors would use a compass. They thought it was bewitched by some magic, and they were afraid to have anything to do with such a thing. Sailors are likely to be superstitious, and they were afraid that if they took the compass on board it might bewitch their ship and bring them bad luck.

The other magic thing was gunpowder.

Never before 1300 had there been such things in Europe as guns or cannons or pistols. All fighting had been done with bows and arrows or swords or spears or with some such weapons. A sword can only be used on a man a few feet away, but with guns an enemy may be killed and walls battered down miles away. After gunpowder was invented, the armor that the old knights wore was of course no longer of any use, for it could not protect them from shot and shell. Gunpowder has changed fighting completely and made war the terrible thing it has become.

Although Marco Polo was supposed to have told about gunpowder and its use in cannons as he had seen it in the East, most people think it was the Arabs who brought the knowledge to Europe. However it happened, we're sure it was in Asia that people first discovered how to put certain ingredients together that resulted in an explosive. It was quite a while, however, before gunpowder was made strong enough to do much damage. In fact, it was over a hundred years before fighting with guns entirely took the place of fighting with bows and arrows in Europe.

60

Thelon Gest Wart Hate Verwas

Is this another Latin heading?

No, it's English.

Don't you understand English?

It was 1338, and Edward III was king of England. He also owned some land in France, which the French king wanted to take away from him. Edward III decided he wanted to rule France as well as England. He said he was related to the former king of France and had a better right to the country than the one who was ruling. So he started a war to take France, and the war he started lasted more than a hundred years. This is known as the Hundred Years' War and it is:

The Longest War that Ever Was!

The English army sailed over from England and landed in France. The first great battle was fought in 1346 at a little place called Crécy.[1] The English army was on foot and was made up chiefly of the common people. The French army were mostly knights clad in armor on horseback.

The French knights on horseback thought themselves much finer than the common English soldiers who were on foot. The English soldiers,

---

[1] Crécy [krās′ sē]

however, used a weapon called the longbow, which shot arrows with terrific force, and they completely whipped the French knights in spite of the fact that the knights were nobles, were trained to be fighters, rode on horses, and were protected by armor.

Cannons were used by the English in this battle for the first time. The cannons, however, did not amount to much nor do very much harm. They were so weak that they simply tossed the cannonballs at the enemy as one might throw a basketball or football. They scared the horses of the French but did little other damage. But this was the beginning of what was before long to be the end of knights and armor and feudalism.

After the battle of Crécy, a horribly contagious disease called *bubonic plague*[2] attacked the people of Europe. It was like the plague in Athens in the Age of Pericles, but this plague did not attack just one city or country. It was supposed to have started in Cathay, and it spread westward until it reached Europe. There was no running away from it. It spread far and wide over the whole land and killed more human beings than any war that has ever been. The bubonic plague was called Black Death, because black spots came out all over the body of anyone who caught it, and he was certain to die within a few hours or a day or two. There was no hope. No medicine had any effect. Many people committed suicide just as soon as they found they had the disease. Many died just from fright, actually "scared to death."

It lasted two years, and millions upon millions caught the disease. One third of the people of Europe died of it. Whole towns were wiped out, and in many places no one was left to bury the dead. Dead bodies lay where they had fallen—on the street, in the doorway, in the marketplace.

The crops in the fields went to waste, for there was no one to gather them. Horses and cows roamed over the country at will, for there was no one to care for them. The plague attacked even sailors at sea, and ships

---

[2] bubonic plague [byōō bon′ ik plāg]

were found drifting about on the water with not a soul alive left on board, with not even one left to steer the ship.

What if it had killed every last man, woman, and child in the world! What then would have been the future history of the world?

As if there were not enough people dead already, the Hundred Years' War still went on year after year. The soldiers who had fought at Crécy had been dead for years. Their children had grown up, fought, and died; their grandchildren had grown up, fought, and died; and their great grandchildren had done the same; and the English army was still fighting in France. The French prince at that time was very young and weak, and the French were almost in despair—hopeless—because they had no strong leader to help them drive out the English after all these many years.

Now, in a little French village there was living a poor peasant girl, a shepherdess, called Joan of Arc. As she watched her flocks of sheep, she had wonderful visions. She heard voices calling to her, telling her she was the one who must lead the French armies and save France from England. She went to the prince's nobles and told them her visions. But they did not put any faith in her or her visions, and they did not believe she was able to do the things she thought she could.

To test her, however, they dressed up another man as the prince and put him on the throne while the prince stood at one side with the nobles. Then they let Joan into the room. When Joan entered the royal hall, she gave one look at the man who was seated on the throne and dressed up as the prince. Then without hesitating she walked directly past him and went straight to the *real* prince. Before him she knelt and said, "I have come to lead your armies to victory." The prince at once gave her his flag and a suit of armor, and she rode out at the head of all the army and had the prince crowned king.

Joan of Arc at the stake

The French soldiers took heart again. It seemed as if the Lord had sent an angel to lead them, and they fought so hard and so bravely that they won many battles.

The English soldiers, however, thought that it was not the Lord but the devil who had sent Joan and that she was not an angel but a witch, and they were very much afraid of her. At last, the English made her prisoner. The French king, whom she had saved, didn't even try to save her, in spite of all she had done for him. Now that things were going his way, he didn't like to have a woman running things, and the soldiers didn't like to have a woman ordering them around, and they were glad to be rid of her.

The English tried her as a witch, judged her guilty of being a witch, and then they burned her alive at the stake.

But Joan seemed to have brought the French good luck, to have put new life into their armies, for from that time on, France increased in strength, and, after more than a hundred years of fighting, at last drove the English out of the country. In more than one hundred years of fighting, hundreds of thousands of people had been wounded and crippled and blinded and killed, and after it all England was no better off, just the same as when it started—all the fighting all for nothing.

61

Print and Powder
or
Off with the Old,
On with the New

UP to this time there was not a printed book anywhere in Europe. There was not a newspaper. There was not a magazine. All books had to be written by hand. This, of course, was extremely slow and expensive, so there were very few of even these handwritten books. Only kings and very wealthy people had any books at all. Such a book as the Bible, for instance, cost almost as much as a house, and so no poor people could own such a thing. Even when there was a Bible in a church, it was so valuable that it had to be chained to keep it from being stolen. Think of stealing a Bible!

Actually, if you remember, the Chinese invented printing. Later, people began to print books in a new way. First the printer put together wooden letters called type, and then smeared them with ink. Then he pressed paper against this inky type and made a copy. After the type was once set up, thousands of copies could be made quickly and easily. Then he could take the letters apart and use them to make the next page. This, as you of course know, was printing. It was printing with movable type. It all seems so simple, the wonder is that no one had thought of this type of printing thousands of years before.

It is generally believed that a German named Gutenberg[1] made the first printed book in Europe. And what book do you suppose it was that he

---

[1] Gutenberg [gōōt′ en bûrg]

printed? Why, the book that people thought to be the most important book in the world— the Bible. It took Gutenberg five years to make such a big book, and he finished it in 1456.

Gutenberg at his press, comparing a printed sheet with a manuscript

The first dated book printed in England was made by an Englishman named Caxton.[2] It was called *Sayings of the Philosophers,* and was printed in 1477.

Before this time few people, even though they were kings or princes, knew how to read. There were no books to teach them how to read and few books for them to read if they had learned. So what was the use of learning?

You can see how difficult it must have been for people throughout the Middle Ages, without books or newspapers or anything printed, to learn what was going on in the world, or to learn about anything that one wanted to know.

Now that printing had been invented, all that was changed. Storybooks, schoolbooks, and other books could be made in large numbers and more cheaply. People who never before were able to have any books could now own them. People could now read all the famous stories of the world and learn about geography, about history, about anything they wanted to know. The invention of movable type was soon to change everything.

The Hundred Years' War had at last come to an end soon after the invention of printing.

---

[2] Caxton [kak′ sten]

At the same time something else that was a thousand years old came to an end.

The Muslims, whom we haven't heard of for a long time, had tried to capture Constantinople in the seventh century but had been stopped, as I told you, by tar and pitch that the Christians poured down on them.

Now in 1453 the Muslims once again attacked Constantinople. This time, however, the Muslims were Turks, and they didn't try to batter down the walls of the city with arrows. They used gunpowder and cannon. Against the power of this new invention the walls of Constantinople could not stand, and finally the city fell. Constantinople became Turkish and the magnificent Church of Santa Sophia,[3] which Justinian had built a thousand years before, was turned into a mosque for Muslim worship. This was the end of all that was left of the old Roman Empire—the other half of which had fallen in 476.

Ever after the downfall of Constantinople in 1453, wars were fought with gunpowder. No longer were castles of any use. No longer were knights in armor of any use. No longer were bows and arrows of any use—against this new kind of fighting. There was a new sound in the world, the sound of cannon—firing: "Boom! boom! boom!" Before this, battles had not been very noisy except for shouts of the victors and the moans of the dying. So some people call 1453 the end of the Middle Ages and the beginning of Modern History.

Gunpowder had put an end to the Middle Ages. The invention of printing and that little magic needle, the compass, did a great deal to start what we call Modern History.

---

[3] Sophia [sō fī′ ə]

62

A Sailor Who Found a *New* World

WHAT book do you like best?

Alice in Wonderland?

Gulliver's Travels?

One of the first books to be printed and one that children at that time liked best was

The Travels of Marco Polo.

One of the boys who loved to read these stories of those far-away countries of Asia with their gold and precious jewels was an Italian named Christopher Columbus. Christopher Columbus was born in the city of Genoa, which is in the top of the *boot*. Like a great many other boys who were born in seaport towns, he had heard the sailors on the wharves tell yarns of their travels, and his greatest ambition in life was to go off to sea and visit all the wonderful lands of which he had read and been told. At last the chance came, and, though only fourteen years old, he made his first voyage. After that, Columbus made many other voyages and grew to be a middle-aged man, but he never got to the countries he had read about in *The Travels of Marco Polo.*

Many sea captains of that time were trying to find a shorter way to India than the long and tiresome one that Marco Polo had taken. They felt sure there was a shorter way by sea, and now that they had the compass to guide them, they dared to go far off searching for such a waterway.

By this time many books had already been printed. Some of these books on travel were written by the old Greeks and Romans. Some had been written by Arabs. The navigators knew that the world was round, even though some uneducated medieval folk believed it to be flat. Columbus had read these books and he said to himself that if the world is really round, one should be able to reach India by sailing toward the west. It should be much easier and shorter that way than if one took a boat to the end of the Mediterranean Sea and then went over land for thousands of miles the way Marco Polo had gone.

The more Columbus thought of the idea, the surer he was that this could be done and the more eager he was to get a ship to try out his idea. Of course, being only a sailor, he had no money to buy or hire a ship in which to make the trials and he could find no one to help him.

First Columbus went to the little country called Portugal. Portugal was right on the ocean's edge. It was to be expected then that the people of Portugal would be famous sailors, and they *were*—as famous as the Phoenicians had been of old. Columbus thought they might be interested and help. Besides, the king of Portugal was extremely interested in discovering new lands.

But the king of Portugal thought, as the others did, that Columbus was foolish and would have nothing to do with him. The king wanted to make quite sure, however, that there was nothing in Columbus's idea. Furthermore, if there were any new land, he wanted to be the first to discover it himself. So he secretly sent some of his sea captains off to explore. After a while they one and all returned and stated that they had been as far as it was safe to go, and that positively there was nothing at all to the west but water, water, water.

Columbus in disgust then went to the next country—Spain—which at that time was ruled by King Ferdinand and his Queen Isabella. King Ferdinand and Queen Isabella were just then too busy to listen to Columbus. They were fighting with the Muslims, who had been in Spain ever since 732, when, you remember, they got as far north as France. At last Ferdinand and Isabella succeeded in driving the Muslims out of their country, and then Queen Isabella became very much interested in Columbus's ideas and plans and finally promised to help him. She even said she would sell her jewels, if necessary, to give him the money to buy ships. So Columbus, with her help, was able to buy three little ships named the *Niña*,[1] *Pinta*, and *Santa Maria*. So small were these three boats that nowadays we would be afraid to go even out of sight of shore in them.

At last everything was ready, and Columbus set sail from the Spanish seaport of Palos[2] with about a hundred sailors. Directly toward the setting sun into the broad Atlantic, Columbus steered. Past the Canary Islands he sailed, on and on, day and night, always in the same direction.

See if you can get this idea—the idea that almost everyone had at that time except a few Scandinavians—that all there was of the world was what we have so far been studying about. Try to forget that you ever heard of North and South America. They, of course, knew of no such lands. Try to think of Columbus on deck scanning the waves in the daytime or peering off in the darkness at night, hoping sooner or later to sight, not a new land—he wasn't looking for a new land—but for China or India.

Columbus had been out for over a month, and his sailors began to get worried. It seemed impossible that any sea could be so vast, so endless,

---

[1] Niña [nēn′ yə]　　　　　　[2] Palos [pä′ lōs]

with nothing in sight before, behind, or on either side. They began to think about returning. They began to be afraid they would never reach home. They begged Columbus to turn back. They said it was crazy to go any farther; there was nothing but water ahead of them, and they could go on forever and ever, and there would never be anything else.

Columbus argued with them, but it was no use. Finally he promised to turn back if they did not reach something very soon. As the days went on still with nothing new,

Columbus arguing with his crew

the sailors plotted to throw Columbus overboard at night and so get rid of him. They would then sail home and tell those back in Spain that Columbus had fallen overboard by accident.

At last, when all had given up hope except Columbus, a sailor saw a branch with berries on it floating in the water. Where could it have come from? Then birds were seen flying—birds that never get very far away from shore. Then one dark night, more than two months after they had set sail, they saw far off ahead a twinkling light. Probably no little light ever gave so much joy in the world. A light meant only one thing— human beings—and land, land—land at last! On the morning of October 12, 1492, the three boats ran ashore. Columbus leaped out, and falling on his knees, offered up a prayer of thanks to God. He then raised the Spanish flag, took possession of the land in the name of Spain, and called it *San Salvador*,[3] which means in Spanish, *Holy Saviour*.

Now, Columbus thought this land was India or nearby islands called the Indies that he had at last reached, though of course we know now that two great continents, North and South America, blocked his way to India. In fact, he had only landed on a little island in the Bahamas off the coast of America.

Columbus and his sailors soon saw that people lived on this island. Columbus claimed the land for Spain. You may wonder how he thought he could do this when the land obviously already belonged to the people living there. One reason was that in those days, Europeans thought that if people were not Christians, then they had no rights. And so Columbus believed that he could simply take over their country and call it his own. Besides that, he hoped that someday the new land might make him rich.

Since Columbus thought that he had reached India, he called the people he found on the island Indians. *We*, of course, know that they were really Native Americans and not Indians. And *we* know that Native Americans had been living there for many centuries before Columbus even thought of sailing out into the Atlantic.

---

[3] San Salvador [san sal′ və dôr]

Columbus went on to other islands nearby; but he found very little gold and few precious stones such as he had expected, or the wonders that Marco Polo had described; and as he had been away so long, he started back again to Spain the way he had come. With him he took several Native Americans to show the people at home, and also some tobacco, which he found them smoking and which no one in Europe had even seen or heard of before.

When he at last reached home safely again, people were overjoyed at seeing him and hearing of his discoveries. Everyone was wildly excited—but only for a while. People soon began to say it was nothing for Columbus to have sailed westward until land was found, that anyone could do that.

One day when Columbus was dining with the king's nobles, who were trying to belittle what he had done, he took an egg and, passing it around the table, asked each one if he could stand it on end. No one could. When it came back to Columbus, he set it down just hard enough to crack the end slightly and flatten it. Of course, *then* it stood up. "You see," said Columbus, "it's very easy if you only know how. So it's easy enough to sail west until you find land after I have done it once and shown you how."

Columbus made three other voyages to America, four in all, but he never knew he had reached the Americas. Once he landed in South America, but he never reached the mainland of North America.

As Columbus did not bring back any of the precious jewels or wonderful things that those in Spain expected him to, people lost interest in him. Some were so spiteful and jealous of his success that they even charged him with wrongdoing, and King Ferdinand sent out a man to take his place. Columbus was put in chains and shipped home. Although he was promptly set free, Columbus kept the chains as a reminder of men's ingratitude and asked to have them buried with him. After this,

Columbus made one other voyage, but when at last he died in Spain, he was alone and almost forgotten even by his friends. What an end for the man who had once been such a hero!

Of all the people of whom we have heard, whether kings or queens, princes or emperors, none can compare with Columbus. Alexander the Great, Julius Caesar, Charlemagne, were all killers. They took away. But Columbus *gave*. He gave us a new world. Without money or friends or luck, he stuck to his ideas through long years of discouragement. Although made fun of and called a crank and even treated as a criminal he never

> gave up,
>
> > gave out, nor
> >
> > > gave in!

63

Fortune Hunters

THE New World had no name. It was simply called *the New World*, as one might speak of *the new baby*.

It had to have a name, but what should it be? Of course if we could have chosen the name, we should have called it *Columbia* after Columbus. But another name was selected, and this is how it happened.

An Italian named Americus Vespucci[1] made a voyage to the southern part of the New World. Then he wrote a book about his travels. People read his book and began to speak of the new land that Americus described as Americus's country. The New World came to be called America after Americus, although in all fairness it should have been named after Columbus; don't you think so? Children sometimes have names given them which they would like to change when they grow up. But then it is too late. We sometimes speak and sing of our country as Columbia, although that is not the name on the map. We call a great many cities and towns and districts and streets Columbus or Columbia in memory of Christopher Columbus.

After Columbus had shown that there was no danger of falling off the world and that there really was land off to the west, almost everyone who had been hunting for India now rushed off in the direction Columbus had taken. "Copy cats!" A genius starts something; then thousands follow—

---

[1] Vespucci [ve spo͞o′ chē]

Map shows limited European knowledge of the continent. Compare with map in story 65.

imitate. Every sea captain who could do so now hurried off to the west to look for new countries, and so many discoveries were made that this time is known as the Age of Discovery. Most of these men were trying to get to India. They were after gold and jewels and spices, which they thought they would find in India in great quantities.

Now we can understand why people might go long distances in search of gold and precious stones, but they also went after spices—such as cloves and pepper—and you may wonder why they were so eager to get spices. You yourself may not like pepper very much, and you may dislike cloves. But in those days they didn't have refrigerators, and meats and other foods were often spoiled. We would have thought such food unfit to eat. However, they covered it with spices to kill the bad flavor, and then food could be eaten that otherwise one could not have swallowed. Spices didn't grow in Europe—only in warmer countries. People paid big prices to get them, and that is why men made long journeys after them.

A Portuguese sailor named Vasco da Gama[2] was one of those who were trying to get to India all the way by water. He did not, however sail *west* as Columbus had done, but *south* down around Africa. Others had tried before to get to India by going south and around Africa but none had gone more than part way. Many frightful stories were told by those who had tried but had at last turned back. These stories were like the tales of Sinbad the Sailor. They said that the sea became boiling hot; they said that there was a magnetic mountain which would pull out the iron bolts in the ship, and the ship would then fall to pieces; they said there was a whirlpool into which a ship would be irresistibly drawn—down, down, down to the bottom; they said there were sea serpents, monsters so large that they could swallow a ship at one gulp. The southern point of Africa was called the Cape of Storms, and the very name seemed to be bad luck, so that it was changed to the Cape of Good Hope.

In spite of all such scary stories, Vasco da Gama kept on his way south. Finally, after many hardships and many adventures, he passed around the Cape of Good Hope. He sailed on to India, got the spices that were so highly prized, and returned safely home. This was in 1497, five years after Columbus's first voyage, and Vasco da Gama was the first modern European to go to India by water.

There's one thing you always have to remember about these *discoveries*. That is this—that there were *some* people who did know about these places all along! The Native Americans knew about America. The Scandinavians or Vikings did, too. The Indians knew about India and so, you will soon see, did a lot of other people.

---

[2] da Gama [də ga′ mə]

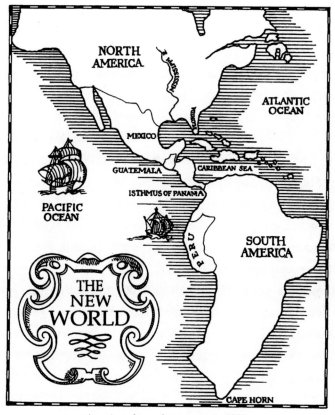

Americas drawn from a map in 1570.

Compare with two maps in story 78.

England did not want to be left out of the search for new wealth across the ocean. In the same year that Vasco da Gama reached India, a man named John Cabot set sail from England on a voyage of discovery. His first trip was a failure, but he tried again and finally came to Canada and sailed along the coast of what is now the United States. These countries he claimed for England, but he returned home, and England did nothing more about his discoveries until about a hundred years later.

Another Spaniard, named Balboa,[3] explored the central part of America. He was on the little strip of land that joined Central and South America which we now call the Isthmus[4] of Panama. Suddenly he came to another great ocean. This strange new ocean he named the South Sea, for although the Isthmus of Panama connects Central and South America, it bends so that one looks *south* over the ocean.

Then came the longest trip of all. A Portuguese named Magellan wanted to find a way to India *through* the New World, for he thought there must be some opening through which he might pass this new land that blocked the way. He tried to get his own country to help him. Again Portugal made the same mistake it had made in the case of Columbus. The Portuguese government would not listen to Magellan. So Magellan went to Spain, and Spain gave him five ships.

With these five ships, Magellan sailed off across the sea. When he reached South America, he sailed south along the shore, trying to find a passage through the land. One place after another seemed to be the passage for which he was looking, but each one turned out to be nothing but a river's mouth. Then one of his ships was wrecked, and only four were left.

With these four ships, he still kept on down the coast until he finally reached what is now Cape Horn. Through the dangerous opening there, since called after him the Straits of Magellan, he worked his way. One ship deserted and went back home the way it had come. Only three were then left.

With these three ships, he at last came into the great ocean on the other side, the same ocean that Balboa had called the South Sea. This Magellan named the *Pacific*, which means *calm*, because after all the storms they had had, it seemed so calm and quiet. However, food and water became scarce and finally gave out. Magellan's men suffered terribly from thirst and hunger and even ate the rats that are always to be found on shipboard. Many of his men were taken sick and died. Still he

---

[3] Balboa [bal bō′ ə]   [4] Isthmus [is′ məs]

kept on, though he had lost most of the crew with whom he had set out. At last he reached what are now the Philippine[5] Islands. Here he and his men got into a battle with the local people, and Magellan was killed. There were now not enough men left to sail three ships, and so one of these was burned, and only two were then left.

Two of the ships, however, of the five with which Magellan had started, still kept on. Then one of these was lost, disappeared and was never heard of again, and only a single ship, named the *Victoria*, remained. It seemed as if not one ship, not one man, would be left to tell the tale.

From an old print of Magellan's Victoria

Around Africa the *Victoria* struggled. Magellan's men, worn out with hunger and cold and hardships, still battled against wind and storm. At last a leaky and broken ship with only eighteen men sailed into the harbor from which it had set out more than three years before. Thus the *Victoria—Victory!*—Magellan's ship, but without Magellan—was the first ship to sail completely around the world. This voyage settled forever the argument that had been going on for ages, whether the earth was round or flat for a ship had actually sailed around the world! In spite of this proof, for many more years thereafter, there were people who still would not believe the world was round.

---

[5] Philippine [fil′ ə pēn]

64

The Land of Enchantment

or the Search for Gold and Adventure

ALL sorts of marvelous tales were told about the wealth and wonders of the New World.

It was said that somewhere in the New World there was a *Fountain of Youth*, and that if you bathed in it or drank of its water, you would become young again.

It was said that somewhere in the New World there was a city called El Dorado[1] built of solid gold.

So everyone who liked adventure and could get enough money together went off in search of these things that might make him famous or healthy, wealthy or wise, or forever young.

One of these men was Ponce de León,[2] a Spaniard. Ponce de Leon was looking for the *Fountain of Youth*. While searching for this lifegiving water, he found Florida. But instead of finding the Fountain of Youth, he lost his life in fighting with the people who already lived in Florida.

Another one of these men was Hernando de Soto. He was searching for El Dorado, the city of gold. While doing so, he discovered the longest river in the New World—the Mississippi. Instead of finding El Dorado, de Soto was taken sick with fever and died. Now, the Spaniards, to make

---

[1] Dorado [də rä′ dō]   [2] Ponce de León [pons də lē ən′]

the Native Americans fear them, had said that de Soto was a god and could not die. In order to cover up the fact that de Soto had actually died, his men buried him at night in the river he had discovered. They then said that he had gone on a trip to heaven and would presently return.

The first country you come to south of the United States is called Mexico. Here lived at that time a nation of Indians known as Aztecs.[3] These Aztecs had a very advanced civilization. They did not live in tents but in houses. They built fine temples and palaces. They made roads and aqueducts, something like those of the Romans. They had enormous treasures of silver and gold. Yet the Aztecs worshiped idols and sacrificed human beings to them. Their king was a famous chief named Montezuma.[4]

A Spaniard named Cortés[5] was sent to conquer these Aztecs. He landed on the shore of Mexico and burned his ships so that his sailors and soldiers could not turn back. The Aztecs had never seen horses, some of which the Spaniards had brought over across the water, and they were astonished at what seemed to them terrible beasts that the Spaniards rode. When the Spaniards fired their cannon, the Aztecs were terrified. They thought it was thunder and lightning that the Spaniards had let loose.

Cortés moved on toward the Aztec capital, the city of Mexico, which was built on an island in the middle of a lake. The people he met on the way fought desperately, but as they had only such weapons as men used in the Stone and Bronze Ages, they were no match against the guns and cannon of the Spaniards.

Montezuma, their chief, wishing to make friends, sent Cortés rich gifts, cartloads of gold, and when Cortés reached the capital city Montezuma treated him as a guest instead of an enemy and entertained him and could not do enough for him. Cortés told Montezuma all about the Christian religion and tried to make him a Christian also, but Montezuma thought his own gods just as good as the Christian God, and he would not

---

[3] Aztecs [az´ teks]
[4] Montezuma [mon tə zōō´ mə]

[5] Hernando Cortés [er nän´ dō kôr tez´]

change. Then suddenly Cortés took Montezuma prisoner, and terrible fighting began. At last Montezuma was killed, and Cortés succeeded in conquering Mexico, for though the Aztecs fought desperately and bravely, shot and shell were too much for them.

In Peru in South America was still another nation of civilized Indians even more wealthy than the Aztecs. They were called Incas, and it was said that their cities were paved with gold.

A Spaniard named Pizarro[6] went to Peru to conquer it as Cortés had conquered Mexico. Pizarro told the ruler, who was called the Inca, that the pope had given the country to Spain. The Inca had never heard of the pope and must have wondered what the pope had to do with Peru and how he could give it away. Naturally the Inca would not give up his country to Spain. Then Pizarro *took* it away. He had but a few hundred men, but he had cannons, and of course the Incas could not stand up against cannon.

Another people found by the Spanish were the Mayas.[7] The Mayas lived on land that today is in Mexico and also Guatemala. The Mayas had a written language that we are only beginning to figure out how to read. They also invented a calendar and had built observatories from which to watch the stars. They built tall pyramids that remind us of the ancient Egyptian pyramids. Like the Incas, the Mayas were conquered by Spanish guns.

The Aztecs, the Incas, and the Mayas—these are only three of many native peoples that were living in America when the Spanish came. And do you know—Incas, Aztecs, and Mayas are still alive today, and you can visit Central and South America and see some of the wonderful things they built.

France and other countries of Europe also sent out explorers to conquer parts of America, and then missionaries to teach Native Americans the

---

[6] Pizarro [pi zär′ ō]   [7] Mayas [mä′ yəz]

Christian religion, but these you will hear more about when you study American history.

Many of the explorers were really pirates, even worse pirates than the Norsemen who raided England and France, because they murdered people who were without equal weapons to fight back. The excuse they often gave for doing so was that they wanted to make the natives Christians. No wonder that the natives did not think much of the Christian religion if it taught murder of people who could not defend themselves. The Muslims made converts with the sword, but the Christians made converts with shot and shell.

65

Along the Coast of East Africa

AMERICA was not the only place where adventurers sailed in search of excitement and wealth. While the Spanish were conquering the Aztecs, Incas, and Mayas in America, the Portuguese went to Africa. Just as Christopher Columbus was looking for a route to India by sailing west, the Portuguese were also looking for a way to sail to India and China. They decided to try sailing around Africa. They didn't know for sure that they could ever find an end to that continent—a way around—but they wanted to try.

Before Columbus got to America, several Portuguese explorers sailed south along the coast of West Africa. They passed the mouth of the Senegal River that had been in Mansa Musa's empire. Then they rounded the corner of the great continent and soon came to Benin,[1] an empire in a part of Africa that is now Nigeria.[2] Benin was ruled by a king called an *oba* and was known for its beautiful artwork. If you visit a large art museum, you can see carvings and statues and ceremonial masks made in Benin. Farther south still, the ships passed an empire called Kongo.[3] One explorer even got as far as the very southern tip of Africa, but then he turned around and headed for home.

---

[1] Benin [be nēn']
[2] Nigeria [nĭ jēr' ē ə]

[3] Kongo [kong' go]

City states of East Africa

Five years after Columbus left Spain, Vasco da Gama left Portugal. He finally succeeded in sailing around that southern tip of Africa and into the Indian Ocean. He sailed up the east side of Africa. Then he traveled on toward India. While he was still in East Africa, he found wonderful cities that he thought nobody knew about.

Way back, in fact, some Europeans *had* known that these cities were there. Greeks and Romans as well as Egyptians all knew their way to East Africa. Soon after the time of Christ, a Greek guidebook for sailors told how to get to the different ports and said that ivory, tortoise shell, and coconut oil were traded there. During these early years, the towns were small, with perhaps one thousand people living in them.

Around 900 A.D. or about one hundred years after Charlemagne, at a time when very few Europeans were doing much traveling and all had forgotten about East Africa, an Arab geographer visited there. He was on his way home from a trip to India and China. He wrote that in East Africa the climate was warm and the land fertile and that gold and many other wonderful things were found there. We know now that a lot of traders visited East Africa during those first thousand years after Christ. Archeologists have found large numbers of coins from Persia, Greece, Rome, Arabia, and even India and China there. They have found pieces of pottery and glassware from China, India, and Arabia too. The Arabs visited East Africa most. In fact, some of the Arabs who went there to trade settled down and made their homes there. Soon the language spoken by the Africans had some Arab words mixed into it. Then Arabs began writing that language in Arabic letters. That language is called Swahili.[4] Swahili is still spoken all through East Africa.

The most famous early traveler to visit East Africa was a Muslim from Tangier, a city in North Africa. His name was Ibn Battuta.[5] He was the Marco Polo of the Muslim world. In fact, he lived about the same time that Marco Polo did, in the 1300s. The stories of Ibn Battuta's travels were written in Arabic, so most Europeans never read them, but he was very famous where people knew how to read Arabic.

That Ibn Battuta really got around! He left home when he was twenty years old to go on the pilgrimage to the Muslim holy city of Mecca. After he got there, he was having such an interesting time traveling that he didn't go back home for twenty-five years. He visited southern Russia, Persia, India, and Indonesia. And just like Marco Polo, he got all

---

[4] Swahili [swä hē′ lē]　　　　　　[5] Ibn Battuta [ib′ ən ba tōō′ tə]

the way to China. His goal was to go everyplace in the world where there were Muslims, and he did.

One of the most interesting places he visited was East Africa. A lot of the people there were Muslims. As you know, some were Arabs. Most were Africans. Sometimes Africans had married Arabs, and their children were a mixture of the two.

By Ibn Battuta's time, the trading towns had grown into cities. They were city states, independent like the earlier Greek city states. Each city had its own ruler, and each was surrounded by countryside where men and women farmed. You can still visit many of these cities in East Africa. The cities had names like Mogadishu,[6] Malindi,[7] Mombasa,[8] and Kilwa.[9] Try saying those names. They may seem strange at first, but soon they will seem easy to you.

Ibn Battuta described Kilwa as the most beautiful town in the whole world. There were fountains and public squares, he said. The main palace was on a high cliff above the Indian Ocean, had one hundred rooms, and an eight-sided swimming pool. How would you like to have been a guest of the ruler in Kilwa?

The cities all had ports where large vessels tied up. Arab ships were sixty to seventy feet long. Even larger ships came from Persia and India. Occasionally Chinese fleets of hundreds of huge ships visited the East African ports. Africans sold gold, iron, and ivory in exchange for silks, glassware, and tools. Once, the city of Malindi sent a wonderful gift to the emperor of China. Can you imagine something—that was not gold—that the ruler of Malindi might think would be a good surprise for the wealthy and powerful Chinese emperor? Something that did not exist in China? It must have made a big impression on the Chinese, because they wrote all about it—and that's how we still know about this gift. Well, have you

---

[6] Mogadishu [mō gä dē′ shoo]
[7] Malindi [mə lin′ dē]

[8] Mombasa [mom bä′ sä]
[9] Kilwa [kil′ wä]

guessed? It was a

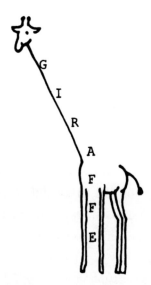

That's certainly something they didn't have in China!

The rulers of those city states must have been pretty smart because one thing that they *didn't* have much of was war. There were some minor squabbles, but most of the cities didn't even have large fortifications except around the ports. They didn't think they needed them because they weren't fighting each other all the time. This meant that they could spend all their energy on trade and farming. I'm sure it's one reason why these cities were so prosperous.

Eventually, though, they were attacked. Then they had a real problem. Can you guess what country decided to take over these cities? I'll give you a hint. There was a country that wanted to take control of the trade routes—that wanted to move in on the trade with India and China. Well, you may have guessed it by now. That country was Portugal. When the Portuguese discovered that not only was there gold in Africa, but that the East Africans already had the trade with the East that both Portugal and

Spain wanted, they were ready to move in.

The Portuguese came with big guns on their ships. When a city didn't just give in to them, they attacked. Mombasa was completely destroyed. All the people there were killed.

The East Africans knew they couldn't defeat the big ships and their cannon. So they used another strategy to get rid of the Portuguese. They stopped the gold trade. The miners stopped mining gold. The merchants stopped shipping gold. Gradually the ports closed down. The people from the cities moved into the countryside and became farmers. Now, the Portuguese weren't interested in farms so—except for keeping a few places where their ships could stop to get fuel and supplies on the long voyage to the Indies—they lost interest in East Africa. The people had lost their cities, but they had won their peace.

66

Rebirth

HERE is a long word for you; it is Renaissance.[1]

It means *rebirth*.

Of course, nothing can be born again. But people call this time we have now reached the Renaissance, the time of rebirth. Here is the reason why they call it that.

You remember the Age of Pericles, don't you, when such beautiful sculptures and buildings were made in Athens? Well, in the fifteen hundreds not everyone was rushing off to the New World in search of adventure. While the voyages that I have told you about were taking place, there were living and working in Italy some of the greatest artists the world has ever known.

Architects built beautiful buildings something like the old Greek and Roman temples. Sculptors made statues that were almost as beautiful as those of Phidias. People began to take an interest once more in the old Greek writers, whose books were now printed for everyone to read. It seemed almost as if Athens in the Age of Pericles had been born again. That is why people speak of this time as the Renaissance.

One of the greatest of these artists of the Renaissance was a man named Michelangelo.[2] But Michelangelo was not just a painter; he was

---

[1] Renaissance [ren′ ə säns]   [2] Michelangelo [mī kəl an′ jə lō]

a sculptor, an architect, and a poet as well. Michelangelo thought nothing of spending years working on any statue or painting that he was doing. When he had finished, he had done something that people even now go from all over the world to see.

Nowadays, sculptors first model a statue in clay and then copy it in stone or cast it in bronze, but Michelangelo did not do this. He cut his figures directly out of the stone, without making a model first. It was as if he saw the figure imprisoned in the stone and then cut away the part that closed the figure in.

A large block of marble had been spoiled by another sculptor. Michelangelo saw a figure of David *in* it, and, setting to work, he cut this young athlete *out*.

He made also a statue of Moses sitting down. It is now in a church in Rome, and when you walk up to it, it is so lifelike that it seems as if you were in the presence of the prophet Moses himself. The guide tells you that when Michelangelo had finished this statue of Moses he was so thrilled by the figure he had created that, feeling it must come to life, he struck it on the knee with his hammer and commanded as he did so, "Stand up!" And then the guide shows you a crack in the marble to prove that the story is true!

The pope wanted Michelangelo to paint the ceiling of the Sistine Chapel. This is the pope's private chapel in Rome. At first Michelangelo didn't want to do the painting. He told the pope he was a sculptor and not a painter. But the pope insisted, and Michelangelo at last gave in. Once having agreed to do the work, however, Michelangelo gave himself to it heart and soul.

For four years he lived in this room—the Sistine Chapel—and hardly ever left it day or night. Beneath the ceiling, he built himself a platform, and lying on this scaffold, he would read poetry and the Bible and work as the spirit moved him. Locking himself in, he would let no one enter, not even the pope himself. He wanted to be alone and to be left alone.

Michelangelo at work

One day the pope, finding a door left open went into the chapel to see how things were getting along. Michelangelo, thereupon, accidentally dropped some of his tools, and they just barely missed hitting the pope on the head. The pope was very angry, but he never returned uninvited again.

People now go from all over the world to see this ceiling, which only can be viewed comfortably by lying on the floor or by looking at it in a mirror.

Michelangelo lived to be nearly ninety years old, yet he had very little to do with people. He could not stand being bored by them. He lived apart, in the company of the gods and angels that he painted.

Raphael[3] was another famous Italian artist. He lived at the same time as Michelangelo. Raphael, however, was just the opposite of Michelangelo in most ways. Michelangelo liked to be by himself. Raphael loved company. He was very popular and constantly surrounded by his friends and admirers, for everybody loved him on account of his genius and kindly nature. Young men swarmed about him, drinking in his words and humbly copying everything he did. He had fifty or more pupils studying and painting under him, and they went along with him whenever he went out even for a walk. They almost worshiped the ground he walked on.

---

[3] Raphael [raf′ ē əl]

Raphael painted many beautiful pictures. One of the best known is *School of Athens*. He painted many pictures of the Virgin Mary with the infant Jesus. These are called *Madonnas*. One of the best known of these pictures of Mary and the Christ child is called *Sistine Madonna*. It was painted for a little church, but it is now in a great picture-gallery.

Raphael died when he was still a young man, but he worked so hard and so continuously that he has left a large number of pictures. He painted only the very important parts of his pictures himself—perhaps only the faces. The bodies and hands and clothing he usually left to be painted by his pupils. They were glad to be allowed to do even a finger of a painting on which their master had worked.

Leonardo da Vinci[4] is another great artist who lived at this time. He could do any number of things exceptionally well. He would be called a jack-of-all-trades, but unlike most jacks-of-all-trades, he was good at everything. He was an artist, an engineer, a poet, and a scientist. He made, however, very few paintings, because he did so many things besides, but these few pictures are beautiful and famous. One of these is *The Last Supper*. It is considered, as is the *Sistine Madonna*, one of the greatest paintings in the world. Unfortunately, it was painted directly on a plastered wall, and in the course of time much of the plaster with the paint has peeled off, so that there was little left of the original painting. Recently this painting was restored. The colors were brightened up so, once again, we can see its full beauty.

Leonardo usually painted his women smiling. One of his most famous paintings is the picture of a woman called *Mona Lisa*. She has a smile that is called *quizzical*. You can hardly tell whether she is smiling *at* you or *with* you.

---

[4] da Vinci [də vin ′ chē]

67

Christians Quarrel

SOME people say young boys and girls can't understand this chapter. They say it is too difficult. But I want to see if it is.

Up to this time, as I have told you before, in Western Europe had been one Christian religion—the Catholic. There was no Episcopalian, nor Methodist, nor Baptist, nor Presbyterian, nor any other denomination. All were just Christians.

In the sixteenth century, however, some people began to think that changes should be made in the Catholic religion.

Others thought changes should not be made.

Some said it was all right as it was.

Others said it wasn't all right as it was. So a quarrel started.

This is the way the trouble began. The pope was building a great church called St. Peter's in Rome. It took the place of the old church that Constantine had built on the spot where St. Peter was supposed to have been crucified head down. The pope wanted it to be the largest and finest church in the world, for Christ had said, "Thou art Peter, and upon this rock [Peter means rock in Latin] I will build my church . . . ." So the Church of St. Peter's was to be the Capitol of the Christian religion. Both Michelangelo and Raphael had worked on the plans for the new church.

In order to get marble and stone and other materials for this Church of St. Peter, the pope did as others before him had done; he tore down other buildings in Rome and used their stone for the new church.

Besides all this the pope needed an enormous amount of money to build such a magnificent church as he had planned. So he started to collect from the people. Now, there was a man in Germany named Martin Luther who was a monk and a teacher of religion in a college. Martin Luther thought that not only this but also other things in the Catholic Church were not right. He made a list of ninety-five things that he thought were not right and nailed them up on the church door in the town where he lived, and he preached against doing these things. The pope sent Luther an order to stop, but Luther made a bonfire and burned it publicly. Many took sides with Luther, and before long there was a great body of people who had left the Catholic Church and no longer obeyed the pope.

The pope called on the king of Spain to help in this quarrel with Luther. The reason he called on him was this: the king of Spain was Charles V, the grandson of the Ferdinand and Isabella who had helped Columbus. He was not only a good Catholic but the most powerful ruler in Europe. The Spanish explorers had claimed large parts of America and so Charles was owner of a large part of the New World. But he was emperor not only of these Spanish settlements in America but of Austria and of Germany as well. It was quite natural that the pope should go to Charles for help.

Charles commanded Luther to come to a city named Worms to be tried. He promised Luther that no harm would be done him, and so Luther went. When Luther arrived at Worms, Charles ordered him to take back all he had said. Luther refused to do so. Some of Charles's nobles said Luther should be burned at the stake. But Charles, as he had promised, let him go and did not punish him for his belief. Luther's friends were afraid, though, that other Catholics might do him harm. They knew Luther would take no care of himself, and so they themselves took him prisoner and kept him shut up for over a year, so that no one could harm him. While Luther was in prison, he translated the Bible into German; it was the first time that the Bible had been written in that language.

The people who protested against what the pope did were called Protestants, and the new churches that grew from this protest are still called Protestant today. The time when these changes were made in the Catholic form of worship was called Re-form-ation, as the old religion was *reformed.*

Now, you may be a Catholic and your best friend may not be a Catholic, but that makes no difference in your friendship. But at that time those who were Catholics were deadly enemies of those who were not, and vice versa. Each side was sure it alone was right and the other side was wrong. Each side fought for the things it thought were right, fought the other side as furiously and madly and bitterly as if the other side were scoundrels and devils. Friends and relatives murdered each other because they thought differently about religion, and yet all were supposed to be Christians.

Charles was greatly worried and troubled by the religious quarrels and other difficulties in his vast empire. He became sick and tired of being emperor and of having to settle all the many problems he had to solve. He wanted to be free to do other things that he was more interested in. Being king did not mean being able to do whatever you wanted, as some people think. Charles then did what few rulers have ever done voluntarily: He resigned—*abdicated,* as it is called—and gave up his throne to his son, who was named Philip II.

Charles, glad to be rid of all the cares of state, went to live in a monastery. There he spent his time doing what he liked—what do you suppose?—making mechanical toys and watches—until he died!

Now, the king of England at this time, when Charles was king of Spain, was Henry VIII. His last name was Tudor. So many kings had first names which were alike that such names were numbered to tell which Charles or Henry was meant and how many of the same name there had

Henry VIII and his second wife Anne Boleyn

been before. Henry VIII was, at first, also a strong Catholic, and the pope had called him Defender of the Faith. But Henry had a wife whom he wanted to divorce because she had no son. Henry wanted a son to succeed him as king and keep England united. In order to divorce her so that he might marry again, he had to have the agreement of the pope because the pope was the only one who could give Henry a divorce. Now, the pope at Rome was head of the Christian Church in all of Europe and the Americas and said what Christians could do or could not do, no matter whether they were in Italy or Spain or England. Henry asked the pope to grant him this divorce. The pope, however, told him he would not give him a divorce.

Now, Henry thought it was neither right nor proper that a man in another country—even if he *were* pope—should say what could be done in England. He himself was ruler, and he didn't intend to let any foreigner meddle in his affairs or give him orders.

Then Henry said that he himself would be head of all the Christians in England; then he could do as he wished without the pope's permission. So he made himself head, and then he divorced his wife. All the churches in England were now told by the king what they should do; the pope no longer had anything to say in the matter; the English churches obeyed the king, not the pope. This made the second big break in the Catholic Church.

After this, Henry VIII had five other wives, six in all; not of course all at one time, for Christians could only have one wife at a time. His first wife he divorced, the second he beheaded, the third died. The same thing happened to his last three wives: the first he divorced, the second he beheaded, and the third survived. Henry died before she did.

Is this too difficult for you to understand?

68

Queen Elizabeth

KING Henry VIII had two daughters.

One was named Mary, and one was named Elizabeth.

Their last name was of course Tudor, the same as their father's although we do not usually think of kings and queens as having last names.

King Henry had a son, also, and he was first to become king after his father died, for though he was younger than his sisters, a boy was supposed to be more fit to rule than a girl. But he didn't live long, and then Mary was the first of the two sisters to become queen.

Mary did not approve what her father had done when he turned against the pope and the Catholic Church. Mary herself was a strong Catholic and ready to fight for the pope and the Catholic Church. She thought that all those who did not believe as she did should be persecuted for heresy, or expressing beliefs opposed to the traditional Catholic Church. Like the queen in *Alice in Wonderland*, she was always saying, "Off with his head!" This seems to us very unchristian, but in those days their ideas about such things were different. Mary had so many people killed that she was called Bloody Mary.

Mary married a man who was just as strong a Catholic as she and even bloodier. He was not an Englishman, but a Spaniard, Philip II of Spain, son of Charles V, who had abdicated.

Philip II was much sterner than his father had been. Philip tried to make those who were Protestants, or who were supposed to be Protestants, confess and give up Protestantism. If they did not do so, they were tortured as the old Christian martyrs had been tortured. This was called the Inquisition.[1] Those suspected of being Protestants were tormented in all sorts of horrible ways. Some were tied up in the air by their hands, like a picture hung on a wall, until they fainted from the pain or else confessed what they were told to confess. Some were stretched on a rack, their heads pulled one way and their legs the opposite way, until their bodies were nearly torn apart. Those who were found guilty of being Protestants were killed outright, burned to death, or put slowly to death, so that they would suffer longer. You should know that Protestants were not the only people who suffered under the Spanish Inquisition. A century earlier, Jews were tortured in the same way. Most left Spain to find new homes in North Africa or Europe.

The people whom Philip chiefly persecuted were the Dutch people in Holland. Holland then belonged to his empire, and a great many of the Dutch people had become Protestants.

Now, there was a Dutchman called William the Silent because he talked little but did a great deal. William was furious at the way his people were treated. He fought against Philip and at last succeeded in making his country free and setting up the Dutch Republic. But William the Silent was murdered by order of Philip.

And that's the kind of man Bloody Mary had for a husband.

After Mary Tudor died, her sister, Elizabeth Tudor, became queen. Elizabeth was the strongest of Henry's three children. Elizabeth had red

---

[1] Inquisition [in kwə zish· ən]

hair and was very vain and loved to be flattered. Many men loved her but she never married, and, as a woman who never marries was called a virgin, she was known as the Virgin Queen.

Elizabeth was a Protestant and was just as bitter against the Catholics as her sister and sister's husband had been against the Protestants.

A relative of Elizabeth was queen of Scotland. Scotland is a country north of England, but at that time it did not have the same ruler as England, and its queen was named Mary Stuart. Mary Stuart, Queen of Scots, was young, beautiful, and fascinating; but she was a Catholic, and so Elizabeth and she were enemies.

Elizabeth heard that Mary Stuart was trying to become queen of England as well as Scotland, so she had her, although a relative, put in prison. In prison Mary Stuart stayed for nearly twenty years and was then at last put to death by Elizabeth's orders. It is hard for us to understand how anyone could have her own relative killed in this cold-blooded way, especially anyone who pretended to be a Christian, but in those times it was a very common custom, as we see when we hear of so many murders committed by the rulers of the people.

Philip II the great champion of the Catholics, made up his mind to punish Elizabeth, his sister-in-law, for killing such a good Catholic as Mary Stuart. So he got together a large navy of very fine ships called the Spanish Armada.[2] All Spain was very proud of this fleet. It was boastfully called the Invincible Armada; *invincible* means *unconquerable*.

The Invincible Armada set forth in 1588 to conquer the English navy. Lined up in the shape of a half-moon, the ships sailed grandly toward England.

The English fleet was composed only of little boats. Instead of going out to meet the Armada in regular sea battle as the Spaniards expected, the English

---

[2] Armada [är mä´ də]

ships sailed out and attacked the Spanish ships from behind and fought one ship at a time. The English were better fighters, and their small boats were quicker and more easily managed. They could strike a blow and get away before a Spanish ship could turn around into position to fire. Gradually the English fleet sank or destroyed the big Spanish boats one by one.

Then the English set some old boats afire and started them drifting toward the Spanish fleet. As all boats at that time were of course made of wood, the Spaniards became frightened at these burning piles drifting down upon them, and part of the fleet sailed away. The rest tried to get back to Spain by sailing the long way round, north of Scotland. However, a terrible storm struck them, and almost all the boats were shipwrecked, and thousands of dead bodies were washed up on shore. The great Spanish Armada was destroyed, and with it ended the power of Spain at sea. Spain was no longer the great nation it had been.

At the beginning of Elizabeth's reign, the largest and most powerful country in the world was Spain; at the end of her reign it was England that was the most powerful. Her fleet, which King Alfred had started far back, became one of the largest.

People at that time thought it impossible for a woman to rule as well as a man, but under Elizabeth's rule England in turn became the leading country of Europe. Elizabeth proved that a woman could rule England better than most kings had.

69

The Age of Elizabeth

THIS story is about the Age of Elizabeth. I'm not going to tell you how old Elizabeth was, though she did live and reign a great many years.

I'm going to tell you some of the things that happened during her long life, for the time when she lived is called the Age of Elizabeth.

There was a young man named Raleigh[1] living when Elizabeth became queen. One day when it was raining and the streets were muddy, Elizabeth was about to cross the street. Raleigh saw her and, to keep her from soiling her shoes, ran forward, took off his beautiful velvet cape, and threw it in the puddle where she was about to step, so that she might cross upon it as upon a carpet. The queen was greatly pleased with this thoughtful and gentlemanly act and she made him a knight, so that he was then called Sir Walter Raleigh, and ever after that he was one of her special friends.

Sir Walter Raleigh was much interested in America. Cabot had claimed a great part of it for England almost a hundred years before, but England had done nothing about it. Raleigh thought something should be done about it; he thought English people should settle there, so that other countries like Spain, which had made so many settlements in America, would not get ahead of England. Raleigh got together several companies

---

[1] Raleigh [rä′ lē]

of English people and sent them over to an island called Roanoke,[2] which was just off the coast of the present state of North Carolina. At that time, however, almost the whole coast of the United States as far north as Canada was called Virginia. It had been named Virginia in honor of the Virgin Queen Elizabeth.

Some of these Roanoke colonists became discouraged with the hardships they had to suffer and so gave up and sailed back home again. Those who remained all disappeared. Where? No one knows. We think they must either have been killed or have died of starvation. At any rate, not one was left to tell the tale. Among these Roanoke colonists was the first English child born in America—a girl, who had been named Virginia Dare, for the queen was very popular and a great many girls were named Virginia after her.

Some tobacco was brought back from Virginia, and Sir Walter Raleigh learned to smoke. This was such a strange and unknown thing at that time that one day while he was smoking a pipe, a servant who saw smoke coming out of his mouth thought he was on fire and, running for a bucket of water, emptied it over his head.

Virginia is still famous for its tobacco. At first tobacco was supposed to be very healthful, for the Native Americans seemed to have very good health, and they smoked a great deal. Afterward, however, in the next reign, King James so hated tobacco that he wrote a book against it and forbade its use. Now we know that James was right and that tobacco can make people sick with deadly diseases.

After Queen Elizabeth died, Raleigh was put in prison, for it was said he was plotting against the new king, James, who came after Elizabeth. The prison where he was placed was the Tower of London, the old castle that William the Conqueror had built. Here Raleigh was kept for thirteen long years, and to pass the time away he wrote a *History of the World*.

---

[2] Roanoke [rō′ ə nōk]

But at last he was put to death as many other great men were also.

During the reign of Queen Elizabeth, there lived the great writer of plays, the greatest writer the world has ever known. This man was William Shakespeare.

Shakespeare's father could not write his name. Shakespeare himself spent only six years at school. As a boy he was rather wild, and he was arrested for hunting deer in the forest of Sir Thomas Lucy at Stratford.

When still a boy, Shakespeare married a girl older than himself named Anne Hathaway. After he had been married a few years he left her and their three children, left the little town of Stratford, and went up to the great city of London to seek his fortune. There, Shakespeare got a job working around a theater, holding the horses of those who came to see the plays. Then he got a chance to act in the theater, and he became an actor, but he did not become a very good one.

In those days the theaters had no scenery. A sign was put up to tell what the scene was supposed to be. For instance, instead of forest scenery, they would put up a sign saying, "This is a forest," or instead of a room scene a sign saying "This is a room in an inn." There were no

Shakespeare reading to Elizabeth

actresses. Men and boys took the parts of both men and women.

Shakespeare was asked to change some of the plays that had already been written, so that they could be better acted. He did this very well; then he started in to write plays himself. Usually he took old stories and made them into plays, but he did it so wonderfully well that they are better than any plays that have ever been written before or since.

Though Shakespeare left school when only thirteen years old, he seems to have had a remarkable knowledge of almost everything under the sun. He shows in his plays that he knew about history and law and medicine. Some of the best known of Shakespeare's plays are *Hamlet*, *The Merchant of Venice*, *Romeo and Juliet*, and *Julius Caesar*.

Shakespeare made a good deal of money for those times—almost a fortune. Then he left London and went back to live in the little town of Stratford where he was born. Here at last he died and was buried in the village church. People wanted to move his body to a greater and handsomer place, to a famous church in London. But someone, perhaps Shakespeare himself, had written a verse which was carved on his tombstone. The last line of this verse said, "And curst be he who moves my bones"; so they never were moved, for no one dared to move them.

70

James the Servant

or

What's in a Name?

WHAT does your name mean? If it is
>Baker or
>>Miller or
>>>Taylor or
>>>>Carpenter or
>>>>>Fisher or
>>>>>>Cook,

it probably means that at some time one of your ancestors was a

>baker, or
>>miller, or
>>>tailor, or
>>>>carpenter, or
>>>>>fisher, or
>>>>>>cook.

If your name is Stuart or Steuart or Stewart or Steward, it may mean that at some time one of your ancestors was a steward, for in olden days people knew very little about spelling, and they spelled the same name in different ways. A steward was a chief servant.

There was a family named Stuart in Scotland, and from chief servants or stewards they had become rulers of the Scots. Mary Stuart, whom Elizabeth had beheaded, was one of them.

As Queen Elizabeth never married, she had no children to rule after her. She was the last of the Tudor family. The English had to look around for a new king, and they looked to Scotland.

Now, Scotland, as I have told you, was then a separate country and not a part of Britain as now. The son of Mary Stuart was then king of Scotland. His name was James Stuart. As he was related to the Tudors, the English invited him to come and rule over them. He accepted the invitation and was called James I. So we speak of his reign and that of his children as the reign of the Stuarts.

The Stuart family reigned for about a hundred years, that is, from 1600 to 1700, all except about eleven years when England had no king at all.

Many times the English must have been very sorry that they had ever invited James to be their king, for he and the whole Stuart family lorded it over the English people. They acted as if they were lords of creation, and the English people had to fight for their rights.

A body of men called Parliament[1] was supposed to make the laws for the English people. But James said that Parliament could do nothing that he didn't like, and if they weren't very careful, he wouldn't let them do any governing at all. James said that whatever the king did was right, that the king could do no wrong, that God gave kings the right to do as they pleased with their subjects. This was called the Divine Right of Kings. Naturally the English people would not put up with this sort of thing. Ever since the time of King John, they had insisted on their own rights. The Tudors had often done things that the people didn't like, but the Tudors were English. The Stuarts, however, were Scottish, and the

---

[1] Parliament [pär′ lə mənt]

people looked on them as foreigners; what they permitted in one of their own family they wouldn't stand in these strangers whom they had invited into their family. So, of course, a quarrel was bound to start. But the real fight came with the next king and not with James.

During King James's reign, the Bible was translated into English. This is the Bible that is called the *King James Bible*.

Nothing much happened in England during James's reign, but in some other countries a great deal did happen although the king had little to do with it. English people made settlements in India, that far-away country that Columbus had tried to reach by going west; and these settlements there grew until India at last belonged to England. England had conquered a large empire and become a wealthy and powerful nation.

Settlements also were made in America; one was made in the South and one, in the North. Raleigh's settlement at Roanoke had disappeared, as I told you; but in 1607 a boatload of English men sailed over to America looking for adventure and hoping to make their fortunes by finding gold. They landed in Virginia and named the place where they settled Jamestown after their king, James. But they found no gold, and as they were not used to work, they didn't want to do any. Their leader, Captain John Smith, took matters in hand and said that those that didn't work shouldn't eat. So then the colonists had to go to work.

Back in England people had learned to smoke, and so the colonists began to raise tobacco for the English people. The tobacco brought the colonists so much money that it proved to be a gold mine—of a different kind—after all. But the colonial gentlemen wanted someone to do the rough work for them. A few years later black people were brought over from Africa and sold to the colonists to do the rough work. This was the beginning of slavery in America, which grew and grew until, on big plantations in the South, almost all the work was done by slaves.

This system of slavery was of course very wrong and cruel, but it lasted for several hundred years. Greed lay at the root of this as well as many other evils.

A little later another company of people left England for America. These people were not looking for fortunes, however, as the Jamestown settlers had been. They were looking for a place where they might worship God as they pleased, for in England they were interfered with, and they wanted to find a place where no one would interfere with them. So this company of people left Plymouth, England in 1620 in a ship called the *Mayflower*, sailed across the ocean, and landed in a place they named Plymouth, in Massachusetts, and there they settled. More than half of them died the first winter from hardship and exposure in the bitter weather that they have in the North; nevertheless, none of those who were left would go back to England. This settlement was the beginning of that part of the United States called New England. You will hear more about both settlements later when you study American history. At present we must see what was going on in England, for there were great goings on following the reign of James Stuart.

71

A King Who Lost His Head

THE next king was King Charles I. He was the son of King James, whom you have just read about, and he was "a chip off the old block." Like his father he believed in the Divine Right of Kings, that he alone had the right to say what should be done or what should not be done, and he treated the English people as King John had; that is, as if they were made simply to serve his pleasure and to do as he said.

But this time the people didn't carry him off, as they had King John, to agree to a paper. They started to fight. The king made ready to fight for what he thought his rights. He got together an army of lords and nobles and those who agreed with him. Those who took his side even dressed differently from those who were against him. They grew their hair in long curls and wore a broad-brimmed hat with a large feather and lace collars and cuffs of lace even on their breeches.

Parliament also got together an army of the people who wanted their rights. They had their hair cut short and wore a hat with a tall crown and very simple clothes. A country gentleman named Oliver Cromwell trained a regiment of soldiers to be such good fighters that they were called Ironsides.

The king's army was made up of men who prepared for battle by drinking and feasting. The parliamentary army prayed before going into battle and sang hymns and psalms as they marched.

At last after many battles the king's army was beaten and King Charles was taken prisoner. A small part of Parliament then took things into their own hands, and though they had no right to do so, they tried King Charles

King Charles I and Oliver Cromwell

and condemned him to death. They found him guilty of being a traitor and a murderer and other terrible things. He was taken out in front of his palace in London in the year 1649, and his head was cut off. People now feel that this was a shameful thing for the parliamentary army to do to the king, and even at that time only a part of the English people were in favor of it. He might have been sent away instead of being killed, or he might have had his office of king taken away from him.

Oliver Cromwell, the commander of the parliamentary army, then ruled over England for a few years. He was a coarse-looking person with very rough manners, but honest and religious, and he ruled England as a stern and strict father might rule his family. He would stand no nonsense. Once when he was having his picture painted—for there were no photographs then—the artist left out a big wart he had on his face. Cromwell angrily told him, "Paint me as I am, wart and all." Cromwell was really a king although he called himself Protector.

When Cromwell died, his son became ruler after him, just as if he were the son of a king, but the son was unable to fill his father's shoes. He meant well, but he hadn't the brains or the ability that his father had, and so in a few months he resigned. Oliver Cromwell had been so strict that the English people had forgotten about their troubles under the Stuarts. So in 1660 when the English found themselves without a ruler, they invited the son of the monarch they had beheaded, and once more a Stuart became king. This was Charles II.

Charles was called the Merry Monarch because all he seemed to think about was eating and drinking, amusing himself, and having a good time. He made fun of things that were holy and sacred. To revenge himself on those who had put his father to death he had those of them who were still living killed in the most horrible way one could think of. Those that were dead already, Oliver Cromwell among them, were taken from their tombs; then their dead bodies were hanged and afterward beheaded.

In his reign that old and terrible disease, the plague, broke loose again in London. Some people thought that God had caused it, that He was shocked by the behavior of the king and his people especially toward holy things, that He was punishing them. The next year, 1666, a great fire started and burned up thousands of houses and hundreds of churches. But the Great Fire, as it was called, cleaned up the disease and dirt and was therefore really a blessing. London had been a city of wooden houses. It was rebuilt of brick and stone.

Only one more Stuart ruler shall I tell you about—or rather a royal pair, William and Mary—because in their reign the fight between the people and their kings was once for all finally settled. In 1688 Parliament drew up an agreement called the Bill of Rights, which William and Mary signed. This agreement made Parliament ruler over the nation, and ever since, Parliament—not the king—has been the real ruler of England. This was called the *Glorious Revolution*.[1] It was glorious because there was no war. I think we have heard enough of the Stuarts for a while.

---

[1] Revolution [rev ə lo͞o′ shən]

72

Red Cap and Red Heels

THE last Louis I told you about was a saint—the Louis who went on the last Crusade.

I'm going to tell you now about two kings named Louis who were not saints—not by any means.

They were Louis XIII and Louis XIV and they ruled France while the Stuarts were reigning in the seventeenth century in England.

Louis XIII was king in name only. Another man told him what to do, and he did it. Strange to say, this other man was a great ruler of the church called a cardinal, who wore a red cap and a red gown. The cardinal's name was Richelieu.[1]

Now, you are probably sick and tired of hearing about wars, but during the reign of Louis XIII, another long war started, and I must tell you something about it, for it lasted thirty years. It was therefore called the Thirty Years' War. It was different from most wars. It was not a war of one country against another. It was a war between the Protestants and Catholics.

Cardinal Richelieu was of course a Catholic and the real ruler of France, which was a Catholic country. Nevertheless, he took sides with the Protestants, for they were fighting a Catholic country called Austria,

---

[1] Richelieu [rish′ ə loo]

and he wanted to beat Austria. Most of the countries in Europe took part in this war, but Germany was the battleground where most of the fighting was done. Even Sweden, a northern country of Europe which we have not mentioned before, took part. The king of Sweden at this time was named Gustavus Adolphus,[2] and he was called the Snow King because he was king of such a cold country, and also the Lion of the North, for he was such a brave fighter. I am mentioning him particularly because of all kings and rulers in Europe at this time he was the finest character. Indeed, most of the other rulers thought only of themselves, and they would lie and cheat and steal and even murder to get what they wanted, but Gustavus Adolphus was fighting for what he thought was right. Gustavus Adolphus was a Protestant, and so he came down into Germany and fought on the side of the Protestants. He was a great general, and his army won. Unfortunately he himself was killed in battle. The Protestants came out ahead in the Thirty Years' War, and at last a famous treaty of peace was made called the Treaty of Westphalia. By this treaty it was agreed that each country should have whatever religion its ruler had; it could be Protestant or Catholic, as the ruler wished.

During the Thirty Years' War, the plague, that old deadly contagious disease we have heard of before, broke out in Germany. A little town named Oberammergau[3] prayed that it might be spared. The townspeople vowed that if they were spared they would give a play of Christ's life once every ten years. They were spared, and so every ten years, ever since then, with only a few exceptions, they have been giving what is called the Passion Play. Tens of thousands of tourists from all over the world travel to this little out-of-the-way town to see the townspeople act the story of Christ's life. The play is given on Sundays during the summer of the tenth year and lasts all day long. About seven hundred people take part. It is a great honor to be chosen to play the part of a

---

[2] Gustavus Adolphus [gus tä′ vōōs ə dol′ fəs]   [3] Oberammergau [ō bər ä′ mər gou]

saint, and it is the highest honor to be selected to play the part of Christ.

The next French king to rule after Louis XIII and Richelieu was Louis XIV.

The people in England had at last succeeded in getting the power to rule themselves through their Parliament. But in France, Louis would let no one rule but himself. He said, "I am the state," and he would let no one have a say in the government. This was the same as the Stuarts' Divine Right of Kings that the English people had put an end to. Louis ruled for more than seventy years. This is the longest time that anyone in history has ever ruled.

Louis XIV was called the Grand Monarch, and everything he did was to show off. He was always parading and strutting about as if he were the leading character in a play and not just an ordinary human being. He wore corsets and a huge powdered wig and shoes with very high red heels, to make himself appear taller. He carried a long cane, stuck out his elbows, turned out his toes, and strutted up and down, for he thought these things made him seem grand, important, imposing.

Louis XIV

All this may sound as if Louis were a strange person with no sense, but you must not get that idea. In spite of his absurd manners, he made France the chief power in Europe. He was almost constantly fighting other countries, trying to increase the size of France and to add to his kingdom, but I have already told you so much about so many fights, that I'm not going to tell you any more about his just now, for you would probably not read it if I did. So France had her turn as leader of all the other countries, as Spain and England had had theirs as well.

Louis built a magnificent palace at Versailles[4] in which were marble halls, beautiful paintings, and many huge mirrors in which he could see himself as he strutted along. The palace was surrounded by a park with wonderful fountains. The water for the fountains had to be brought a long distance, and it cost thousands of dollars to have the fountains play just for a few minutes. Even today sightseers visit Versailles to see the magnificent palace rooms and to watch the fountains play.

But Louis surrounded himself not only with beautiful things. He also surrounded himself with all the most interesting men and women of his time. All those who could do anything exceptionally well, all those who could paint well or write well or talk well or play well or look well, he brought together to live with him or near by him. This was called his *court*. They were the chosen few who looked down on all the others.

Louis XIV getting ready for bed

This was all very fine for the people who were lucky enough to be in Louis's court. But the poor people of France, ordinary farmers and the men and women who worked in the towns, were the ones who had to pay Louis's expenses and those of his court. They were the ones who had to pay for his parties and balls and feasts and for all sorts of presents that he gave his friends. We shall soon see what happened. The poor people would not stand that sort of thing forever. "The worm will turn," we say.

---

[4] Versailles [ver sī']

73

A Self-Made Man

WHO was the Father of his Country?

I know what you will say:

"George Washington."

But there was another man called *The Father of His Country* before Washington was born, and he was not an American.

In the northeast of Europe and in northern Asia, there is a great country twice as large as our own. Its name is Russia. Very little had been heard of Russia before the Year 1700, for although it was the largest country in Europe, its people were relatively isolated—that is living apart from the rest of Europe. The Russians were a branch of the large Indo-European family called Slavs. Genghis Khan and the Mongols had conquered Russia in the thirteenth century and ruled over the land. So, although the Russians were Christians, they were in some ways more like the people of the East than like Europeans. The men had long beards and wore long coats. The people counted on an abacus as the Chinese did. Long after serfdom had ended in Western Europe, a great many Russians still were serfs.

Well, just before 1700 there was born a Russian prince named Peter. When a small boy, Peter was very much afraid of the water. But he felt so ashamed that he, a prince, should fear anything that he forced himself to get used to the water. He would go to it and play in it and sail boats on it, although all the time he was almost scared to death. At last he not only got over this great fear but he came to like the water and boats more than any other playthings.

When Peter grew up, the thing he wanted more than anything else in the world was to make his country important in Europe, for before this time it had not been. It was big but not great. He wanted his people to share the culture and wealth that other Europeans enjoyed. But before he could teach his own people, most of whom were very poor and ignorant, he had to learn himself. As there was no one in Russia who could teach him what he wanted to know, he disguised himself as a common laborer and went to the little country of Holland. Here he got a job in a shipbuilding yard and worked for several months, cooking his own food and mending his own clothes. While he was doing this, however, he learned all about building ships and studied many other things besides, such as blacksmithing, cobbling shoes, and even pulling teeth.

Then he went to England, and everywhere he went he learned all he could. At last he returned to his own country with the knowledge he had gained and set to work to make Russia over. First of all, Peter wanted Russia to have a fleet of ships as other nations had. But in order to have a fleet, he had to have water for his ships, and Russia had almost no land bordering on the water. So Peter planned to take a seashore away from the neighboring country of Sweden.

Now the king of Sweden at this time was Charles. He was the twelfth king named Charles that Sweden had had. Charles XII was hardly more than a boy, and Peter thought it would be an easy matter to beat this boy and help himself to whatever land he wanted on the water. But Charles was not an ordinary boy. He was an extraordinary boy, extraordinarily bright and gifted, and he had been unusually well educated besides. He knew several languages; he had learned to ride a horse when he was four years old and how to hunt and to fight. Besides all this, he feared neither hardship nor danger. Indeed, he was such a dare-devil that people called him the Madman of the North. At first Peter's army was beaten by Charles.

But Peter took his beating calmly, simply remarking that Charles would soon teach the Russian army how to win. Indeed, so successful was Charles at first in fighting Peter and all others who threatened him that the countries of Europe began to think of him as Alexander the Great come to life again, and they feared he might conquer them all. But at last the Russians did win against Charles, and Peter got his seashore. Peter then built the fleet for which he had been working and planning for so many years.

The capital of Russia was Moscow.[1] It was a beautiful city but near the center of that country and far from the water. This didn't suit Peter at all. Peter wanted a fine city for his capital, but he wanted it right on the water's edge, so that he could have his beloved ships close to him. He picked out a spot not only on the water but mostly water, for it was chiefly a marsh. Then he put a third of a million people to work filling in the marsh, and on this he built a beautiful city. This city he called St. Petersburg in honor of his patron saint, the apostle Peter, after whom he himself had been named. The name of St. Petersburg was later changed to Petrograd[2] and still later to Leningrad; and now it is again called St. Petersburg. After a revolution, which you will read about later, the capital was moved back to Moscow.

Peter improved the laws, started schools, and built factories and hospitals and taught his people arithmetic. He made his people dress like other Europeans. He made the men cut off their long beards, which he

---

[1] Moscow [mos' kou]   [2] Petrograd [pe' trə grad]

thought looked countrified. The men thought it indecent to have no beards so some saved them to be placed in their coffins in order that at the day of resurrection they could appear before God unashamed. He introduced all sorts of things that he found in Europe but which were unknown in his own country, and he really made Russia over into a great European nation. That is why he is called Peter the Great, the Father of his Country.

Peter fell in love with a poor peasant girl, an orphan named Catherine, and married her. She had no education, but she was very sweet and lovely and bright and quick-witted, so the marriage turned out happily. The Russians were shocked at the idea of having a queen who was not a princess and was so low-born. But Peter had her crowned, and after he died she ruled over Russia.

74

A Prince Who Ran Away

IF you put a P in front of Russia it makes—Prussia. This was the name of a little country in Europe that was later a part of Germany. Russia was big, and Peter made it great. Prussia was small, but another king made it also great. This king was named Frederick. He, too, lived in the eighteenth century, but a little later than Peter, and he, too, was called "the Great"—Frederick the Great.

Frederick's father, who was the second king of Prussia, had a hobby for collecting giants as you might collect postage stamps. Wherever he heard of a very tall man, no matter in what country and no matter what it cost to get him, he bought or hired him. This collection of giants he made into a remarkable company of soldiers, which was his special pride.

He was a very cranky, cross, and bad-tempered old king. He treated his children terribly, especially his son Frederick, whom he called Fritz. Fritz had curls and liked music and poetry and fancy clothes. His father didn't like this, for he wanted a son who would be a soldier and fighter. His father, when angry, used to throw dishes at him, lock him up for days at a time, and feed him on bread and water and whip him with a cane. Finally Fritz could stand it no longer, and he ran away. He was caught and brought back. His father was so angry with his son for disobeying and acting as he had done that he was actually going to have him killed—yes, put to death—but at the last minute was persuaded not to do it.

But here is a strange thing: When Fritz grew up to be Frederick, he turned out to be just what his father wanted him to be—a great soldier and fighter. He still loved poetry and even tried to write poems himself, and he was very fond of music and he played the flute very well indeed. But Frederick wanted above everything else to make his country important in Europe; for before his time it was of little account, and no one paid much attention to it.

Now, the neighboring country to Prussia was Austria. Austria was ruled over by a woman named Maria Theresa.[1] Maria Theresa had become ruler of Austria at the same time that Frederick had become king of Prussia. Some people said that a woman should not rule a country and they wanted to use this as an excuse to start a war. Frederick's father had promised to let Maria Theresa alone—he had promised not to fight just because she was a woman—but when Frederick became king, he wanted to add a part of Austria to his own country, so he simply helped himself to the piece of Maria Theresa's country that he wanted. He didn't care if she was a woman or what his father had promised. Of course this started a war. Before long almost every country in Europe was fighting either with Frederick or against him. But Frederick not only succeeded in getting what he was after; he succeeded in holding on to it.

Maria Theresa, however, would not give up. She wanted to get back what had been wrongfully taken away from her. She began quietly and secretly to get ready for another war against Frederick. Quietly and secretly she got other countries to promise to help her. But Frederick heard of what she was doing, and suddenly he attacked her again, and for seven long years this next war went on. This was called the Seven Years' War. Frederick kept on fighting until he had beaten Austria for good and

---

[1] Maria Theresa [mə rē′ ə tə rā′ sə]

until he had gained his purpose, which was to make his little country of Prussia the most powerful country in Europe. He still held on to the part of Austria that he had at first taken away. Maria Theresa was a great queen, and she would have won against Frederick had he been an ordinary king. But she had too strong a ruler against her. Frederick was one of the world's smartest generals and too much for her.

The Seven Years' War, strange to say, was fought out not only in Europe but in far-off America, also. England had taken Frederick's side. France and other countries had taken sides against him. The English settlers in America, who were on Frederick's side, fought the French settlers, who were against him. When Frederick won in Europe, the English in America also won against the French in America. I am telling you all this because that is why we in America speak English instead of French today. If Frederick had lost in Europe and the English had lost in America, France would have won, and we here in America would probably now speak French instead of English.

Frederick, like some other kings we have heard of before, thought nothing of lying or cheating or stealing if he had to in order to get the better of other countries. Fair means or foul means made no difference to him. But his own people he treated as if they were his children and did everything he could for them. Like a lioness with her cubs, he fought for his family, even with the world against him.

There was a mill close by Frederick's palace that belonged to a poor miller. As it was not a pretty thing to be so near, the king wanted to buy it in order to tear it down and get rid of it. But the miller would not sell. Although Frederick the Great offered a large sum of money, the miller refused. A great many kings would simply have taken the mill and perhaps put the miller in jail or put him to death. Frederick did neither, for he thought his lowliest subject had his rights and that if he didn't want to sell he shouldn't be made to. He left the miller undisturbed, and the mill stands today as it did then, close to the palace.

Though Frederick was a German, strange to say, he hated the German language. He thought it the language of the uneducated. He himself spoke French and wrote in French and only spoke German when he had to talk to his servants or those who did not understand French.

75

America Gets Rid of Her King

DID you know that we once had a king?

His name was George.

No, George Washington wasn't a king.

This was another George.

You remember the Stuarts in England—James, Charles, and the rest of the family who ruled England for a hundred years from 1600 to 1700. Well, about 1700 England ran out of Stuarts—there were no more Stuart children.

As England had to have another king, they asked a distant relative of the royal family over from one of the German states to rule England. Yes, from Germany to rule England. His name was George, and the English called him George I. George couldn't even speak English. He was German and loved his own country much better than England. You can imagine what sort of king he was. His son, George II ruled after him, although he, too, was more German than English. But when the grandson, George III, came to the throne he was a born and bred Englishman. It was in this grandson's reign, in the reign of George III, that our country, the United States, was born.

When a wheel turns over, we call it a *revolution*, which is a big name for a little thing.

When a *country* turns around, we also call it a revolution, which is a big name for a big thing.

Our country had started with the two little settlements, or *colonies*, as they were called, of Jamestown and Plymouth. It had grown and grown until there were a number of settlements along the coast of the Atlantic Ocean. Most of the people who had settled here first were English, and the king of England ruled over them. Soon people from other countries like Germany, Holland, Scotland, and Ireland came here. Africans were brought against their will to work as slaves. The king of England ruled over all these people, too. The king asked these people to send him money, which was called *taxes*. Now, the money collected from taxes was not, of course, for the king to put in his pocketbook to use as he liked. It was supposed to be spent on the people who were taxed, to be used for roads, schools, police, and such things that are for the good of all.

These people along the coast, who were paying money or taxes to the king far off across the water, thought they ought to have a vote to say how this money should be spent and on what it should be spent. But they did not have a vote, and they thought they ought not to have to pay taxes to the king away off in England.

One of the leading citizens of America at this time was a man named Benjamin Franklin. He was the son of a candlemaker, but from a poor boy, who had once walked the streets of Philadelphia with a loaf of bread under each arm, he had risen to a very honored position in the country. He had learned to be a printer and had started one of the first and best newspapers in the United States. He was a great thinker and had invented a stove and a lamp and had succeeded in getting electricity from the lightning in the clouds by flying a kite with a wire during a storm. He was one of the Wise Men of the West.

Map of the thirteen original states

Franklin was sent over to England to try to get the king to change his mind about taxing the colonies or to bring about some sort of agreement with him. But King George was hardheaded, and Franklin was unable to stop the king from doing what he had made up his mind to do.

The people in America, finding that talking did no good, started in to fight. They raised an army. Then they tried to find a good man to command the army. Such a leader must be honest and brave; he must have a good mind; he must love his country; and he must be a good fighter. They looked around for a man who had all these qualities, and they found one. The man they picked was honest and brave. A legend grew up that when this man was a boy, he had cut down a favorite cherry tree of his father's just to try a new hatchet he had been given. When this boy was asked by his angry father if he had done it, he answered honestly and bravely, "I cannot tell a lie; I did." Of course, now you know who it was—George Washington. We know now that this story was made up by a man who wrote a book about George Washington. It's not true, but it makes a good story, doesn't it?

George learned to be a surveyor—that is, a man who measures land—and when only sixteen years old he was employed to survey the large farm of Lord Fairfax in Virginia; that showed he had a good mind. He then had been a soldier and

George Washington surveying Lord Fairfax's farm

had fought bravely and well in the French and Indian War, as the Seven Years' War was called here. That showed that he loved his country and was a good fighter. George Washington was chosen to lead the American army against the English.

The Americans did not at first think of starting a new country. They simply wanted the same rights that Englishmen in England had. They soon found out that there was only one way to get those rights, and that was to start a new country, independent of England. So a man named Thomas Jefferson wrote a paper which was called a Declaration of Independence—can you say it?—because it declared that the colonies were going to be independent of England. There were fifty-six Americans chosen by the people to sign it. Each one of the signers would have been put to death as a traitor to England if the United States had not won, and each signer knew it, yet he signed it nevertheless. But just signing this paper didn't make England give up the colonies. Oh, no! King George's armies tried to stop the colonies from getting away from the rule of England.

Washington had a very small army with which to fight the English army, and very little money with which to pay the soldiers or to supply them with food or clothes or powder and shot. One winter the soldiers nearly froze and starved to death, for they had little clothing and hardly any food but carrots, and it seemed as if the war could not go on unless they got help. Yet Washington kept up their spirits.

Benjamin Franklin was sent across the ocean, not to England this time of course, but to France to see if he couldn't get some help from that country. France hated England, because France had lost part of America, Canada, in the Seven Years' War, but at first France would not help. France took little interest in the fight, for Washington's army had lost a number of battles against the English, and people don't like to back a loser. The year after the Declaration of Independence, the American army beat the English badly at a place called Saratoga[1] in New York State. The king of France then became more interested, and then he sent

---

[1] Saratoga [sar ə tō′ gə]

help to the colonies to carry on the war. A young French nobleman named Lafayette hurried over from France and fought under General Washington and did so well that he made a great name for himself.

England, seeing that things were going against her, now wanted to make peace with the Americans and give them the same rights that English citizens had, but it was then too late. At the beginning of the war, the Americans would have agreed to this and been glad to agree, but now they would agree to nothing less than complete independence from England; and so the war went on, for England would not let the colonies go.

The English had been beaten by the Yankees, as they called them, in the North, at Saratoga. Then they sent their general, Lord Cornwallis, to the south of our country to see if he could beat the people there. General Greene was put in command of the southern American soldiers. Lord Cornwallis tried to fight Greene, but Greene led Cornwallis a merry chase around the country until he was all tired out and finally went into a little place called Yorktown on the coast of Virginia. Here, Cornwallis and his army were caught fast so that they could not get out. On the side of the land was the American army, and on the ocean side were the French warships that had been sent over to help. Cornwallis had to surrender.

King George then said, "Let us have peace"; and in 1783 the war was ended by a treaty of peace, eight years after it had started, and the colonies were independent of England. This was called the Revolutionary War, and after it was over our country was called the United States.

There were just thirteen of these original colonies that joined as partners in this Union. That is why there are just thirteen stripes in our flag. Some people think thirteen is an unlucky number; but our flag with its thirteen stripes still waves over the land, and it has brought us good luck; don't you think so?

Washington was made the first President, and so he is called the Father of his Country; the First in War, the First in Peace, and the First in the Hearts of his Countrymen.

76

Upside Down

MEASLES and Mumps are very catching.

So are Revolutions.

Just a little later than the Revolution of the thirteen colonies, the people in France had a Revolution, too. They saw how successful the Americans had been in their fight against the king of England, and so they rebelled against their own king and queen in France. This was called the French Revolution.

The reason the French people rebelled against their king was that they had very little, and the king and his royal family and nobles seemed to have everything. Both the Americans and the French rebelled against paying taxes. Although the English taxes were not very high, the Americans thought them unjust. The French taxes, however, not only were unjust but they took almost everything away from the people.

I have already told you how bad things were under Louis XIV, and they got worse until the people could stand it no longer.

At this time the king of France was Louis XVI, and his queen was named Marie Antoinette.[1] The people were so poor that they had hardly anything to eat except a very coarse and bad-tasting kind of bread called black bread. They were compelled to pay the king and the nobles money

---

[1] Marie Antoinette [mə rē′ an twə net′]

so the king and nobles could live in fine style and have parties; and they had to do all sorts of work for nothing or next to nothing. If anyone complained, he was put in a great prison in Paris called the *Bastille*[2] and left there to die. In spite of the fact that all the people were so terribly poor, the king and the queen and their friends lived in luxury and extravagance with everything in the world they wanted, all paid for by the poor people.

Neither the king nor his wife was really wicked. They were simply young and thoughtless. They meant well, but like a great many well-meaning people they lacked common sense and did not know how others lived. They didn't seem to understand that people *could* be poor, for they had so much themselves. Marie Antoinette was told that her subjects had no bread to eat. "Let them eat cake," she said.

To right the wrongs of the people, a body of many of the best men from all France gathered together and, calling themselves the National Assembly, tried to work out some plan to do away with all the injustice the people had been suffering. They wanted to make everyone free and equal and give everybody a say in the government. Their slogan was, *Liberté, égalité, fraternité*. In English this means, *Liberty, equality, brotherhood*.

The poor had become so furiously angry at the way they had been treated by the rich that they would stand things no longer, and a wild and angry mob of them attacked the old prison of the Bastille. They battered down the walls and freed the prisoners and killed the guards of the Bastille simply because they were servants of the king. Then they cut off the heads of the guards and stuck them on poles and, carrying them aloft, paraded through the streets of Paris. There were only seven prisoners in the old jail, so that freeing them didn't matter much, but this attack was to show that the people would no longer allow the king to imprison them.

---

[2] Bastille [ba stēl´]

The Bastille was stormed on July 14, 1789. This was the beginning of what is called the French Revolution, and this day is celebrated in France in almost the same way that our Fourth of July is, for it was the French Declaration of Independence against their kings.

Lafayette, who was now back in France, the same Lafayette who had helped the Americans fight their king, sent the key of the Bastille over to George Washington as a souvenir that his own country had now overthrown its king and declared its independence.

The king and queen were living in the beautiful palace at Versailles, the palace that Louis XIV had built. Many of the king's nobles, when they heard what was taking place in Paris, became frightened and, deserting their king and queen, took to their heels and left the country. They knew pretty well what was going to happen, and they didn't wait to see.

Meanwhile the National Assembly drew up what was called a Declaration of the Rights of Man, which was something like our Declaration of Independence. It said that all men were born free and equal, that the people should make the laws, and that the laws should be the same for all.

Soon after the Declaration of Rights had been made, the angry mob from Paris, ragged and wildlooking, carrying sticks and stones, and crying, "Bread, bread!" marched the thirteen miles to Versailles, where Louis and Marie Antoinette were still living. Up the beautiful grand staircase of the palace they rushed. The few guards remaining round the king were unable to hold them back. They captured the king and queen and took them prisoners to Paris. There they kept Louis and Marie Antoinette prisoners. Once the king and queen tried to escape in disguise but were caught before they could get out of the country, and they were brought back.

Then it was that the National Assembly drew up a *constitution*—a set of rules by which the country should be justly governed. This the king agreed to and signed.

That still wasn't enough. The people wanted no king at all to rule over them. So about a year later they started a real republic like our own, and the king was sentenced to death. A Frenchman had invented a kind of machine with a big knife for chopping off heads. This was called the *guillotine*, and it was used instead of an ax, for it was quicker and surer.

French revolution crowd and guillotine

The king was taken to the guillotine, and his head was cut off.

But the people did not settle down quiet and contented when they had got rid of their king. They were afraid that those who were in favor of kings might start another kingdom. The people chose red, white, and blue as their colors and the *Marseillaise*[3] as their national song; and everywhere they marched they carried the tricolor, as they called the three-colored flag, and as they marched they sang the *Marseillaise*.

Then began what is called the Reign of Terror, and that is a tale of blood. A man named Robespierre[4] and two of his friends were leaders in

---

[3] Marseillaise [mär sə lāz′]   [4] Robespierre [rōbz′ pēr]

the Reign of Terror. Anyone whom the people suspected of being in favor of kings they caught and beheaded. The queen was one of the first to have her head cut off. If anyone even whispered that there was a man, or a woman, or even a child who was in favor of kings, that man, woman, or child would be rushed to the guillotine. If anyone hated another and wished to get rid of him, all he had to do was to point him out as in favor of kings, and off he would be taken to the guillotine. No one was sure of his life for a day. He never knew what moment some personal enemy might accuse him. Hundreds, then thousands, of suspected people were beheaded, and a special sewer had to be built to carry off the blood. The guillotine, fast as it was, was too slow for the terrorists. It could cut off but one head at a time, and so prisoners were lined up and shot down with cannon.

People seemed to have gone wild, crazy, mad! They insulted Christ and the Christian religion. They put a pretty woman called the Goddess of Reason on the altar of the beautiful Church of Notre Dame and worshiped her instead of the Lord. They pulled down statues and pictures of Christ and the Virgin Mary. In their places they put statues and pictures of their own leaders. The guillotine was put up in place of the cross. They did away with Sundays. They made a week ten days long, and every tenth day they made a holiday instead of Sunday. They stopped counting time from Christ's birth, because they didn't want anything that had to do with Christ, and they began to call the year when the republic was started in 1792 the *Year 1*.

But Robespierre wished to rule alone, and he plotted against his two friends. One of these he had beheaded, and the other was killed in his bathtub by a girl named Charlotte Corday,[5] who was in a rage at what he had done. So Robespierre was left alone. At last the people, in fear of this man who was such a monstrous and inhuman tyrant, rose up against

---

[5] Corday [kor day']

him. When he found that he too, was to be put to death, he tried to commit suicide, but before he could do so, he was caught and taken to the guillotine, where he went to the same death to which he had sent countless others, and the Reign of Terror was ended.

77

A Little Giant

AT last the Revolution was stopped.

It was stopped by a young soldier only about twenty years old and sixty inches tall.

The Government was holding a meeting in the palace while an angry mob in the streets outside were trying to attack the palace. A young soldier had been given a few men and told to keep the mob away. The young soldier pointed cannons down each street that led to the palace, and no one dared to show himself. The young soldier was named Napoleon Bonaparte.[1] He made such a fine record that people wanted to know who he was and where he came from.

Napoleon had been born on a little island called Corsica in the Mediterranean Sea. He was born just in time to be a Frenchman, for the island of Corsica had belonged to Italy and had only just been given to France a few weeks before he was born. As soon as he was old enough, he was sent off to a military school in France. There, his French schoolmates looked upon him as a foreigner and didn't have much to do with him. But Napoleon made high marks in arithmetic, and he loved hard problems. Once he shut himself up in his room to work over a hard problem, and there he stayed for three days and nights until he had found the answer.

---

[1] Napoleon Bonaparte [nə pō lē′ ən bō′ nə pärt]

Napoleon showed early in his career that he was going to be a fine soldier, and when he was only twenty-six years old he was made a general.

Now, at this time all the other countries of Europe had kings. France had caught the fever of revolution from the Americans all the way across the ocean and had got rid of her kings. The kings of these other countries were afraid their people might catch the fever of revolution, too. All of these other countries became enemies of France because France had put an end to her kings. Besides that, the French army was invading France's neighbors to help them get rid of their kings. So, once again, war was on.

Napoleon was sent off to fight Italy. He had to cross the Alps, which Hannibal in the Punic Wars had crossed long before. But Hannibal had no heavy cannons when he crossed; it seemed impossible for Napoleon's army to cross with cannons. Napoleon asked his engineers, the men who were supposed to know about such things, if it could be done. They said they thought it was impossible.

"Impossible," Napoleon angrily replied, "is a word found only in the dictionary of fools." Then he shouted:

"There shall be no Alps!" and went ahead and crossed them. His army won in Italy, and when he returned to France he was greeted by the people as a conquering hero. But the men who were then governing France were afraid of him. They feared he might try to make himself king because he was so popular with the people. Napoleon, however, asked to be sent to conquer Egypt because he had an idea he could get the better of the English there. He thought he might then cut England off from India, the colony that they had won in the reign of James I. England had lost America and didn't want to lose India, too.

The French Government was very glad to get rid of Napoleon, and so they sent him off to Egypt as he asked. He quickly conquered Egypt as Julius Caesar had done, but there was no Cleopatra to upset his plans.

While he was conquering Egypt, his fleet, which was waiting for him at the mouth of the Nile, was caught and destroyed by the English fleet under a great admiral, if not the greatest that ever lived. His name was Lord Nelson.

Napoleon had no way to take his army back to France. He left his army in Egypt under command of another. He himself, however, managed to find a ship to take him back home. When he reached France, he found that the men who were supposed to be governing were quarreling among themselves, and, seeing his chance, he had himself made one of three men chosen to rule France. He was called first consul; and there were supposed to be two assistant consuls but the assistants were little more than clerks to do Napoleon's bidding. It was only a very short time before he was next made first consul for life. Then, not long after that, he became emperor of France and also king of Italy.

The other countries of Europe began to fear that Napoleon would conquer them, too, and make them also a part of France. All the other countries joined together to beat him. Napoleon planned to conquer England first, and he got ready a fleet to cross over to England. But his fleet was caught off Spain near a point called Trafalgar[2] by the same English admiral, Lord Nelson, who had beaten him in Egypt. Before this battle, Nelson said to his sailors, "England expects every man to do his duty," and they did it. Napoleon's fleet was utterly destroyed, though Nelson himself was killed.

Napoleon then gave up the idea of conquering England, and he turned his attention in the opposite direction. He had beaten Spain and Prussia and Austria. Almost all Europe either belonged to him or had to do what he said. He then attacked Russia. It was a great mistake he made, for Russia was far off and very large, and it was wintertime and very cold. Still, he managed to reach Moscow way off in the center of Russia with

---

[2] Trafalgar [trə fal′ gər]

Europe in 1815

his army. But the Russians burned the city and destroyed all the food, so that Napoleon had nothing with which to feed his army. It was terribly cold; there were deep snows; and, in retreating, his army suffered enormous losses. Napoleon himself soon made a beeline to Paris, leaving his soldiers to get back the best way they could. Men and horses died of cold and hunger by the thousands. Napoleon reached Paris, but his fortune had turned. All of Europe was getting ready to put an end to the tyrant, and it was not long after this that he was hemmed in and beaten by his enemies.

When Napoleon saw that he was beaten, he signed a paper saying that he would give up and leave France. This he did, sailing away to a little island called Elba, just off the coast of Italy, not far from the island where he was born.

But Napoleon, on the island of Elba, got an idea that all was not lost and that he might return to France and get back his power again. All of a sudden, to the surprise of France and the rest of the world, he landed on the coast of France. The French government at Paris sent an army of his old soldiers against him with orders to meet him and bring him to Paris in an iron cage. But when his old soldiers met their old general, they went over to his side, and so with them he marched on to Paris. The English and German armies were north of France and preparing to fight. Napoleon quickly got together an army and went forth to meet them. At a little town called Waterloo, Napoleon fought his last battle, for there he was utterly beaten by an English general named Wellington. This was the year 1815. We still speak and probably always will speak of any great defeat as a *Waterloo*.

There is a peculiar sentence which reads backward the same as forward. It is what Napoleon might have said after all was over. It is

ABLE WAS I ERE I SAW ELBA.

After Napoleon was beaten at Waterloo, the English took him away and put him on a little island far off in the ocean where he could not possibly escape. It was a lonely spot named St. Helena after the mother of Constantine. Here he lived for six years before he died.

Napoleon was probably the greatest general that ever lived, but that does not mean that he was the greatest man. Some say he was the worst, for just to make himself great, he killed hundreds of thousands of people and brought destruction and ruin to the whole of Europe wherever he fought his battles.

This brings us up into the nineteenth century, for Napoleon died in 1821. How long ago is that?

Napoleon at St. Helena

78

Latin America and
the Caribbean Islands

WHEN you think about places like Mexico and South America and the Caribbean[1] islands, you may think about wonderful beaches or the celebration of Carnival that is like Mardi Gras in New Orleans. But did you know that the first university in North America opened in Mexico before Jamestown was even thought of? Or do you know the name of Simon Bolívar,[2] a hero in South America, who is known there as well as George Washington is known in the United States?

Mexico, which is part of North America, along with Central and South America and the island nations of the Caribbean all have long histories just as we do. Most people from the United States don't know those stories and usually don't know very much at all about the other countries in this hemisphere. So I'm going to tell you a little about these neighbors of ours, especially about several of their heroes. When you know these stories, you will know more about our neighbors to the south than most adults do! Try it out on your family. See if I'm right.

You remember that the Spanish conquered most of the islands of the Caribbean and then Central and South America and Mexico in the years after Columbus first crossed the Atlantic. The Spanish took over lands where many different groups of Native Americans like the Mayas, the

---

[1] Caribbean [kar ə bē′ ən]   [2] Simon Bolívar [sī mən′ bol ē′ vər]

Incas, and the Aztecs had been living. They found lots of gold and silver. They made the native people work in the gold and silver mines so that the precious metals could be shipped to Spain to make that nation richer. When other European countries saw the fabulous wealth, they wanted some too. Soon the Spanish had to share the "New World" with other people. Portugal occupied the land that we call Brazil today. England and France claimed the eastern part of North America. England, France, Holland, and even Denmark snatched up some of the islands and a little land along the coast of Central and South America, but Spain continued to control most of the land that we call Latin America today. The Spanish language spoken by the colonists is still the most common language in Latin America, which includes all the lands in the Americas south of the United States. And the Roman Catholic religion, followed by most of the Spanish settlers, is still the largest religion there.

Most of the early Spanish settlers were men. Many of them married Native American women. Soon there were a lot of people whose parents and grandparents were both European and Native American. These people are called *Mestizos*.[3] People whose ancestors were only Europeans were called *Creoles*.[4] In some places land owners brought slaves from Africa to do their work for them. Some people with African ancestors married Creoles or Mestizos. Soon people in Latin America came not only in all sizes and shapes but in all colors as well. The king and queen in Spain sent out officials to rule over all these people. The officials collected taxes, but they didn't let any of the people have much say in how they would be ruled.

You can imagine that there were a lot of unhappy people in the colonies in Latin America and the Caribbean! The Creoles thought that they should run the government and keep all the gold and silver and other wealth found in America. The Native Americans and the Mestizos

---

[3] Mestizos [me stē′ zos]   [4] Creoles [krē′ ols]

Colonial Latin America showing Native American civilizations

both believed that they should have as much power as the Creoles or the officials sent from Europe. And, of course, the slaves didn't like being slaves, and they wanted very much to be free. This was true not only in the Spanish colonies but everywhere throughout Central and South America and the Caribbean.

Can you guess what happened next?

If you guessed revolution, you are right. In fact, a lot of revolutions broke out all over the place. These came not too long after the American Revolution and the French Revolution that you already know about.

Each revolution had its own battles and its own heroes. Here are just a few of the stories.

The first big revolution took place in Haiti.[5] Haiti is an island nation in the Caribbean and was a French colony. When the revolution began in France in 1789, people in Haiti heard all about it. They heard the famous slogan, *Liberté, égalité, fraternité*. Do you remember what that means? Well, the people in Haiti wanted their share of that liberty, equality, and brotherhood that everyone was talking about. But the Haitians didn't exactly agree on what that meant! The wealthy Creoles who owned most of the land thought it meant that they should be equal to French people in France. Ordinary people in Haiti, some of whom had a mixed racial background (whose ancestors were part French and part African) thought it meant that they should be equal to the wealthy Creoles. Slaves believed that it meant slavery should be abolished and all the former slaves should be full citizens with the same rights as all citizens. Before long, everybody was fighting everybody else.

One part of this fighting was a slave rebellion that began on the northern part of the island. As so often happens, a strong leader took charge and led his people to victory. This man was Toussaint L'Ouverture.[6] Toussaint, as he is called, had been born a slave. He is said to have been the grandson of an African king. He could read and write, and he knew all about the revolution in France and the ideals of liberty and equality. He also knew how dreadful it was to be a slave. So he and his followers fought hard until the French government abolished slavery in Haiti, and then he continued to fight until he was put in charge of the government. He ruled well for several years. He asked black people and white people to work together to rebuild the country that had been torn apart by war, and Haiti began to recover. Then Napoleon came to power in France, and Napoleon didn't like this strong ruler named Toussaint.

[5] Haiti [hā′ tē]   [6] Toussaint L'Ouverture [tōō san′   lōō ver tyr′]

You might say that Napoleon was jealous of Toussaint. Or maybe Napoleon just decided that he wanted to control the island. In any case, Napoleon sent soldiers to Haiti. The general in charge of the French army played a mean trick on Toussaint. He invited Toussaint to be his guest for dinner. Then, when Toussaint came, the French general took him prisoner. Toussaint was sent to a prison all the way across the Atlantic in France. He died there a year later. But all was not lost. Soon a new leader named Jean-Jacques Dessalines[7] took over the fight, and Haiti became an independent country. This is not a story with a completely happy ending though. After independence, a civil war broke out and Haiti had no real peace for many years.

In Spain's American colonies, there were a lot of unhappy people, too. Like the Haitians, they knew about the revolutions in the United States and in France. And they also had a lot of complaints about the conditions of their own lives. The Creoles were angry because people sent by the king from Spain had all the power, and they had none. All the people living in the Spanish colonies resented paying high taxes to the king of Spain. The Mestizos were angry with Spain just as the Creoles were. Native Americans knew that the Spanish had taken away their land, made them perform forced labor like slaves and killed many of their people. Most of all, these native peoples wanted their land back. Slaves in Latin America, like slaves everywhere, wanted to be free.

The first revolt against Spanish rule took place in South America, in what is now the nation of Peru. It was led by a man named Tupac Amaru,[8] a Mestizo who was descended from Inca kings. The Spanish troops came and killed him and his followers, and that was the end of that. Latin America would have to wait a while for things to change.

A little after 1800, things really began to happen. First, in Europe, Napoleon conquered Spain, threw out the king, and made his own brother

---

[7] Jean-Jacques Dessalines [zhän zhäk′ dā sa lēn′]   [8] Tupac Amaru [tōō′ pak e mä′ rōō]

Countries of Latin America and the Caribbean

the new king of Spain. What do you think of that? Well, the people in Latin America saw it as a good excuse to declare independence. After all, their old king was no longer on the throne and clearly, they figured, Napoleon had no right to rule them. So the fighting began.

First, in Argentina, an army organized and won independence. The leading general, José de San Martín[9] then decided on a dangerous plan. He led his armies across the high Andes mountains into Chile and later on to

___

[9] José de San Martín [ho zä' dā san mär tēn']

Peru to fight for independence in those places, too. Look at the map and see where those countries are. About one third of San Martín's soldiers were slaves to whom he had promised freedom for joining his army.

The best known hero in all Latin American history is Simon Bolívar. Just as I told you at the beginning, he is as famous in South America as George Washington is in the United States. Simon Bolívar was born in Caracas, Venezuela.[10] He was the youngest of four children. His parents were wealthy Creoles who owned several houses, silver and copper mines, large herds of cattle, and large farms where sugar and cocoa were grown. You probably think that Simon must have been a very lucky little boy but, in fact, he was not. Simon's father died before he was three, and his mother died two weeks before his ninth birthday. The children all went to live in different places. Simon went to live with an uncle. This man was cold to Simon, and Simon missed the rest of his family very much.

When Simon was eleven, his uncle hired a young man to come tutor him. In those days, wealthy boys did not go to school. They had private tutors who came to their homes. Simon's new tutor was also named Simon—Simon Rodriguez.[11] This young teacher taught Simon Bolívar all the new ideas that educated people were talking about. He taught him about the revolutions in the United States and France. He told him to look around him at the sad lives of the Native Americans and the slaves in Venezuela and to see how the Spanish wouldn't let people in their colonies rule themselves. With all this, it's not surprising that Simon Bolívar grew up to be a revolutionary.

In 1811, Creoles in Venezuela declared their independence from Spain. Just as we had to fight the British after we declared independence, the people of South America had to fight the Spanish to make their independence real. Simon Bolívar became one of the highest ranking officers in the rebel army. The next year, there was a terrible earthquake

---

[10]Caracas, Venezuela [kə rä′ kəs, ven ə zwā′ lə]   [11] Rodriguez [rō drē′ gə z]

in Caracas that killed ten thousand of the rebel soldiers. A lot of people would have given up, but Simon Bolívar did not. He formed a new army and fought on. Finally he liberated Venezuela and then Colombia, Bolivia, and Ecuador. Bolívar was chosen president of the newly independent lands. He called this new country Gran Colombia in honor of Christopher Columbus.

Bolívar hoped to unite all the states of Latin America. But his plans never worked out. The places that broke away from Spanish rule split into the many separate countries of modern Central and South America. One country is named for the famous leader Bolívar. Can you pick it out on the map?

In most of the new countries, the wealthy people would not share the power with ordinary people, and they also refused to return any land to the Native Americans. Nor would they end slavery as Simon Bolívar wanted them to do. So all of Latin America's problems were not solved after independence. Still, Simon Bolívar is a hero in all the countries of South and Central America. He is known throughout the region as *El Libertador*[12]—the Liberator.

Our nearest southern neighbor is Mexico. Take a minute and find Mexico on the map. Mexico used to be called New Spain, and it included such places as Texas, Arizona, New Mexico, and California. Mexicans rebelled against Spain just as the people in South America did. The first uprising was led by a Creole priest named Father Miguel Hidalgo.[13] He led a small group of Native Americans and others who joined him. They wanted to take some of the land from the few very wealthy people who owned it all and give some of it back to the native people from whom it had been taken, and to other poor people as well. The Spanish and the wealthy Creoles all went after him and, of course, they defeated his rebels. After Hidalgo was captured and executed, a Mestizo priest named

---

[12] Libertador [lē ber tä dôr']   [13] Miguel Hidalgo [mi gel' hi dal' gō]

Father José Maria Morelos[14] led the fight. He, too, was captured and executed. In the end, the Creoles led the fight for independence from Spain, but they kept all the power in the hands of rich people. A general named Agustín de Iturbide[15] actually declared Mexican independence in 1821. Soon after that, he was declared emperor, and the history of modern, independent Mexico had begun.

You can see from all this that there is a lot of history in the Americas south of the United States. All these new names may seem hard at first but, if you just think of them as people like George Washington, Benjamin Franklin, and Thomas Jefferson, you will understand what important people they are.

Now, you go try out some of those names on an adult you know and see how little most people from the United States know about our southern neighbors.

---

[14] José Maria Morelos [hō zā′ mər rē′ ə mô re′ lôs]   [15] Agustín de Iturbide [a goos tēn′ dā ē tōor′ vēd]

79

From Pan and His Pipes
to the Phonograph

Frogs croak.

Cats meow.

Dogs bark.

Sheep bleat.

Cows moo.

Lions roar.

Hyenas laugh.

But only birds and people *sing*.

And people can do what birds cannot.

They can also make music out of *things*.

HAVE you ever made a cigar-box fiddle or a pin piano or musical glasses? In the long-ago story-book times, Apollo took a pair of cow horns and fastened between them seven strings made from the cow's skin. This was called a *lyre*. These strings he picked with his finger or with a quill, making a little tinkling sound that could hardly have been very beautiful. Yet Apollo's son, Orpheus,[1] is said to have learned from his father to play so beautifully on the lyre that the birds and wild beasts and even trees and rocks gathered around to hear him.

---

[1] Orpheus [ôr′ fē əs]

Pan, the god of the woods, who had goat's horns, and ears and legs and feet, tied together several whistles of different lengths and played on these as you might on a mouth organ. This instrument was called *Pan's pipes*.

The lyre and Pan's pipes were two of the earliest musical instruments. The first was a stringed instrument, the second a wind instrument. The long strings and long pipes made low notes; the short strings and short pipes made high tones.

From Apollo's lyre we get the piano with its many, many strings. Did you ever look at the inside of a piano and see the many strings of different lengths? They are, however, not picked as the strings of a lyre or harp are picked, but hammered by little felt-covered blocks as you touch the keys.

From Pan's pipes we get the great church organ with its pipes like giant whistles. You don't, of course, blow the pipes with your mouth as you do a whistle. The pipes are so big you must blow them with a machine.

We know what the instruments in olden times were like, but we don't know what the music that people made was really like; there were no phonographs or tapes to bottle up the sounds and, when uncorked a thousand years later, to pour forth the old notes once again. The music went off into thin air and was lost.

It was not until about the Year 1000 A.D. that music could even be written down. Before then all music was played *by ear*, for there was no written music. A Benedictine monk named Guy, or, in Italian, Guido, thought of a way to write down musical notes, and he named the notes do, re, mi, fa, and so on. These were the first letters of the words of a hymn to St. John which the monks sang like the scale.

Another Italian is sometimes called the Father of Modern Music. His name is Palestrina,[2] and he died in 1594. He set the church service to music, and the pope ordered all churches to follow it, but the people

---

[2] Palestrina [pal ə strē′ nə]

didn't like his music very much; that is, it was not what we call *popular*.

It was not until a hundred years later—that is, about 1700—that the first great European musician lived who wrote music that was really popular, that the people in Europe and America loved, and that we still love today.

He was a German named Handel. His father was a barber, a dentist, and doctor, and he wanted his boy to become a great lawyer. But the only thing the boy liked was music.

In those days there were no pianos. There was a little instrument with strings which was played by touching keys. This was called a clavichord. Sometimes it had legs like a table. Sometimes it had no legs and was just laid on a table.

Handel, though only six years old, got hold of one of these instruments, and, without anyone finding out about it, he had it put up in his room in the attic of his house. After everyone had gone to bed at night, he would practice on this clavichord until late, when he was supposed to be in bed. One night his family heard sounds up under the roof. Wondering what it could be, they took a lantern, and, quietly climbing the attic stairs, they suddenly opened the door, and there sat little Handel in his nightclothes on a chair with his feet reaching only half way to the floor, playing on the clavichord.

Handel is found in the attic

After that, Handel's father saw it was no use trying to make his son a lawyer. He got teachers for him, and before long the boy amazed the world with his playing. He went to England, lived there, became an Englishman, and when he died the English people buried him in Westminster Abbey, a church in which famous Englishmen were buried.

Handel set parts of the Bible to music. These songs with the Bible words to be sung by a chorus of voices were called *oratorios*, and one of these oratorios named *The Messiah* is sung almost everywhere at Christmas time. In addition to his religious music, Handel wrote forty-six operas!

Living at the same time as Handel was another German musician named Bach.[3] Bach played divinely on the organ as Handel did on the clavichord and wrote some of the finest music for the organ that ever had been written. Strange that both Handel and Bach went blind in their old age, but to them it was sound, not sight, that counted most. Which do you think "counts more"?

Almost all musical geniuses have been musical wonders when they were still babies. They have been great musicians even before learning to read and write.

One such genius was born just before Bach and Handel died. He was an Austrian named Mozart.

Mozart, when only four years old, played the piano wonderfully. He also wrote music—composing, it is called—for others to play.

Mozart's father and sister played very well, so the three went on a concert tour. Mozart, the boy wonder, played before the empress, and everywhere he went he was treated like a prince, petted and praised and given parties and presents.

He grew up and married, and ever after he had the hardest kind of time trying to make a living. He composed all sorts of things, plays with

---

[3] Bach [bäkh]

music called *operas*, and *symphonies*, which are written for whole orchestras to play; but he made so little money that when he died he had to be buried where they put people who were too poor to have a grave for themselves alone. People afterward thought it a shame that such a great composer should have no monument over his grave, but then it was too late to find where he was buried. A monument was put up, but to this day no one knows where Mozart's body lies.

A German named Beethoven[4] had read the stories of the boy wonder, Mozart, and he thought he, too, would like to have a boy wonder to play before kings and queens. When his son was only five years old, he kept the boy practicing long hours at the piano until he became so tired that the tears ran down his cheeks. But Ludwig Beethoven, as he was named, finally came to be one of the greatest musicians who have ever lived. He could sit at the piano and make up the most beautiful music as he went along—*improvise*, as it is called—but he was never satisfied with it when written down. Time and time again he would scratch out and rewrite his music until it had been rewritten often a dozen times.

But Beethoven's hearing began to grow dull. He was worried that he might lose it entirely—a terrible thing to happen to anyone, but to one whose hearing was his fortune, nothing could be worse. At last he did become deaf. This loss of his hearing made Beethoven hopelessly sad and bad-tempered, cross with everything and everybody. Nevertheless, he didn't give up; he kept on composing just the same, even after he could no longer hear what he had written.

Another great and unusual German musician named Wagner lived until 1883. Though he practiced all his life, he never could play very well. But he composed wonderful operas, and he wrote not only the music but the words, too. He took old Germanic myths and fairy tales and made them into plays to be sung to music. At first some people made fun of his

---

[4] Beethoven [bā′ tō vǝn]

music, for it seemed to them so noisy and "slam-bangy" and without tune. Now people make fun of those people who don't like it!

I have told you in other places of painters and poets, or architects and wise men, of kings and heroes, of wars and troubles. I have put this story of music of all ages in one chapter, which I have tucked in here between the acts, to give you a rest for a moment from wars and rumors of wars.

When I was a boy I never heard any great musicians play. Now you and I can turn on the record, tape, or CD player anytime and hear the music of Palestrina or Mozart, of Beethoven or Wagner, of dozens of other masters, played or sung to us whenever we wish. No caliph in the *Arabian Nights* could command such service for his pleasure!

80

The Daily Papers of 1854–1865

IF you could go up into your grandmother's attic or the attic of somebody else's grandmother, or could dig down into some old trunk, you might find some of the newspapers that were printed during the years from 1854 to 1865. You might actually read in these daily papers the happenings that I am now going to tell you about. Under the heading, *Foreign News*, you would probably find some of the following things told about:

ENGLISH NEWS. At this time the queen of England was named Victoria. She was much beloved by her people because she had such a kindly nature. You may have seen a picture of her surrounded by her many children. Victoria had five daughters and four sons. So you can see that she was a mother as well as a queen. She was more like a mother to her people than a queen. She ruled for more than half a century, and the time when she ruled is called the Victorian Age.

The English news of 1854 would tell about a war that the English were then fighting with Russia. Russia was a long way off, and so the English had to send their soldiers in boats through the Mediterranean Sea to the end, then past Constantinople into the Black Sea. There, in a little spot of land that jutted out from Russia into the Black Sea, most of the fighting was done. This little spot of land was called the Crimea,[1] and the war therefore was called the Crimean War. In this war in that far-off land, thousands of English soldiers died from wounds and disease.

Now, there was living in England at the time of this war a lady named Florence Nightingale.[2] She was very tender-hearted and always looking out for and taking care of those who were sick. Even as a little girl, she had played that her dolls were sick with a headache or a broken leg, and she would bandage the aching head or broken leg and pretend to take care of her sick patient. When her dog was ill, she nursed him as carefully as if he were a human being.

Florence Nightingale heard that English soldiers were dying by the thousands in that distant land far away from home and that there were no nurses to take care of the wounded. She got together a number of women, and they went out to the Crimea. Before she arrived, almost half the soldiers who were wounded died—fifty soldiers out of a hundred; after she and her nurses came, only two in a hundred died. She went about through the camps and over the battlefields at night carrying a lamp, looking for the wounded. The soldiers called her the Lady of the Lamp, and they all loved her.

When at last the war was over and she returned to England, the government voted to give her a large sum of money for what she had done. She, however, refused the money for herself but took it to found a home for training nurses. Nowadays professional nurses are thought almost as necessary as doctors, and anyone who is sick can call in a trained nurse to take care of him, but at that time there were no professional nurses. Florence Nightingale was the first to start teaching nursing, and she is looked upon almost as a saint today.

In one battle in the Crimea, a company of soldiers mounted on horseback were given by mistake an order to attack the enemy. Though

---

[1] Crimea [krī mē′ ə]   [2] Nightingale [nīt′ n gāl]

they knew it meant certain death, they never hesitated but charged, and two-thirds of them were killed or wounded in less than half an hour. Lord Tennyson, the English poet, has told this story in verse which you may know. It is called *The Charge of the Light Brigade.*

JAPANESE NEWS. Japan is a group of islands near China. Although I have not told you about it before, it was an old country, settled in its ways even before Rome was founded. In Europe there have been constant

Florence Nightingale searching out the wounded

changes of kings and rulers and people and countries. But in Japan they have had the same line of kings since before Christ.

Japan was very lucky in one way. In all the years, the Japanese islands were never occupied by a foreign army. But in 1853, the year before

England began the Crimean War, an American naval officer named Commodore Perry sailed into Tokyo Bay, an important Japanese harbor, with American warships. The Japanese emperor then allowed Americans to come in and do business in Japan.

These are some of the things you might read about in those old newspapers. Such news would probably have taken up little space. Perhaps they would have been found down at the bottom of a column if the newspaper were American. But if the paper were printed between 1861 and 1864, the greater part of it would be about a war that was going on in our country at that time. This was a war between our own people, a family quarrel, which we call the Civil War, or the War between the States.

Two parts of our country, the North and the South, did not agree on several matters, chief of which was the question whether southerners could own slaves. So they went to war with each other. Thousands upon thousands of Americans died in this war. The war lasted for four years, from 1861 to 1865, before it was decided that no one could ever again own slaves in the United States.

Some of you who read these pages may be descended from men who fought in this Civil War. Some of these fought for the South; some fought for the North. Black men and white men and even some women fought. You should ask your parents or grandparents if any of your ancestors fought in the Civil War.

The president of the United States at that time was a man named Abraham Lincoln. Lincoln was a very poor boy who had been born in a log cabin. He had taught himself to read by the light of a blazing knot of wood at night after his day's work on his father's farm was done. As he was very poor, he had only a few books, and these he read over and over again. One of these books was the same *Aesop's Fables*[3] that you read.

---

[3] *Aesop's Fables* [ē' sopz fā' b əlz]

When Lincoln was a young man, he became a storekeeper. One day he found that he had given a poor woman a smaller package of tea than she had paid for, and he closed the store and walked many miles to her house in order to return the change. People began to call him Honest Abe after that, for he was always very honest and kind-hearted.

Lincoln visiting camp and shaking hands with the soldiers

He studied hard and became a lawyer and at last was elected president of the United States. While he was president, he declared that slavery should be abolished. One evening, Lincoln was watching a play from a private box at Fords Theater. Suddenly, John Wilkes Booth, who thought Lincoln had not done right in freeing the slaves, broke into the president's box and shot Lincoln, who died the next day.

Lincoln was one of our greatest presidents. Washington started our country; Lincoln prevented its splitting into two parts and kept it together as one big united land to grow into the great country it now is.

81

Three New Postage Stamps

LET us look backward a minute to see what had been going on in Europe since the time of Napoleon.

After Napoleon was sent to Elba, the French had to have another ruler. They wanted their old kings back again. The family name of their old kings was Bourbon,[1] and the French thought they ought to have a Bourbon ruler over them. Accordingly they tried out three Bourbons— one after the other—all relatives of their last king, whom they had beheaded.

All of them proved no good. The French people had given the Bourbon family a good tryout, and so at last they stopped worrying with kings and started another republic.

Now, a republic has a president instead of a king, so the people had to choose a president; and whom do you suppose they picked out? Why, the nephew of Napoleon. The nephew of Napoleon was named Louis Napoleon. He had planned and plotted again and again to make himself king of France, but again and again he had failed. And now he was elected president! But Louis Napoleon didn't want to be *only* president. He wanted to be like his uncle the great Napoleon. He dreamed of being emperor and conquering Europe, and so it was not

---

[1] Bourbon [bo͞or′ bən]

long after this before he had himself made emperor, and called himself Napoleon III.[2]

Napoleon III was jealous of the neighboring country of Prussia. It was getting to be too strong, he thought. Prussia had a king at this time named William who was very able himself, and he had an able assistant or prime minister named Bismarck,[3] who was looking for an excuse to fight France. Presently a war was started between the two countries in 1870. Napoleon soon found he had made a bad mistake in picking the war with Prussia. Prussia was not *getting* too strong; it was already too strong.

Napoleon III was completely beaten by Prussia, and he with a large army had to surrender. Then in disgrace he went to live in England.

The Prussians marched into Paris and made the French agree to pay them a billion dollars. When some of the French towns said they couldn't pay, Bismarck lined up the leading citizens of the place and told them they would be shot if they didn't raise the money that was demanded. France paid, and, to the wonder and amazement of everybody, they paid this immense sum in two years' time. But it took France a long time to forget the way they were made to pay and the way they were treated by the Prussians, and for a long time there was deadly enmity between these two countries. This war was called the Franco-Prussian War,[4] as it was between France and Prussia.

There were a number of little countries near Prussia. They were called German states. But though their people were related and spoke the same language, the countries or states were separate. As a result of the war, Prussia was able to join all these German states together and to make for the first time one big, strong, powerful nation called Germany, feared by other countries on account of its great army of fighting men. William was made emperor of all Germany and

---

[2] Napoleon I had a young son who might have been Napoleon II if he had lived. The story is, that when Napoleon III was made emperor his name was printed simply with three exclamation marks after it— Napoleon!!!—and this was by mistake read Napoleon III.

[3] Bismarck [biz′ märk]

[4] Franco-Prussian War [frang′ kō prush′ ən]

called kaiser. He was crowned in the French palace that Louis XIV had built at Versailles.

The French thought the Germans had been able to win this war because they had public schools in which all their children were trained and because of the way their soldiers were drilled. So France set to work and started public schools everywhere in France and imitated the German way of drilling their army so that they would be prepared in the next war.

France became a republic with a president and an assembly chosen by the people. The French wanted no more emperors.

At that time Italy was not a single country as it is now. It was a collection of small states, as Germany had been. Some of these were independent; some were owned by France; some were owned by Austria. The king of one of these Italian states was Victor Emmanuel. He wanted all the Italian states to unite and become one single country like our United States. He was helped by his prime minister, a very able man named Cavour,[5] and by a rough but romantic popular hero named Garibaldi,[6] who was called the Hero of the Red Shirt.

Garibaldi, who had been a candlemaker in New York City, was always poor and seemed not to care for money. He was so popular that whenever he called for soldiers to fight with him for his beloved Italy, they at once flocked around him, ready to fight to the death.

At last these three, Victor Emmanuel, Cavour, and Garibaldi, succeeded in making their country one big nation. The Italians erected monuments to them and named streets after them. To honor Victor Emmanuel, they built a magnificent building on a hill in Rome overlooking the city, a building that was intended to be more beautiful than anything built in Athens during the time of Pericles, or in Italy during the Renaissance.

[5] Cavour [kä vo͞or´]   [6] Garibaldi [gär ē bôl´ dē]

If you collect postage stamps it would be interesting for you to get, if you can, stamps of these countries at that time, the New French Republic, United Germany, and United Italy.

82

The Age of Miracles

You may think the Age of Miracles was in Biblical days.

But if a man who lived at that time should come back to earth *now* he would think this the Age of Miracles.

If he heard you talk on a telephone to a person thousands of miles away, or even a hundred feet away, he would think you a magician.

If you showed him people moving and talking on a movie screen or a television screen, he would think you a witch.

If he heard you start a band playing by turning on a tape player or a radio, he would think you a devil.

If he saw you fly through the air in an airplane, he would think you a god.

We are so used to the telephone, television, and tape recorders, to automobiles and huge trucks and jet planes, to electric lights and moving pictures and radios and marvelous cameras that it is hard to imagine a world in which none of these things existed—absolutely none of these things. Yet in the year 1800, not a single one of these inventions was known.

Neither George Washington nor Napoleon ever saw an airplane or an automobile. They never used a telephone or a radio or even a bicycle. They never heard of a gasoline engine or a diesel engine or an electric light. They never even imagined men walking on the moon, or close-up photographs of Mars, or television sets, or even typewriters. And as for computers and radar and X-rays—well!

More wonders have been made in the last hundred years than in all the previous centuries of the world put together.

A Scotsman named James Watt was one of the first of these magicians whom we call inventors. Watt had watched a boiling kettle on the stove and noticed that the steam lifted the lid. This gave him an idea that steam might lift other things as well as the lid of a teakettle. So he made a machine in which steam lifted a lid called a piston in such a way as to turn a wheel. This was the first steam engine.

Watt's steam engine moved wheels and other things, but it didn't move itself. An Englishman named Stephenson put Watt's engine on wheels and made the engine move its own wheels. This was the first locomotive. Soon funny-looking carriages drawn by funny-looking engines were made to run on tracks in America. At first these trains ran only a few miles out, from such cities as Baltimore and Philadelphia.

Then a young fellow named Robert Fulton thought he could make a boat go by putting Watt's engine on board and making it turn paddle wheels.

Riverboat with steam-driven paddle wheel

People laughed at him and called the boat he was building *Fulton's Folly*, which means *Fulton's foolishness*. But the boat worked, and Fulton had the laugh on those who had laughed at him. He called his boat the *Clermont*, and it made regular trips up and down the Hudson River.

No one had ever before been able to talk to another far off until the telegraph was invented. The telegraph makes a clicking sound. Electricity flows through a wire from one place to another place which may be a long distance off. If you press a button at one end of the wire, you stop the electricity flowing through the wire, and the instrument at the other end makes a click. A short click is called a dot, and a long click is called a dash. These dots and dashes stand for letters of the alphabet so you can spell out a message by dots and dashes.

A is	• —	dot-dash
B is	—• • •	dash-dot-dot-dot
E is	•	dot
H is	• • • •	dot-dot-dot-dot
T is	—	dash

An American painter named Morse invented this wonderful little instrument. He built the first telegraph line in America between Baltimore and Washington, and this was the first message he clicked across it: "What hath God wrought!"

A schoolteacher named Bell was trying to find some way of making deaf children hear, and in doing so he invented the telephone. The telephone carries words as the telegraph carries clicks. You do not have to know a special alphabet or spell out words by dots and dashes as you do on the telegraph. With the telephone, anyone can talk from one side of the world to the other, and with ships at sea and planes in the air.

Many inventions now in everyday use have been partly invented by several people, so that it is hard to say just which one thought of the invention first. Several people thought of a way to run a machine by feeding it electricity. This was the electric motor. Then others thought of a way to run a machine by exploding gas. This was the motor used in automobiles.

Automobiles, as you know, became very popular. At first, people didn't need a license to drive and there were no traffic controls—like stop signs or traffic signals—on the streets. You can imagine some of the problems this caused. An African American named Garrett Morgan invented the three-color traffic signal and patented it in 1923. This helped make the streets safer for cars and for people walking too.

Electric lights were invented by Thomas Alva Edison. Edison was called a wizard, because in the Middle Ages, wizards were supposed to be able to do and to make all sorts of wonderful and impossible things, to turn lead into gold, to make people invisible, and that sort of thing. But Edison has done things that no wizard of a fairy tale had ever even thought of. Edison was a poor boy who sold newspapers and magazines on a train. He was interested in all sorts of experiments and fitted up a place in the baggage car where he could make experiments. But he made so much of a mess in the car that at last the baggageman kicked Edison's whole outfit off the train. Edison invented many things connected with the phonograph and the movies, and he has probably made more useful and important inventions than any other man who has ever lived, so that he is much greater than those mere kings who have done nothing but quarrel and destroy—without whom the world would have been much better off if they had never lived!

Thousands of people who lived in the past ages tried to fly and failed. Millions of people have said it was impossible to fly and foolish to try.

Some have even said it was wicked to try, that God meant that only birds and angels should fly. At last, after long years of work and thousands of trials, two American brothers named Wright did the impossible. They invented the airplane and, in 1905, the plane flew 24.2 miles in 38 minutes 3 seconds!

An Italian named Marconi invented the radio, and others every day are still making wonderful inventions, but you will have to read about these yourself, for this book isn't big enough for me to tell you all about them.

Here is a good subject for an argument or debate: Are we any happier *with* all these inventions than people were a thousand years ago *without* them?

Life is faster and more exciting; but it is more difficult and more dangerous. Instead of singing or playing the violin, or piano, we turn on the stereo or the radio and miss the chief joy in music, the joy of making it ourselves. Instead of the jogging drive in an old buggy behind a horse that goes along through the countryside almost by himself, we speed on in dangerous autos, to which we must pay constant, undivided attention or be wrecked. Instead of pure air, we often have pollution.

83

A Different Kind of Revolution

JAMES Watt's steam engine and Robert Fulton's steam powered ship were part of a revolution—a different kind of revolution. Usually we think of a revolution as being like the American Revolution or the French Revolution when people fought a war against a government. But this revolution took place slowly and without any armies. Yet it certainly did change the world. It is called the Industrial Revolution.

In the last chapter, I told you about some of the wonderful inventions like cars, airplanes, radios, and televisions that we have because of the Industrial Revolution. That's the fun part. But a lot of other things happened, too. This peaceful revolution changed the world every bit as much as the big wars—maybe more! Here's how.

All those wonderful new things were made in factories. The first factories were built in England. They made cloth and then clothing. Later they made railroad cars and tracks. Soon English factories were making all sorts of good things, and England began to grow very rich and powerful.

In some ways countries are just like boys and girls. You know that sometimes, when one student in a class brings in a new toy or wears a new jacket, everybody else wants one, too. Well, soon other countries wanted to be like England and they began building factories so they would be rich and powerful, too. A lot of European countries like France, Germany, and Italy did this. So did the United States and Japan. Soon all these places were making lots of things in their factories. They made clothes and furniture. They made cars and even candy. This was called the Industrial Revolution.

We all know that now we can go to the store and buy these things that are made in factories. But would that be enough of a change to call it a REVOLUTION? Well, maybe yes, maybe no. But there were other things that began happening as soon as the factories were built. All of these things together really were a revolution.

One big change happened like this. A lot of people came to work in the new factories. You wouldn't have much of a factory if nobody worked there, would you? It took a lot of men and women to work in the factories. Families left the countryside. They stopped farming and became factory workers. The men who built the factories wanted so many workers that they even paid children to work there. This wasn't very good for the children, though, because they didn't get to go to school. It also wasn't very good because those early factories had a lot of unsafe machines and sometimes the children and the grownups, too, got hurt. Despite all that, lots of men, women, and children came to work. So one big change is that many people stopped farming and became factory workers. Which would you rather do? Why?

Some people had been making things at home—like candles or soap or sweaters to sell. When a family does this, it's called a *cottage industry* because they work in their cottage. After the Industrial Revolution, factories made many of the same things. Since a factory made so many sweaters, for example, so fast, it could sell them for less money than an individual could. Because of this, many people who had worked at home had to go to work in factories.

Most of the factories were built in cities. Coming to work in the factory meant coming to live in a city. Soon the cities got very crowded. In those early days people had to live close together, because they had to live near their jobs so they could walk to work.

How far would you be willing to walk to work or school? People often walked a mile or two each way. After trolley cars were invented, people could live farther away from work. At first, trolleys were pulled along tracks on city streets by horses, and they were slow. By the end of the nineteenth century, electric trolleys became common, and people could live even farther away. So the cities grew larger. Here's a second big change then. Cities grew big like the ones we know today.

Way around the world, even in countries where there weren't any factories yet, people's lives changed, too. You have to stop and think about this for a minute. It may seem hard to believe that the life of a child in Africa, India, Korea, or Hawaii could change just because men in England, America, or Japan built factories. But that's what happened. Here's how.

You know that when you make anything, you have to make it out of *something*. So the factories that made clothes and furniture, cars and candy had to make these out of something. Some factories made clothes out of cotton that grew in India. Other factories made furniture out of the wood from trees that grew in forests in Africa, Asia, and the countries around the Caribbean Sea. Cars have to have tires, and they are made out of rubber that comes from rubber trees that grow in forests in Africa, Asia, and South America. To make candy, you use sugar that comes from plants that grow in places like Hawaii and Cuba. Now you can begin to see why the Industrial Revolution was felt around the world.

The countries that built the factories needed supplies from all around the world. Those countries were strong and had the advantage of modern ships and weapons built in their factories, so the *industrialized* countries soon moved in and took over a lot of places that had the supplies they wanted—the places where cotton grew, where trees like mahogany and rubber grew, where sugar cane grew. England, France, Germany, and other European countries made colonies of most of Africa and a lot of Asia as well. Japan conquered Korea and some other places nearby. Even the United States came to own places like Hawaii and the Philippines although we didn't call these our colonies.

Now the people who lived in all these places weren't very happy to have foreigners coming in and taking over. They felt the same way about them that you might feel about a bully at school. They didn't like that big guy who wanted to push all the little guys around. Sometimes the conquerors brought good things, like modern medical care. But, still, nobody really wants to be bossed around by somebody else. So, less than a hundred years later, the colonies around the world rose up, just as we did during the American Revolution, and fought to become independent. You'll read more about this later.

You know that sometimes changes aren't always all good. One bad thing that happened because of the Industrial Revolution was the taking of colonies by the rich industrialized countries. Another bad result of the Industrial Revolution is still troubling us today. That is pollution. Also, many natural resources are being used up or destroyed. Pollution and the loss of natural resources are called environmental problems.

We know that factories that make wonderful things sometimes discharge poisons into the air that we breathe and the water we drink. That is pollution. People can get sick from breathing polluted air and drinking polluted water.

We know that over the years, many of the earth's forests have been cut down so the wood from the trees could be used for building houses and furniture and for making paper. When a forest is destroyed or an ocean is polluted, then the animals that live there have no place to live any more, and so they die out. When there are no more animals of any

Urban factories spewing smoke

given kind, we say that they are *extinct*. Today, a number of animals are in danger of becoming extinct, either because they are being killed or because their homes are being destroyed. Can you name any of these animals?

These are some of the problems caused by the Industrial Revolution that we have not yet solved. Do you have any ideas how they could be solved? There's something for you to talk about.

There are four big things to remember about the Industrial Revolution. A lot of people worked in factories instead of on farms. The towns grew into the large cities that we know today. The industrialized nations became so rich and powerful that they could control most of the rest of the world. And we still have to solve environmental problems that were caused by the Industrial Revolution.

84

A World at War

Now, I must tell you about a fight so big that the world was at war.

There was a little country in Europe called Serbia.[1] It was next door to the big country of Austria. But though little Serbia and big Austria were next-door neighbors, they were not good neighbors. Each was always saying mean things about the other. This was because Austria ruled over several other kinds of people besides Austrians, and some of these people were related to the Serbians. The Serbians used to say that Austria treated these people unfairly. But the Serbians did more than *say* things. They formed secret societies to send people into Austria to stir up trouble. Austria said that Serbia was trying to break up the kingdom of Austria by making the people discontented and unwilling to be ruled by Austria.

Then a young man who lived in Serbia shot an Austrian prince, the prince who was to have been the next king of Austria.

Of course Austria was furious and blamed Serbia. The Serbs said they were very sorry but they had nothing to do with the death of the prince. However, Austria wouldn't accept Serbia's apology. Austria thought the time had come to punish Serbia for all the trouble Austria was having. In spite of everything the other countries in Europe could do to stop this, Austria declared war on Serbia.

---

[1] Serbia [sûr′ bē ə]

Europe in 1914

The trouble started to spread just like fire in a field of grass. Russia took the side of Serbia and ordered its army to get ready to fight. Germany took the side of Austria. Ever since the time of the Franco-Prussian War and Bismarck and William, the big countries of Europe had been training for a fight. Nearly all these countries had been getting together in two groups, one made up of the friends of Germany; the other, friends of France.

Russia was a friend of France and so when Russia got ready to fight, France ordered its armies to get ready to help Russia. That meant Germany would be between two big enemies, France on one side and Russia on the other. Germany decided to strike quickly and destroy France before Russia could hit hard from the other side.

To get at France quickly, Germany had to go through the little country of Belgium.[2] Germany and France had agreed that neither would march armies through Belgium but when the war began German armies marched in anyway and pushed aside the Belgians, who tried to stop them. Germany's armies rushed on toward the capital of France, Paris. They got as far as a river called the Marne,[3] only twenty miles from Paris. There, the French under General Joffre[4] stopped the German army. This battle of the Marne is probably one of the most famous of all the battles you have heard about so far in this history, for though the war went on for four years after this battle, if the Germans had won at the Marne, they would have captured Paris and probably made France a German country.

By this time, England had come into the war on the side of France and Belgium and Russia. England had the strongest navy in the world. The German navy wasn't strong enough to beat the English navy, so Germany kept its battleships at home. Germany had to fight from under the sea with submarines, which were hard for the English ships to catch. It was the first war in history in which battles were fought not only on land and on sea but up in the air and down under the water.

The German submarines sometimes sank ships belonging to countries that weren't in the war. That, of course, made these countries very angry with Germany, and so before the war was over, almost all the countries of the world were in the fight. That is why we call it a World War. Later there was another World War, so we call this World War I just as we call a king George I so as not to confuse him with George II.

Millions of people had been killed, millions of soldiers had been wounded, billions of dollars had been spent, and still the war went on, with neither side able to win. All of a sudden Russia had a revolution. Russia was so poor that some of its soldiers received no ammunition and

---

[2] Belgium [bel´ jəm]   [4] Joffre [zhôf´ rə]
[3] Marne [märn]

no medical supplies. The Russian people killed their ruler, the czar, and his family, and refused to fight any longer. Things began to look pretty bad for the Allies.

The United States did not enter the war until 1917, almost three years after it had begun; it did so after German submarines began sinking American ships and killing Americans.

America was so far off—three thousand miles away and across an ocean—that it seemed impossible that we could do much in the war. However, in a very short time, the United States had sent two million soldiers across in ships. Under General Pershing they fought great battles.

At last, Germany and its friends surrendered and on November 11, 1918, Germany signed a paper agreeing to do everything the Allies asked. The first World War in history was ended. The kaiser went to live in Holland, and Germany became a republic. Big Austria became little Austria, for all its lands and many of its people were taken away and

Surrender of Germans

made into independent countries. Little Serbia disappeared altogether. In its place was formed the new country of Yugoslavia, which included Serbia and several other small states.

85

A Short Twenty Years

How long is a piece of string? That's a silly question and probably would get a silly answer.

How long is twenty years? That sounds like a silly question too, but it's not as silly as it sounds. To a dog twenty years is a long time, more than a lifetime. To a man, twenty years is not so long. In the history of the world, twenty years is just a tiny moment.

It was twenty years—twenty years and a few months—between the end of World War I and the start of World War II. Now, twenty years between two huge world wars is a very short time. Most countries had not fully recovered from World War I before World War II began. This chapter is about those twenty years of peace.

When World War I ended, people everywhere hoped and prayed that there would be no more wars. World War I was even called the "War to End All Wars." When World War I ended, the leaders of the Allied governments met at Versailles in France and drew up a peace treaty known as the Treaty of Versailles.

The treaty said that Germany should have a little army big enough to keep order in Germany but not big enough to make war with. There were to be no army or navy airplanes in Germany, no army tanks, and no submarines. The treaty also said that Germany would have to pay large sums of money to the Allied nations to help pay for what it had destroyed in the war.

Then to try to keep the peace, a League of Nations was set up with headquarters in Switzerland. The greatest invention I can think of would be some thing or some way to keep wars from starting. People hoped the League of Nations would be the great invention that would keep wars from breaking out. Each country was to send men to act for that country at the meetings of the League. When war threatened, the League would warn the warlike country and ask it to bring its case before the judges of a World Court and let them settle the trouble there instead of having the question decided by war.

The League of Nations tried, but it didn't succeed. There were several reasons for this. One was that the United States decided not to join the League. The United States did not want the League to be able to say when the United States would have to send soldiers to help stop another country from making war, in case war started in spite of the World Court's decision.

Another reason that the League didn't work was that there was no way it could make nations do what it told them. It could only ask that the nations do what it wanted them to do. It could not make them do it.

A sign may say "KEEP OFF THE GRASS." If you walk on the grass in spite of the sign, the sign can't stop you, but a nearby policeman can. The League of Nations was like a "KEEP OFF" sign without a policeman.

Never before, I suppose, did so many people hope and pray that wars could be stopped. Other ways to stop wars, besides the League of Nations, were tried, too.

People thought that if nations were not so heavily armed, it might help. The countries with the biggest navies held a conference in Washington and agreed to limit the size of their navies. People thought, too, that if all the countries of the world solemnly promised not to make war, it might help. So an anti-war treaty was made. More than fifty countries signed this treaty and promised to give up war.

Yet wars did break out again, in spite of the League of Nations, in spite of limiting the navies, in spite of the anti-war treaty. There was no force in the world that could be used to stop a war when one started. When a building catches fire in a city, someone calls the fire department. Firemen come rushing with their fire engines and put the fire out. When a fist fight starts in a city, someone calls the police department, and policemen are sent to stop the fight.

But there was no fire department or police department to put out a war when it started. Before long, wars started again. Even the twenty years of peace between world wars were not free from wars. The first new war was in Asia.

After Commodore Perry had opened Japan to foreign trade, Japan had quickly become an industrial nation. Japan had learned the bad things as well as the good things of our civilization. It had built a large war-making modern army and navy. In 1931, Japan used that army to take the northern part of China, called Manchuria,[1] away from China. Later the Japanese started to take over all of China. Of course the Chinese fought to keep the Japanese from doing this. Other countries wrote letters to the Japanese government saying they did not like to see Japan using its armies against China.

"What about that anti-war treaty you signed?" these other countries said to Japan.

But as no other country tried to stop the Japanese by force, the war continued. The Chinese fought hard, but they had very few army supplies and soon Japan had taken all the eastern coast of China and

---

[1] Manchuria [man chōōr′ ē ə]

driven the Chinese government into western China. The League of Nations didn't know how to stop the war, and this war was still going on when World War II started.

While this was going on in Asia, another war had started in Africa. The Italian army marched into the ancient country of Ethiopia. Ethiopia was the same country as the ancient Axum. Do you remember Axum's famous king, who became a Christian in 350 A.D.? That's right. His name was Ezana.

Since the time of King Ezana, Ethiopia had always been independent and ruled by a king. Italy had tried to conquer Ethiopia fifty years earlier and had failed. Now the Ethiopian king's army had a few guns, but his soldiers were mostly armed with spears. The Italian army used airplanes, bombs, artillery, and even poison gas, and so it soon conquered the Ethiopians.

Then a civil war broke out in Spain, in Europe. One set of Spaniards fought another set of Spaniards about which group would govern Spain. Instead of trying to stop the war, Russia sent soldiers to help one side, and Germany and Italy sent soldiers to help the other side.

One, two, three—war, war, war—China, Ethiopia, Spain. The League of Nations hadn't been able to stop the Japanese from attacking China. It couldn't keep Italy from taking Ethiopia though it tried to punish Italy by stopping other countries from sending supplies to Italy. But Italy took Ethiopia anyway. The League had not stopped the war in Spain. As an invention for stopping wars, the League of Nations hadn't worked.

There were other important happenings besides wars in this twenty years of peace. For the first ten years of the peace, people were busy making and selling and buying and using the peacetime things that they could not enjoy while World War I was going on. In the United States, almost everyone who wanted to work could get a job. Factories were busy turning out everything from automobiles to clothespins. Business was booming. People were making money and spending it. Many people thought these booming times would go on forever. But they were wrong. The boom didn't last. What businessmen call a *depression* followed the boom. Good jobs became scarce. Millions of people could not get jobs at all. Factories could not sell as many things as they could make. Many factories had to close. This caused more people to be without jobs. How can a man or woman get money to buy food or clothes or anything if he or she can't find a job? Thus the last ten years of the peace were a troubled time of depression.

The depression had been going on for several years and people were getting desperate when a new president, Franklin Delano Roosevelt, was elected. He became president just when the depression seemed hopeless, when everything looked black and gloomy. People were afraid of what would happen to them. The first day he was president, Roosevelt said, "The only thing we have to fear is fear itself." Roosevelt seemed to know what to do. He asked that laws be passed so money could be given to people who could not find work.

Then the government hired thousands of people to work in any way they could. Artists painted pictures, musicians gave concerts, writers wrote books, laborers raked leaves, dug ditches, built parks, and did many other kinds of work; and all these people were paid for their work by the government. Roosevelt tried out many new ways of running the country. His way of being president became known as the New Deal.

Roosevelt helped the poor people at the expense of the rich people. And yet Roosevelt's family had always been rich, and Roosevelt himself was a rich man. When he was thirty nine years old, he had become ill with polio that left him with his legs paralyzed. After that he could stand only with the help of canes and with steel braces on his legs. He couldn't walk at all but could take a few steps leaning on someone's arm. But in spite of such a handicap, Roosevelt twice became governor of the state of New York and at last president of the United States.

A president of the United States is elected for four years. Every four years the people vote for their next president. Roosevelt was elected for a second four years. The Father of his Country, George Washington, had been made president for two terms of four years each. Washington had refused to be elected for three terms. Since George Washington had refused a third term, no president had ever been elected three times. But when Franklin D.

*President Roosevelt about to address
the nation on the radio*

Roosevelt's eight years were up, he became president a third time—for four more years, four years longer than any president had been before. And when twelve years were up, Franklin D. Roosevelt was elected president a fourth time. That would have made sixteen years as president for Roosevelt if he had not died before his fourth term was over. Roosevelt was president from 1933 to 1945. No other man had been president more than eight years, nor been elected more than twice. Roosevelt had been elected four times in a row.

Roosevelt wasn't able to stop the depression right away. He did show people that everything wasn't hopeless, and he did keep people from going hungry and perhaps starving. But it cost the American people millions and millions of dollars.

Before Roosevelt's third term had begun, the twenty years of peace were over. World War II had started in Europe. The people of the United States hoped their country could keep out of this war. But Roosevelt felt that America might be attacked even though the war was far away across the ocean. He led the country into getting ready for war in case it came to us. And when we were attacked, Roosevelt led the country through the war to victory against Germany, Japan, and Italy. He died a month before the Germans surrendered.

Twenty years of peace—twenty years of an invention-to-stop-wars that didn't work—a boom and depression, and then the biggest and worst war of all. How long is twenty years? It was a short time indeed between two world wars.

86

Modern *Barbarians*

ITALY had a king, but the real ruler of the country was not the king but a dictator named Mussolini.[1] He became dictator some years after the end of World War I. It was Mussolini who led Italy into war with Ethiopia.

Do you remember the story of Cincinnatus in the days of ancient Rome, and how he was made a dictator and saved Rome? And after the enemy was defeated how he gave up being a dictator and went back to being a simple farmer again?

Well, Mussolini was a dictator quite different from Cincinnatus. He did not give up being a dictator. Mussolini made himself more and more powerful all the time.

Now, the people of a country run by a dictator are seldom really happy because they have to do whatever the dictator tells them to do whether they like it or not. What the people think, they must not say for fear of saying something the dictator might not like. People may be imprisoned without a trial. They cannot read about both sides of a question in their newspapers, for the newspapers only print what the dictator wants them to print. People are always afraid in a dictatorship, for the dictator's spies are always listening and watching and waiting for someone to make a

---

[1] Mussolini [mōōs ə lē′ nē]

slip—to say something against the dictator or do something he might not like. It's then goodbye to that person.

The short twenty years of peace after World War I were long enough for several dictators to come to power in Europe.

Mussolini was bad enough. He took away the liberties of the people in Italy. He made war on the Ethiopians just because he wanted their country.

But Mussolini was "small potatoes" to another dictator who also came to power in Europe. This was Adolf Hitler, who became the dictator of Germany. Hitler's gang called themselves Nazis. The word NAZI was made up of the initial letters of the German words for National Socialist German Workers' Party, but most people think NASTY would be a better way to spell it. You might think when you hear the word *party* that it had something to do with a good time like a birthday party. But the party of the Nazis meant a society or group of people who were the followers of Hitler, Hitler's gang.

The Nazis were brutal and cruel. They did horrible things that even Alaric and his Goths, or Attila and his Huns, would not have done. I think the Nazi gang was worse than the Goths or the Huns because the Goths and the Huns were living at a time in history when almost the whole world was ignorant and more primitive. The Nazis lived in a civilized Christian country, with schools and universities and churches, amid the science and knowledge and rules of good behavior of the twentieth century.

The Nazis were against all Jews. They began to persecute the Jews of Germany. Some of the Jews escaped to other countries, but those who could not get away were put in concentration camps where most of them were tortured and killed. The Nazis built large gas chambers, which were big rooms into which poison gas could be piped. They would crowd the

Jews—men, women, and children—into these chambers and turn on the gas. In this way the Nazis murdered millions of Jews.

Not only Jews but thousands of other people in Germany who were thought to be against the Nazis were put in the concentration camps, where many of them died.

Hitler became chancellor and dictator of Germany in 1933. He was a powerful speaker and by his speeches he could move his listeners to do anything he wanted. He did not depend only on his speeches. His Nazi spies were everywhere and whoever said a word against him was apt to be arrested by the Nazi secret police.

Hitler planned to make Germany the most powerful nation in the world. To do this he started to build a huge army. Everyone in Germany was supposed to help make the Germans a warlike nation. Even boys and girls belonged to Nazi clubs and learned to drill and work for the nation. Those men who weren't in the army or navy or air force were put in labor battalions to build forts and military roads and fighting equipment.

I told you that the Treaty of Versailles did not allow the Germans to have a big army or an air force. How about that? But Hitler said that Germany was not bound by the Treaty of Versailles, even though it had been signed by the German government. Before long the Germans had a huge army and air force. Then the Germans started to take lands that were not theirs. Their army marched into Austria and made Austria a part of Germany. Then they began seizing other pieces of land around them.

Now, England had a treaty or agreement with Poland, which was the next country to Germany on the east. This treaty with Poland said that England would protect the independence of Poland. When Germany threatened to attack Poland, England warned Germany about the treaty and said it was England's duty under the treaty to protect Poland. Hitler went ahead anyway and attacked Poland. First he sent his airplanes over

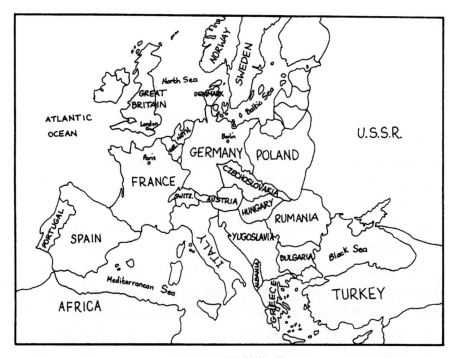

Europe in World War II

Poland and bombed the Poles. Then came the German army, and in a few days it was all over for the Polish army. So England declared war on Germany. It was in 1939 when this happened and World War II began.

Russia was on the other side of Poland, and Russia marched into Poland from the eastern side. There wasn't any Poland left.

Next Germany attacked Norway and Denmark. Norway was seized by German soldiers, who were carried by airplanes and were helped by a few traitors in Norway.

Then Germany attacked France and Belgium and Holland. The German airplanes and tanks were too much for the French, Belgian, and Dutch armies and for the English army that had been sent to France to help them. As soon as Mussolini saw the Germans were winning, he brought Italy into the war on the side of Germany. Soon Holland and Belgium and most of France were taken by the Germans. The German army marched into Paris. Thousands of Frenchmen were sent to work as slaves in Germany, and only England was left to fight the Nazis.

You remember I told you that Parliament was the real ruler of England and not the king. The leader of Parliament, and the man who carries out the laws Parliament makes, is called the prime minister. The prime minister at this time of great danger for England was Winston Churchill. Winston Churchill was a brave and stubborn man. Although England's army had lost its weapons in France, and there were fewer than one hundred tanks in all England and the English had fewer airplanes and a much smaller army than the Germans, Churchill refused to give up. Churchill made speeches over the radio to the people to encourage them to fight on in spite of all the odds against them. Churchill said, "We shall defend our island, whatever the cost may be. We shall fight on the beaches, we shall fight on the landing grounds, we shall fight in the fields and in the streets, we shall fight in the hills: we shall never surrender."

Does that remind you of the answer Leonidas gave to the Persians before the battle of Thermopylae over two thousand years ago? Leonidas said, "Come and take us." Churchill's speech was not short and *laconic* but it meant the same thing.

The Nazis got ready to invade England.

They brought more than three thousand barges to the coast of Europe opposite England. These were to carry the Nazi soldiers across the English Channel. But first Hitler wanted to defeat the English air force, so his troops could land in England more easily. Nazi planes were sent over in great fleets to bomb the English airfields and seaports.

Then Hitler met his first defeat. The English had many fewer planes, but they were able to outfight the Nazi planes. This was called the Battle of Britain. In the first ten days of this air battle, the English shot down 697 planes and lost only 153 themselves!

When Hitler found his planes could not destroy the English air force, he sent fleets of airplanes day and night to bomb London. Thousands and thousands of London civilians were killed by these German bombs. However, the English pilots of the Royal Air Force kept shooting down so many German planes that at last the Germans were afraid to send planes over England except at night. All during the war these night raids on English cities kept up, but Hitler had lost his best chance to invade England. The English had had a few more months to get some weapons and build up their army. Prime Minister Churchill said of the English airplane pilots, "Never in the field of human conflict was so much owed by so many to so few."

87

Fighting the Dictators

THE story of the biggest war that ever was cannot be told all in one chapter.

So this chapter is about World War II, too.

After France was taken, only the British Empire was left unconquered of all those countries that Germany had attacked. Even after the Battle of Britain, no one was sure that the Nazis would not try to invade England. But just keeping the Germans out of England would not win the war. No one believed that the English by themselves could beat the Germans. That is, no one believed it except the English. They refused to give up and they kept right on trying to beat the most powerful, the best trained, and best equipped army in the world.

Other parts of the British Empire sent soldiers to help England. But these other countries (Canada, Australia, South Africa, New Zealand, and India) were far away across seas in which German submarines hunted for ships to torpedo.

Mussolini had brought Italy into the war on the side of Germany. Japan was burning, killing, and bombing in China, and Japan was friendly to Germany.

No country could be sure it would be safe from attack. Who would be next on the list?

Even the United States, three thousand miles across the ocean from Europe, felt its defenses should be strengthened. The very small American army was made into a very large army and American factories were put to work making tanks and airplanes and other war supplies. New ships began to be built for the navy. A large modern army, however, cannot be raised and trained and equipped in just a few days. It takes not a few days, nor months, but years. Warships take even longer than an army. Luckily for us the president, Franklin D. Roosevelt, led the country to prepare itself for war when he did, for just about a year later we were attacked. Even then we weren't ready. But that comes later in the story.

Now, while the Germans were still busy setting up their rule in France and Denmark and Norway and trying to subdue England with their airplanes, Italy tried to capture Greece and Egypt. But the Italians were not as good fighters as the Germans. A brave little Greek army held off the Italians there while an English general in North Africa, using soldiers from all parts of the British Empire, beat two Italian armies that had five times as many soldiers as he had. This freed Ethiopia from the Italians.

But then the Germans sent an army that conquered Greece in three weeks. They sent an army also to North Africa, which fought the British there for the next three years.

Suddenly Hitler attacked Russia. Now, you might think this was a foolish thing for Hitler to do. Russia was a huge country with a large army. Even Napoleon had been unable to take Russia. But Hitler knew that if he conquered Russia, Germany would gain great quantities of oil, wheat, lumber, and minerals. Besides, he thought Russia might attack Germany, for Russia had been building up a big army ever since the Nazis had started their conquests. Hitler had by now brought fifteen European countries under Nazi rule and his armies had never been beaten, though his air force had not been able to make England surrender.

Into Russia rushed the Nazis. They hoped to destroy the Russian armies quickly. Far into Russia the Nazis fought, but the Russian armies, though driven back, were not destroyed. Finally the Nazis reached Moscow and attacked the city on three sides at once. Hitler announced that the battle of Moscow would be the death blow of the Russian armies. But he spoke too soon. The Russians held Moscow for weeks against Germans, who were attacking with thousands of tanks and airplanes. Russian soldiers and the civilians of the city fought side by side to defend it. Finally the Russians pushed back the German army. Moscow was saved.

However, keeping the Germans from taking Moscow would not win the war, just as keeping them out of England wouldn't win the war. Germany and Italy still held almost all of Europe.

Then just as the Russians were driving back the Nazis from Moscow, Japan struck. Japanese airplanes without warning bombed the American fleet at Pearl Harbor in Hawaii. This was on December 7, 1941. All the American warships there were sunk or damaged and more than two thousand Americans were killed. The next day Britain and the United States declared war on Japan. Four days later, Germany and Italy declared war on the United States.

The United States was still not ready to fight both Germany and Japan at the same time. Our new armies were not yet trained, and a new fleet was not yet ready to take the place of the ships bombed at Pearl Harbor. It was lucky that Russia was fighting so fiercely in Europe, for this kept millions of Nazis occupied there and gave us another year to get ready. As fast as our factories could make them and ships could carry them, we sent tanks and trucks and other supplies to Russia and to the British army in Egypt.

Japan, however, could not be stopped at first. The Japanese captured

Pacific areas in World War II

the Philippine Islands, which belonged to the United States. They captured the great British naval base of Singapore in Asia. They captured the islands of the East Indies, which belonged to Holland. They captured Siam and Burma and pushed on toward India. They captured the Malay Peninsula. They had already seized French Indo-China and a lot of China.

You probably have a map of Asia in your atlas or geography book. If you look these places up on the map, you'll see how far Japan's armies went in Asia. On a map of the Pacific Ocean, you can find the islands they captured far from Japan, islands with strange names you would never hear about in a history book except for the battles that were fought there in World War II:

GUAM AND WAKE

NEW GUINEA[1]

BOUGAINVILLE[2] AND GUADALCANAL[3]

KISKA[4] IN THE ALEUTIANS[5]

Many of the places the Japanese captured were defended bravely. The Philippines were taken only after the American and Philippine soldiers were all either killed or captured, except the few that escaped to the hills, where little bands of men kept on doing what damage they could to the Japanese conquerors.

President Roosevelt and Prime Minister Churchill had decided to try to beat Hitler first and then clean up the Japanese. So American and British soldiers were sent to North Africa and fought and beat the German army there. Then they attacked Italy.

Great numbers of American and British soldiers were assembled in England. From England their airplanes bombed the Germans and fought the German airplanes. Finally, in June, 1944, all was ready for the attack on the main German armies. A huge force of American and British soldiers, under the command of General Dwight Eisenhower, crossed the English Channel and landed on the coast of Normandy in France. They fought the Germans in fierce and bloody battles and chased them back across France to Germany. France and Belgium and Holland were made free and became again independent countries.

Meanwhile, the Russians who had been fighting the Germans all this time on the other side of Germany, put on a tremendous drive and pushed the Germans back into Germany. They captured Berlin, the capital. Mussolini had been caught and shot by the Italians themselves in Italy,

---

[1] Guinea [gin′ ē]
[2] Bougainville [boo gan vēl′]
[3] Guadalcanal [gwäd l kə nal′]

[4] Kiska [kis′ kə]
[5] Aleutians [a loo′ shənz]

and now Hitler, with his armies defeated, committed suicide. He could not stand the thought of defeat.

The terrible Nazis were at last beaten, but thousands of people were still homeless and hungry and had to be fed with food shipped in from other countries.

On the other side of the world, the war against Japan was still going on. Many battles had been fought against the Japanese—airplane battles, sea battles, and land battles. One after another, the islands Japan had overrun were recaptured, not easily but by fierce and bloody fights often with the heat and diseases of tropical jungles to add to the difficulties of our soldiers. In the Pacific war, General Douglas MacArthur was the commanding general. His armies with the help of the navy recaptured the Philippines. They were ready to invade Japan itself, when a terrible new weapon was used against the Japanese, and Japan surrendered.

This new weapon was the atomic bomb. Just two of them were dropped from American airplanes onto two Japanese cities. They caused such awful destruction that only two were needed.

Germany surrendered in May, Japan in August of 1945. The biggest and most terrible war in the history of the world was over.

88

A New Spirit in the World

AFTER World War II was over, a lot of people everywhere were talking about making the world a better place. After World War I you remember, most countries of the world joined in a League of Nations to keep new wars from starting; but wars kept right on happening anyway.

After World War II, the countries of the world decided to try again to provide a way for countries to talk with each other to try to solve their differences peacefully rather than by fighting. So they formed the United Nations. The headquarters of the United Nations is right here in the United States, in New York City. Have you ever visited the U.N. headquarters? If you go to New York, you can take a tour of the building and meet people from all over the world who work there.

The United Nations has been more successful than the League of Nations was. Still, there have been a lot of problems that the world has had to face since the end of World War II. I guess it would be too much to expect that the world could get by for very long without any problems. But we can always hope.

Here is one problem that did get solved, at least partly solved, after World War II. The United Nations helped. After the war was over, a lot of people everywhere were talking about making the world a better place. During the war, people had said that it was wrong for Germany and Japan to conquer and rule other countries and their people. After the war was over, some men and women began to ask why some other nations still had the right to rule countries they had conquered earlier. Remember how the industrialized nations had taken colonies to provide their factories with supplies like wood, rubber, cotton, and sugar? Well, after World War II they still had those colonies. In fact, the British colonies were so widespread that the English bragged that, "The sun never sets on the British Empire." Do you know what this means?

Imagine owning so much of the rest of the world that the sun was always shining on a part of the world you owned. The British owned countries like Ghana and Kenya in Africa, big countries like India, and small islands like the Bahamas and Jamaica. The British were very proud of their big empire. But a lot of people in Africa, India, and the islands of the Caribbean weren't so happy about the British. In fact, they had been talking for a long time about getting rid of those foreigners! And after World War II the British were tired from having fought so hard against the Germans and the Japanese. Besides that, people all over the world were saying that every nation should be able to choose its own government. In this discussion, it was hard for the Americans to take the side of their old ally, the English. Why do you suppose this was true? Do you suppose it's because we remembered our own American Revolution?

Leaders in different colonies worked in different ways to win independence for their people. In some places, men organized armies just as George Washington had organized the American army. In other places, men and women organized less violent protests, like marches and speeches. One of the best known heroes of this time was a man in India named Gandhi.

Mohandas Gandhi[1] didn't look much like the hero of a revolution! He was small and thin. He didn't talk much like a revolutionary leader. He said that people should not be violent in their protests. Now, India was a British colony. Gandhi had decided that the British were, at heart, a moral people, so he felt that he just needed to make them, as well as the rest of the world, see what was right. Then they would grant India its independence without a lot of people being killed.

Gandhi was very clever in thinking up things to do to draw attention to India's desire to become independent. He knew that England kept India to make money from the resources that India provided for England's factories and from the taxes that Indians paid. So he decided to make it harder for England to make money from India.

You know that the English in India had been buying cotton to ship to factories in England. This cotton was made into cloth and clothing. Some of the clothing was then shipped back to India and sold at very high prices. The English, of course, kept the profits. Now, before I tell you what Gandhi did, let me tell you what he *didn't* do. He

Gandhi spinning

---

[1] Mohandas Gandhi [mō hən däs′ gän′ dē]

didn't shoot the English living in India. He didn't burn the fields of cotton. He didn't try to sink the English ships that carried the cotton and later the cloth and clothing. He didn't do any of those violent things to drive the English away. What he did do was this. He asked all Indians to spend several hours a day spinning and weaving their own cloth. This way, they would have plenty of cloth without ever having to buy any more from England. So the English wouldn't be making money, but they also wouldn't have any excuse to come and shoot the Indian protesters either. Wasn't Gandhi a clever revolutionary?

Here's another thing he did. The English collected a big tax on salt. Indians had to have salt to preserve their food because most of them had no refrigerator. So the English had a sure source of tax money. Remember how Americans felt about the taxes they paid to England before the American Revolution? Well, the Indians felt the same way about the taxes they had to pay to England. Gandhi figured out a way to avoid paying the tax on salt without breaking the law. He led a great march to the sea. We all know that ocean water is very salty. Gandhi knew this too. So he led thousands of Indians to the edge of the sea. Once there, he taught them how to make the sea water evaporate. This would leave them lots of salt. This way his people could have all the salt they needed—without paying the tax and without breaking any law! When soldiers beat the people making salt, people everywhere, even in England, said that the soldiers were wrong.

Gandhi became very famous all around the world. People thought that it was marvelous that he could make such a strong protest without using violence. Finally the pressure on England became too great, and England gave up. Soon after World War II was over, Indians had won their independence.

Once India was independent, other countries followed quickly. Leaders in Africa, like Kwame Nkrumah[2] in Ghana and Jomo Kenyatta[3] of

---

[2] Kwame Nkrumah [kwä′ mē ən krōō′ mə]   [3] Jomo Kenyatta [jō′ mō ken yä′ tə]

Kenya, won independence for their countries. Algeria became independent from France, but only after a long war. The United States agreed to give the Philippines independence . . . and so it went all over the world. Country after country in Africa and Asia became independent. Large and small islands in the Pacific and Caribbean became independent. Many of these countries were poor and really had to struggle. Many of them are still struggling, but at least they are no longer ruled by foreigners. Do you know what? They almost all celebrate their Independence Day just as we celebrate the Fourth of July. Wouldn't it be fun to travel all around the world and visit every country on its national holiday? Now that almost every country is independent, that would make a very long trip! Do you suppose they all have fireworks?

89

A New **BIG POWER** in the World

AFTER World War II and all its killing and destruction, only two really strong countries were left in the world. These were both very

BIG COUNTRIES.

One of the reasons these two countries were strong is that they were

SO BIG.

On all that land they had lots of the resources a country needs to make it strong: land to grow food; lots of water; wood to build things; and minerals like iron, coal, and oil. These all help make a country strong.

Have you guessed which two big countries I'm talking about? One is very easy to guess. It's the United States. The other is Russia.

During World War II, you remember, these two giants were friends. They were allies. They fought on the same side. After the war was over, they became rivals. They competed to see which would be the stronger. This made for a lot of trouble in the world.

Let me tell you what had been happening in Russia since you last read about that country.

Peter the Great was a ruler of Russia called a czar or emperor. Russia was ruled by a czar or czarina (as a Russian queen was called) for almost two hundred years after Peter the Great. Then the Russians had a big and bloody revolution. This began in 1917. The czar who was ruling then and all of his family were shot.

The reason for the Russian Revolution was about the same as for the French Revolution. The czar and his nobles had great riches and power, but most of the people were very poor and they had no hope of life ever getting better for them.

In 1917 Russia had been fighting in World War I for three hard years. The war had made the misery of the people even more hopeless. When the revolution started, the soldiers stopped fighting and came home to help overthrow the rulers.

A Russian named Lenin had been working and plotting for many years to start the revolution, and he and his friends took charge. Soon Lenin was the head of the revolutionary government and the ruler of Russia.

In 1922, after the revolution, Russia was called the Union of Soviet Socialist Republics, shortened to U.S.S.R., the Soviet Union, or the Soviets. The U.S.S.R. included not only Russia, but eventually fourteen other republics in Europe and in Asia that had been conquered by Russia.

Lenin believed in a kind of government called communism. In communism everything was supposed to belong to the state for the good of all the poor people. Most of the big farms, for instance, were taken away from their rich owners and made into collective farms. A collective farm is a large farm where everybody works together to raise the crops and the profit goes partly to all the people on the collective farm.

All the factories and stores in a communist country are owned not by private people, as they mostly are in our country, but by the state. The communist state itself is supposed to be owned by all the people together. This was a great change from the rule of the czars where most of the wealth and power was in the hands of the czar and his nobles. The communists felt they had to be sure that the new government would work, so they gave a great deal of power to the head of the Communist party. He became as powerful as a dictator.

After the revolution there was much suffering at first. Many people even starved to death, and many who were not in favor of communism were shot. But more and more schools were built, and this was good, for few people had been able to go to school when the czars had ruled. The poor people were still poor, but they felt now that there was a great difference from being poor under the czar with no hope of life ever becoming better for them. Now there was hope of better things to come. Great dams were built across the rivers to supply electricity for steel plants and tractor factories. The nobles' palaces were turned into museums for the people. Subways were built in Moscow. The army was given good leaders and was well trained.

The communists did two things that worried other countries a great deal. They made religious practice unlawful so that all houses of worship were closed. And they believed that communism should be spread all over the world. Even in countries where the people were not ill-treated and were satisfied with their own kinds of government, the communists hoped to get revolutions going so that communism could be made the form of government everywhere.

When Lenin died, the man who took his place as the ruler of the Soviet Union had a long name which would be very hard for you or me to pronounce because we are not used to the Russian language. But luckily he was called by his nickname, Stalin,[1] which is quite easy and means "man of steel." Stalin[2] had first studied as a young man to be a priest. But then, instead of becoming a priest he had become a communist. It was of course very dangerous to be a communist under the czar's government, and Stalin had been put in prison and had often had to hide from the czar's men for trying to stir up a revolution. His experiences had made him hard and tough and that's why he was nicknamed Stalin.

Under Stalin, the Soviets built more factories and large new cities. When Germany suddenly attacked the U.S.S.R. in World War II, the Soviet armies under Stalin fought desperately against the Germans. Finally, as you know, the Soviet armies drove the Germans out of the Soviet Union and entered Germany from the Soviet Union, while the American and British armies were coming in from France.

After World War II, other countries found it hard to get along with the U.S.S.R. because the Soviets had ideas about government and freedom so very different from the ideas of democracies like the United States and England.

The Soviet Union was run by a dictator. People were not allowed to do or say what they wanted but only what the government let them. The newspapers in the U.S.S.R. were never free to print what they wanted to print but only what the government told them to print. Visitors from other countries were not welcome in the U.S.S.R., and very few Soviets were allowed to visit other countries.

The biggest country in Europe, and the biggest country in Asia, and the biggest country in the whole world had now become also one of the most important and powerful countries in the whole world. It also soon became the most dangerous country in the world. I'll tell you why in the next chapter.

---

[1] Stalin [stä′ lin]
[2] His real name was Iosif Vissarionovich Dzugashvili.

90

Trying to Keep Peace

"IF at first you don't succeed try, try again."

After World War I you remember, most countries of the world joined in the League of Nations to keep new wars from starting; but wars kept right on happening anyway.

After World War II, most countries of the world joined together in a United Nations to try again to keep new wars from starting.

This time the United States was quite willing to be a member of the United Nations and this helped because the United States had become just about the most powerful and important country in the world. The Soviet Union was strong and powerful, too, and it also joined the United Nations.

Almost right away, trouble began. Most countries after the war let most of their soldiers leave the armies and go back to their peacetime jobs. But the Soviets kept a huge army always ready to fight. Also, the U.S.S.R. started right away trying to upset the governments of other countries and have communists take over other countries. Almost every country touching the U.S.S.R. was seized by communists. These communists weren't always Soviets, but many of them had been trained in the Soviet Union and did whatever the Soviet Union wanted them to do. Even the huge country of China was conquered by Chinese communist armies who drove out the republican government. Whenever communists took over a country, the people of that country lost most of their rights. They became almost like slaves. They could not own property. They were not free to move around, and if they spoke against the communists, they did become slaves—or were shot.

In the United Nations' meetings, the Soviet communists talked and talked and talked, blaming everything wrong in the world on the countries that were not communist countries and saying that only the communist countries really wanted peace. But all the time they were trying to spread communism in other countries and were building up their huge army. Whenever the

United Nations flag and headquarters

United Nations wouldn't do what the Soviets wanted, the Soviet members acted like spoiled children, who sulk and won't play when they can't have everything their own way.

Here is another area of the world where a problem developed with the Soviet Union. There is a little country in Asia across from Japan called Korea. Korea had been ruled by the Japanese. After Japan was beaten in World War II, the United States and the Soviet Union said they would help Korea until the Koreans could get a government of their own working. The United States helped the southern part and the Soviet Union helped the northern part of Korea. The Soviets trained a North Korean communist army and then suddenly this North Korean army came pouring across into South Korea with its tanks and guns and began fighting the South Koreans. A war had started. What would the United Nations do?

What the United Nations did was this: They asked all United Nations countries to send soldiers to Korea to form a United Nations army to help the South Koreans. The United Nations asked an American soldier, General Douglas MacArthur, to be the leader of this army. The United States sent many soldiers and ships and planes. Other countries sent soldiers and ships and planes also. Of course the U.S.S.R. sent no soldiers, for it really started the war by telling the North Koreans what to do.

At first the United Nations army was driven back, but when it got enough soldiers, it finally chased the North Korean communists out of South Korea and back into the farthest mountains of North Korea.

The United Nations hadn't been able to keep this Korean war from starting, but they had shown that they could and would punish a country that started a war. Would this keep other wars from starting? Sadly to say, the answer is no.

Another very murderous war broke out in an Asian nation called Vietnam. Vietnam had been a colony of France before World War II. After the war, like so many other colonies, the Vietnamese struggled to gain their independence. The French fought hard to keep them but were losing. The Vietnamese leader, a man named Ho Chi Minh,[1] was a communist. He managed to win enough battles that Vietnam was divided into two parts: an independent North Vietnam under Ho Chi Minh and an independent South Vietnam under the rule of men who were friends of the French and against the communists. Ho Chi Minh hoped to unite all Vietnam under his rule.

Because the Americans did not want a communist to rule there, they took over the fight that the French had been unable to win. This is how the United States got involved in a long and brutal war in a small country far away in Asia.

Some Americans believed that the U.S. had to fight in this war to help prevent the spread of communism. Other Americans believed just as strongly that it was wrong to let American soldiers be killed fighting in a little country that was so far away. They felt that if the Vietnamese wanted to be ruled by Ho Chi Minh, then it was their business, not ours.

Finally this war did end, but only after thousands and thousands of people had been killed on both sides. In the end, the American armies withdrew and the North Vietnamese communists united the country under their rule.

The wars in Korea and Vietnam had been very costly. Many men, women, and even children lost their lives. Many other people were injured. All the countries involved had to spend a lot of money on guns and ammunition, airplanes and bombs, and all the equipment they needed to fight. This was money that they could not spend on other things—like food and homes and schools and hospitals.

---

[1] Ho Chi Minh [hō chē min]

These years of the rivalry between the United States and the U.S.S.R. lasted until the early 1990s. Then, very suddenly, a strange thing happened. It happened in the U.S.S.R. It was a surprise ending to this competition which was called the Cold War. The Soviet people had really suffered while their government built up its army. They often couldn't buy fresh fruits or meat to eat. Even winter boots were sometimes hard to find. That is a big problem in a country that gets as cold as the U.S.S.R. does.

The Soviet leaders realized that their communist system wasn't working very well. They realized that their people couldn't have both "guns and butter," as the saying goes. So they said that they were going to give up communism and let people own homes and farms and businesses, just as we do in the United States. They also let go of all their neighbors, the countries that they had controlled since the end of World War II. Then, the Union of Soviet Socialist Republics even split up into smaller republics, each one an independent country. This means that the old Russia isn't too BIG any more. Now what do you think of that?

91

Yesterday, Today, and Tomorrow

THERE is a candy shop near where I live. On its sign it says, "Made Fresh Every Hour." History is being made every day. It is being made fresh every hour. We read about it in the newspapers and the magazines, or hear about it on the radio or television.

Up to this time, history has been marked by the story of one war after another—some big, some small, some short, some long. Almost always a fight has been going on somewhere. It has been War, War, War—Fight, Fight, Fight. Children scratch, kick, and bite. But the older we get, the less do we use our fists and feet to settle quarrels. Fighting seems to be a sign of childhood—that we are *kids*—and our fights, that we call wars, a sign of how young the world really is and we really are—a sign that the world is still but a minute or two old.

Now we admire and praise as heroes Horatius, Leonidas, Joan of Arc, General Eisenhower, and those who have defended their countries against the attacks of the enemy, as we would admire a man who stops a burglar or a murderer who attacks his family in the night. But those, whether kings, generals, or princes, who do the attacking and take life with no other excuse than to add to their power or wealth or glory, are no better than burglars, who go forth with a gun and a blackjack to waylay, rob, and murder for the same purpose. War kills, war destroys, war costs millions of lives and billions of dollars—money that could be used to make us happy, to make the world a better place, instead of causing bitterness, suffering, misery, and unhappiness, widows, and orphans. No one is better off, not even the winner. War is a terrible game, in which even the winner loses.

This is certain: If wars do not end, they will be fought with weapons so deadly that all the people of a country or even of a continent may be killed. Already atomic bombs explode with such a blast that one bomb can blow a whole city to smithereens. Perhaps, if wars continue, there won't be anyone left alive in the whole wide world; and that will be the end of human history.

Perhaps wars can be stopped. Many people everywhere go on trying and hoping to end the danger of another war. It isn't easy to prevent wars, but if the United Nations can act like a fire department to put out wars like fires before they get burning too fiercely, then the world can go on with years of peace. New inventions will be used for peace instead of war.

Already man's inventions seem more magical than magic itself. Airplanes and helicopters and spaceships take the place of flying carpets. They're much better, too, than flying carpets for there really are airplanes, but magic carpets never flew except in man's imagination. Whatever you can imagine, no matter how wild your imagination is, will probably someday be invented—if wars can be prevented. You can imagine an invention to prevent all wars and you can be pretty sure it will someday be in use—if another war doesn't spoil everything first.

Inventions are not quite the same as discoveries. If a thing was there all the time but people didn't know about it, it became a discovery, not an invention.

Discoveries and inventions! Discoveries have been just as important as inventions in the last hundred years and seem just as magical. Of course there are no more continents to discover, but there are still wonderful discoveries being made all the time.

Some of the most important discoveries have been about diseases and how to prevent them. These discoveries have long names like:

Vaccination! Smallpox used to be everywhere. It was a deadly disease. The discovery of how to prevent it by vaccination has saved maybe as many lives as war has taken.

Pasteurization[1] of milk! Do you know what that is? It was named for the Frenchman who discovered how to kill deadly germs. You can guess his name. Yes, it was Pasteur.

Inoculation![2] Do you know what that is? Has the doctor ever given you an injection from a needle to protect you from tetanus or typhoid?

Anesthetics! Do you know what that is? Anesthetics put you to sleep if you have to have an operation. Think of the suffering the discovery of anesthetics has prevented.

Penicillin![3] Do you know what this is? It was discovered just in time to save the lives of many wounded men in World War II.

I wish I could tell you about inventions like the electric eye and radar and jet propulsion. I wish I could tell you about famous scientists like Charles Steinmetz and Albert Einstein. I wish I could tell you about all the inventions and discoveries—from vacuum cleaners to cyclotrons, from air conditioners to electron microscopes, from dynamos to lasers and quasars and human-heart transplants. And blood plasma—an African American, Charles Drew, figured out how to store this in blood banks so it, too, could be used to save the wounded fighting men. You see, scientists can be war heroes just as much as the soldiers! I wish I could tell you about all of them, but I can't. There isn't room in this book for the story of these and dozens of other wonderful things; and besides, I'd never catch up, for new discoveries and inventions are being made all the time—"Made Fresh Every Hour."

---

[1] pasteurization [pas chə riz′ ā shən]
[2] inoculation [i nok yə lā′ shən]

[3] penicillin [pen ə sil′ in]

This story ends here, but only for the moment, for history is a continuing story and keeps going on and on. Even while you are reading this line, scientists are working on inventions and discoveries that may be in the history books of the future.

If you were living in the year 10,000 A.D., as some boy or girl will be, your history would only be just begun when you had reached where we are now. Even World War II would then seem as long ago as the fights of the Stone Age men seem to us. You might think of us and all our wonderful inventions in the same way that we now think of the discovery of copper and bronze.

Perhaps then people will no longer use trains, boats, automobiles, or even airplanes, but go from place to place as on some magic carpet, simply by wishing. Perhaps then they will no longer use letters, telephones, radio, television, or even computers, but read each other's thoughts at any distance.

Perhaps by then people will know how to build factories that don't poison the air and water and to use earth's resources wisely so we don't run out. And perhaps people will have learned to share, so that everyone in the whole wide world has enough food to eat and a decent place to live. Perhaps, best of all, people by then will know how to settle their problems without fighting wars.

And so on—World without end—AMEN!

Index with Pronuciation Guide
PRONUNCIATION KEY

This list of the most important names in the book tells you on what page you may find each name and how to sound those you may not know.

Sound	In These Words	Sound	In These Words
a	map, pat	o	pot, stop
ā	ate, face	ō	over, go
â	care, pair	ô	order, all
ä	far, farther		
		u	cut, butter
e	pet, west, head		
ē	we, meet	oi	boil, voice
		ou	shout, house
i	in, bit		
ī	nice, tiger	o͝o	pull, put
		o͞o	rule, move, use, music

ə represents:

a	in about	o	in lemon
e	in token	i	in happily
	u	in circus	

Index

A

B

Index

Index

F

G

Index

I

J

Index

N

A Child's History of the World

Index

Index

T

Index

Index

Recommended Readings

- Siddhartha by Hermann Hesse, www.bnpublishing.net

- The Anatomy of Success, Nicolas Darvas, www.bnpublishing.net

- The Dale Carnegie Course on Effective Speaking, Personality Development, and the Art of How to Win Friends & Influence People, Dale Carnegie, www.bnpublishing.net

- The Law of Success In Sixteen Lessons by Napoleon Hill (Complete, Unabridged), Napoleon Hill, www.bnpublishing.net

- It Works, R. H. Jarrett, www.bnpublishing.net

- The Art of Public Speaking (Audio CD), Dale Carnegie, wwww.bnpublishing.net

- The Success System That Never Fails (Audio CD), W. Clement Stone, www.bnpublishing.net

CPSIA information can be obtained at www.ICGtesting.com
Printed in the USA
BVOW05s2230120715

408382BV00009B/160/P